Tucker, Legal Environment Pamph. MCB

PREFACE

A nation's legal system is in part shaped by the problems which confront its people and their fears, values, and aspirations. Since law deals with particulars rather than abstractions and with matters of real rather than imaginary concern, procedural and substantive rules have a relevant time frame. A body of law suitable for a sparsely populated nation reliant on a simple agrarian economy would be of little if any value to a people who live in a densely populated area and whose economy is keyed to a highly refined technology.

For centuries the people who inhabited the North American continent were shielded from the horrid and formidable environmental problems which plagued those who live on other parts of the earth's surface. To a great extent this favorable state of affairs can be attributed to a vast land area; a superabundance of lakes, rivers, and streams; a plentiful and wide assortment of wildlife; a multitude of sites of great scenic beauty or historical import; a seemingly endless supply of natural resources; a relatively small population of which a goodly portion was composed of rural dwellers; and industrial techniques, processes, and equipment which posed but a local or minor danger to life-sustaining processes. By the beginning of the twentieth century, however, environmental considerations invited serious attention. In the United States a small core of conservationists took to the hustings. They decried the wanton depletion of the nation's natural resources, the reckless despoilment of nature's diverse offerings, the pollution of mankind's only known home, and the labyrinth of problems generated by a burgeoning urban and suburban population. While their outcries were often shrill and persuasive, for the most part they were sporadic. Few governmental officials and a paltry number of citizens reacted affirmatively. The overall response was limited and of little immediate consequence. But ultimately their call to action prevailed. By the end of the 1950's their urgings had penetrated the outer perimeter of the threshold of interest of the collective psyche of the American people. Official response was now massive. What began as a trickle of legislative, executive, judicial, and administrative involvement soon became a river, if not a sea, of reaction.

At present all levels of government, many governmental institutions, private groups, and individuals are taking part in a pervasive search for appropriate means to resolve local, state, national, and worldwide environmental problems. Less than a decade ago environmental law attracted but scant attention. Today it attracts intense and almost universal interest. Its mandates, few in number prior to the mid-1960's, now are many and continue to multiply. More and more persons, appreciatively aware of the urgent need to protect and improve man's habitat, desire to familiarize themselves with the demands and quality of environmental law.

This book is designed to assist one who has an interest in environmental law to appraise its contents and effectiveness and to become acquainted with (1) the legal framework within which environmental law operates; (2) the governmental institutions involved in the formulation, interpretation, and application of environmental law; (3) the nature of the legal procedures and substantive principles currently being invoked to resolve environmental problems; (4) the types of hazards to the environment presently subject to legal constraints; (5) the impact that the mandates of environmental law have had, and will have, on personal liberties and property rights; and (6) the role individuals and groups can play within the context of our legal system to protect and improve man's terrestrial habitat and the earth's atmosphere.

I am indebted to my wife Gladys for her watchful perceptive assistance. Her wise counsel made lighter the task of accommodating time and space constraints. She helped me to stay on course. My son Sherwin asks the difficult and the pointed questions. His queries made it clear to me that one interested in studying environmental law would best be served by my pursuing a balanced rather than an advocatory approach. My daughter Pamela, who has a teenager's insatiable interest in everything that takes place about her, continuously queried me on content. She forced me to pay special attention to concepts and points of view which I might have otherwise left unchallenged or unmentioned. A great deal of the text, a large number of the cases, and many of the problems found in the chapters which follow were presented over the course of two semesters in my classes which were made-up of undergraduate and graduate students. Their incisive probes and the challenges they made to legislative, executive, judicial, and administrative behavior were of immeasurable help to me.

Environmental law must be of special concern to the young—the under thirty generation. I have selected materials which I believe will be of greatest value and interest to them. I will consider my work a success if it helps them to better understand the function of the law and how it operates and what the legal process can and cannot do to protect the environment.

EDWIN WALLACE TUCKER

Storrs, Connecticut
October, 1972

TABLE OF CONTENTS

*

TABLE OF CASES

The principal cases are in italic type. Cases cited or discussed are in roman. References are to Pages.

TABLE OF CASES

†

TEXT, CASES AND PROBLEMS
on
LEGAL REGULATION
OF THE
ENVIRONMENT

Part One

JURISPRUDENCE AND ECOLOGY

Chapter 1

LAW AND THEORIES OF LAW

Primitive and civilized societies alike use law as a tool to regulate the relationship between government and the individual, to resolve disputes between private persons, and to guard and champion selected policies.

Law may be defined as the body of behavioral norms imposed by and enforceable by government. Justice Oliver Wendell Holmes espoused this description, when he said that law is "a statement of the circumstances in which the public force will be brought to bear upon men through the courts." If he were writing today, Justice Holmes would have to allude to administrative agencies which now share with our courts the power to impose sanctions upon those whose conduct runs counter to government's prescribed directives.

A less restrictive definition of law would include reference to extra-governmental demands and means of enforcement. It would take into account directives and sanctions which emanate from such groups as the family, community, college or university, commune, business enterprise, trade association, or professional organization. Each demands individuals behave in a prescribed fashion. A member of the group who does not may be censured, shunned, or expelled. Those who prefer an elastic encompassing meaning of law might define it as any body of principles, regardless of their source, formulated for the purpose of ordering of human conduct, whether or not there is available any formal procedure through which such principles may be enforced. Note that this definition omits the requisite of governmental involvement spoken of by Holmes. For the purpose of studying environmental law, this more inclusive concept of "law" is more useful. Significant constraints on individual behavior in the area of environmental control are based on other than officially generated and enforceable mandates.

Man probes those forces which affect him. He seeks to understand that which restricts his freedom to do as he pleases. He investigates those means which he believes may assist him to attain selected objectives. So it is not surprising to find that a great deal of thought and writing has been devoted to responding to the query: "What determines the law's ultimate dictates?" For ages men have framed and tested hypotheses as to the origin of law and the forces which determine its content. The hunt continues.

Those who think and write about law are invariably influenced by the prevailing temper of the law and the beliefs and practices of contemporary society. Legal philosophers who lived at a time when slavery was a legally protected relationship invariably found themselves extolling its virtues or speaking of the heinousness of this form of human degradation. In an age of despotism one who reveres tyranny might expound upon the reasons why a despot's laws should be obeyed. Those who oppose despotism would vilify the despot and deride the sanctity of his laws. In a theocracy, lawmakers evaluate their laws in terms of their consistency with the assumed wishes of the deity. Those whose religious beliefs clash with those of the lawmakers or who are agnostics or atheists would insist that the lawmakers use a different frame of reference to evaluate their legislation. At a time when a society is struggling to maintain stability unquestioned adherence to established rules is viewed with favor. When a society is in a state of flux, established norms of behavior may have little or no influence on those who make or administer the law. Instead, they are prone to focus exclusively on the impact of their decisions, thinking in terms of ends rather than means.

Legal philosophers who share like views are said to belong to the same "school" of legal philosophy. Schools are labeled so as to identify the theme which is central to the thinking of its members. The tenets of the following eight generally recognized schools illustrate the diversity of ideas which exist about the nature and function of law.

Natural Law. Proponents of natural law maintain that there exists in nature a paramount body of universally acceptable standards of right and wrong. Any man-made law which contravenes this body of law is unenforceable. They acknowledge that a formal body of natural law principles is not to be found. The demands of natural law are arrived at on a case by case basis. Subjective rather than objective criteria must be employed to test the validity of a challenged legal principle. When passing on the rights of parties, given a particular factual pattern, individual advocates of natural law may differ as to what would be the correct legal outcome. Some members of this school, to test the correctness of a man-made law, would use as their guide what they assume to be generally accepted truths. Others would rely on announced religious doctrine. American courts have used natural law precepts to strike down legislation which, while violative of no precise constitutional prohibition, contravenes what the tribunal regards as a natural prohibition on the law-making power. Natural law philosophy generally serves to vindicate the liberty of the individual and to curb the power of government. When courts invoke natural law philosophy, they seldom expressly make mention of it.

Positivism. Positivist philosophy is based on the proposition that law is any command of the sovereign and all commands of the sovereign must be enforced by those who administer the state's legal system. Positivism bars a jurist from refusing to enforce an order of the sovereign regardless of the jurist's belief as to its propriety. Only express restrictions on the sovereign proscribe the law-making power. Judicial acceptance of positivism during Hitler's reign facilitated court enforcement of his decrees, however diabolic they were.

Analytical Jurisprudence. Akin to, yet distinct from positivism, is the school of analytical jurisprudence. Like positivists, members of this school begin their search for a decision as to rights and duties with an analysis of the sovereign's commands. They insist that the decision-maker's thinking be precise, clear, and logical. They part with the positivists in that they reject robot-like application of a sovereign's directives. They insist that a tribunal must evaluate the results such directives call for. Should the end product prove to be undesirable, it is incumbent upon the tribunal to once again apply the sovereign's dictates but this time in a fashion which would avoid an unwanted result. While positivism and analytical jurisprudence each stress enforcement of the sovereign's commands without measuring them against a higher body of law, the latter, unlike the former, rejects a result militated by bare logic if it proves to be emotionally or intuitively unsatisfactory. Analytical jurisprudence has a natural law dimension since it does recognize that at some point judicial evaluation must occur and at that juncture the jurist must look beyond bare commands precisely, clearly, and logically applied and employ subjective criteria to arrive at what he regards as an acceptable result.

Historical School. Basic to this school is the premise that law is a function of the yardsticks of right and wrong which a particular people has arrived at over a period of time. Prescribed forms of behavior are good if old, bad if new. This school finds merit in making use of past solutions to resolve contemporary problems. Its members look askance at abrupt changes in legal norms and approve of judicial respect for precedent. Custom is regarded as a vital source of court enforceable rules of conduct. Law is seen as of parochial rather than universal worth. Legal principles which prove to be serviceable for one society, in the absence of convincing evidence to the contrary, are not viewed as necessarily useful for another.

Pragmatic Jurisprudence. A proponent of pragmatic juris- prudence sees law as a judicial tool, to be used to attain a meritorious end. In each case the tribunal scrutinizes the facts and a variety of possible solutions. It then selects as its judgment that result which it finds to be the most practical under the circumstances. Pragmatic philosophy rejects the existence of immutable and timeless rules of right and wrong. What is right and what is wrong is determined by the setting in which the behavior in question took place and the use- fulness of each of the options open to the court in terms of prevailing values and desires.

Sociological School. Followers of the sociological school believe that a tribunal has the obligation to familiarize itself with the mores and goals of the group it serves. Courts should fashion the law so that it reflects society's customs and chosen objectives. The aspira- tions and demands of the people play a critical role in determining the content of the law. Since this school anchors judicial decisions to how people generally behave and what they commonly desire it is said to cultivate "living law."

Sociological Jurisprudence. Some of the guidelines espoused by this school resemble those which mark pragmatic jurisprudence and the sociological school. Like the former, it maintains that the judi- ciary should in each case seek out the best of the available alterna- tives. Like the latter, it acknowledges that the milieu in which courts operate must be taken into consideration in the judicial decision-mak- ing process. It differs from these two schools in that it calls upon those who are charged with making and administering the law to utilize the results of research conducted in accordance with social science techniques to determine the forms of behavior courts should demand of government and the citizenry. Jurists must take into consideration the impact of conceivable decisions on society and the individual. They must reject a suggested result if it does not satisfy the realities and needs of the people. This school shuns mechanical application of established norms. It emphasizes the need for judicial evaluation of the desirability of a proposed outcome in terms of con- temporary desiderata. The difference between a good and a bad de- cision is that the good decision is consistent with present-day societal and individual interests; a bad one is not.

Legal Realism. Advocates of legal realism recognize that bene- fits inure to individuals when courts abide by precedent. Persons are able to predict how courts will treat various sorts of behavior. This allows them to plan, confident that so long as they comply with announced norms their acts will be dealt with in the proclaimed fashion. But legal realists are loath to judicial reliance solely on logic and precedent. This can lead to worthless and even injurious decisions. They recognize changes occur in society which necessitate responsive variation in legal principles. Law should be used to promote the realization of existent values. This school calls for a scientific approach to judicial problem solving. It places emphasis on empirical methods. Those who belong to this school insist that studies should be made of what is transpiring among the people. The acquired information should be utilized by the courts in their formulation and application of acceptable rules of conduct. Solutions to new problems should be predicated on fruits of empirical research. Legal realists insist that a form of behavior should not be prescribed when it is obvious that it will not be generally obeyed. Unique to this school is its insistence that attention be paid to why and how those who are charged with making, administering, and enforcing the law think and behave as they do.

One who examines the salient features of each of the described schools quickly becomes aware of the fact that the line of demarcation between a number of schools is indistinct. While each has at least one distinguishing characteristic, several incorporate one or more tenets of one or more of the other schools. This overlapping not only marks the writings of legal philosophers but is also found in executive, legislative, judicial, and administrative agency behavior. Many procedural and substantive principles show acceptance of an eclectic philosophy of law. Judges, for example, freely draw upon a variety of views as to the function of law in the course of arriving at their decisions. At times a single court opinion makes use of two or more schools of thought. Not every judicial opinion is predicated on concepts which may be identified as falling within the parameters of thought commonly ascribed to one of the named schools. The concepts which underlie a court's determination may be unique to the judge or jurists who staff the tribunal. They may be reacting to one or more tests which as yet have not been categorized as belonging to a distinct school. Classification ordinarily follows a long period of judicial use of a new test of right and wrong. One recently recognized school bears the name *egalitarian jurisprudence*. Its essential premise is that in arriving at a decision it is the duty of the court to design and make use of principles which promote equality and eradicate differences in the way people are treated by one another and by those who make and administer the law.

Those involved in devising and administering adjective and substantive principles of law having to do with the control of the environment make use of a variety of philosophical doctrines. These doctrines and the use made of them are considered in the chapters which follow.

UNITED STATES v. INTERNATIONAL MINERALS
& CHEMICAL CORP.

Supreme Court of the United States, 1971.
91 S.Ct. 1697, 402 U.S. 558, 29 L.Ed.2d 178.

[Title 18 U.S.C.A. § 834(a) gives the Interstate Commerce Commission power to formulate regulations for the safe transportation of corrosive liquids. Section 834(f) states that whoever "knowingly violates any such regulation" may be fined or imprisoned. A Commission regulation required shippers to specify "Corrosive Liquid" on shipping papers when shipping such a liquid. Appellee was charged by information with shipping sulfuric acid and hydrofluosilicic acid (each a corrosive liquid) in interstate commerce and knowingly failing to place on its shipping papers the classification "Corrosive Liquid." The District Court dismissed the information, holding that it did not charge a "knowing violation" of the regulation. The United States appealed.]

MR. JUSTICE DOUGLAS delivered the opinion of the Court.
* * *

Here as in United States v. Freed, which dealt with the possession of hand grenades, strict or absolute liability is not imposed; knowledge of the shipment of the dangerous materials is required. The sole and narrow question is whether "knowledge" of the regulation is also required. It is in that narrow zone that the issue of *"mens rea"* is raised; and appellee bears down hard on the provision in 18 U.S.C. § 834(f) that whoever "knowingly violates any such regulation" shall be fined, etc.

* * *

The principle that ignorance of the law is no defense applies whether the law be a statute or a duly promulgated and published regulation. In the context of * * * [§ 834(f)] we decline to attribute to Congress the inaccurate view that that Act requires proof of knowledge of the law, as well as the facts, and intended to endorse that interpretation by * * * the word "knowingly." We conclude that the meager legislative history * * * makes unwarranted the conclusion that Congress abandoned the general rule and required knowledge of both the facts and the pertinent law before a criminal conviction could be sustained under this Act.

So far as possession, say, of sulfuric acid is concerned the requirement of *"mens rea"* has been made a requirement of the Act as evidenced by the use of the word "knowingly." A person thinking in good faith that he was shipping distilled water when in fact he was shipping some dangerous acid would not be covered. * * *

There is leeway for the exercise of congressional discretion in applying the reach of *"mens rea."* United States v. Balint, * * * closely confined the word "wilfully" in the income tax law to include a purpose to bring about the forbidden result:

* * *

In *Balint* the Court was dealing with drugs, in *Freed* with hand grenades, in this case with sulfuric and other dangerous acids. Pencils, dental floss, paper clips may also be regulated. But they may be the type of products which might raise substantial due process questions if Congress did not require, * * * *"mens rea"* as to each ingredient of the offense. But where, as here and as in *Balint* and *Freed*, dangerous or deleterious devices or products or obnoxious waste materials are involved, the probability of regulation is so great that anyone who is aware that he is in possession of them or dealing with them must be presumed to be aware of the regulation.

Reversed.

* * *

APPEAL OF GIRSH

Supreme Court of Pennsylvania, 1970.
263 A.2d 395, 437 Pa. 237.

[Nether Providence Township's zoning ordinance classified approximately 75% of the land in the township either R–1 or R–2 residential. These classifications permitted the construction of one-family dwelling units on areas of not less than 20,000 and 14,000 square feet respectively. An apartment building could not be built without a variance authorizing such construction. Girsh, having entered into an agreement to purchase a 17½ acre tract of land, requested the Township Board of Commissioners to amend the zoning ordinance so as to permit him to build a high-rise apartment house. After his request was denied, he sought a building permit to erect two 19 story 280 unit luxury apartment buildings. He was refused a permit. He appealed to the Zoning Board of Adjustment, contending that the ordinance was unconstitutional. The Board sustained the ordinance. The trial court affirmed the Board's action. Girsh appealed.]

ROBERTS, JUSTICE. * * * it is plain that appellee's zoning ordinance * * * makes no provision for apartment uses. * * * In theory, an apartment use by variance is available, * * *.

* * * It is settled law that a variance is available *only* on narrow grounds, i. e., "where the property is subjected to an unnecessary harship, unique or peculiar to itself, and where the grant thereof will not be contrary to the public interest. The reasons to justify the granting of a variance must be 'substantial, serious and compelling.'" * * * In light of this standard, appellee's land-use restriction in the case before us cannot be upheld against constitutional attack because of the *possibility* that an *occasional* property owner may carry the heavy burden of proving sufficient hardship to receive a vari-

ance. To be constitutionally sustained, appellee's land-use restriction must be reasonable. If the failure to make allowance in the Township's zoning plan for apartment uses is unreasonable, that restriction does not become any the more reasonable because once in a while, a developer may be able to show the hardship necessary to sustain a petition for a variance. * * * for the purposes of this case, the failure to provide for apartments anywhere within the Township must be viewed as the legal equivalent of an explicit total prohibition of apartment houses in the zoning ordinance.

* * *

* * * In refusing to allow apartment development as part of its zoning scheme, appellee has in effect decided to zone *out* the people who would be able to live in the Township if apartments were available. * * * "The question posed is whether the township can stand in the way of the natural forces which send our growing population into hitherto undeveloped areas in search of a comfortable place to live. We have concluded not. A zoning ordinance whose primary purpose is to prevent the entrance of newcomers in order to avoid future burdens, economic and otherwise, upon the administration of public services and facilities can not be held valid."

* * * "The constitutionality of zoning ordinances which totally prohibit legitimate businesses * * * from an entire community should be regarded with particular circumspection; for unlike the constitutionality of most restrictions on property rights imposed by other ordinances, the constitutionality of total prohibitions of legitimate businesses cannot be premised on the fundamental reasonableness of allocating to each type of activity a particular location in the community." * * * we today hold that appellee cannot have a zoning scheme that makes no reasonable provision for apartment uses.

Appellee argues that apartment uses would cause a significant population increase with a resulting strain on available municipal services and roads, and would clash with the existing residential neighborhood. But we [have] *explicitly* rejected both these claims * * * : "Zoning is a tool in the hands of governmental bodies which enables them to more effectively meet the demands of evolving and growing communities. It must not and can not be used by those officials as an instrument by which they may shirk their responsibilities. Zoning is a means by which a governmental body can plan for the future—it may not be used as a means to deny the future. * * * Zoning provisions may not be used * * * to avoid the increased responsibilities and economic burdens which time and natural growth invariably bring." * * * we reaffirm * * * that protecting the character—really the aesthetic nature—of the municipality is not sufficient justification for an exclusionary zoning technique. * * *

* * * people are attempting to move away from the urban core areas, * * * most jobs that are being created * * * are in the suburbs. * * * formerly "outlying", somewhat rural communities, are becoming logical areas for development and population growth * * *

* * * Nether Providence Township may not permissibly choose to only take as many people as can live in single-family housing, in effect freezing the population at near present levels. Obviously if every municipality took that view, population spread would be completely frustrated. Municipal services must be provided *somewhere*, and if Nether Providence is a logical place for development to take place, it should not be heard to say that it will not bear its rightful part of the burden. Certainly it can protect its attractive character by requiring apartments to be built in accordance with (reasonable) set-back, open space, height, and other light-and-air requirements, but it cannot refuse to make any provision for apartment living. * * *

* * * If Nether Providence is located so that it is a place where apartment living is in demand, it must provide for apartments in its plan for future growth; it cannot be allowed to close its doors to others seeking a "comfortable place to live."

* * * reversed.

* * *

PROBLEMS

1. A city hospital established a program under which men and women, married and unmarried, agreed to genetic manipulation, sterilization, or abortion as directed by a board of physicians. Plaintiff, a taxpayer, asked the court to ban the program on the ground that public funds should not be used to demean the sanctity of life and the right of the yet to be born to be free from tinkering. Which jurisprudential theories would counsel for the parties rely upon in support of their respective positions?

2. Plaintiff brought suit to enjoin the defendant municipality from destroying trees more than 25 feet in height located on municipally owned property on which a low income housing project was being built. Preservation of the trees would increase the cost of the housing by 5%. A municipal ordinance provided: "Nature's bounties should in all cases be taken into account in the construction of low-income housing." Which theories of law would plaintiff and defendant make use of?

3. "When the pollution is caused by a new and extraordinary method of using * * * [a stream], hitherto unknown in the state, and such method renders * * * [the stream] so salty at times that cattle will not drink [from] it unless forced to by necessi-

ty, fish are destroyed in great numbers, vegetation is killed and machinery rusted, such use as a matter of law is unreasonable and entitles riparian owners to [injunctive] relief." Which legal theories are consistent with this statement? Which are not?

4. "Ecosystem protection has as much a place in our common law as the protection of life and property. A special statute is not needed to entitle persons who wish to make use of a lake for recreational purposes to obtain a court order barring the dumping of untreated sewage into the lake. Courts must take judicial notice of the horrendous danger raw sewage poses to our ecosystem." Which legal theories would support the role this statement assigns to the courts? Which would not?

5. "The evidence establishes that defendant's cement plant spews dirt, soot, and minute particles into the air which have caused, and will continue to cause, damage to plaintiff's property. The particles represent some danger to plaintiff's health. The total damage to plaintiff's property is $182,000. Current technology cannot prevent the emissions. The plant represents an investment of $45,000,000. It supplies full-time employment for 400 persons. The defendant is a significant employer in the locality. Injunctive relief is denied. Plaintiff shall pay defendant $182,000 for past, present, and future property damage. This decision shall not constitute a bar to federal or state regulatory authorities seeking further relief." Which jurisprudential theories support the court's position? Which do not?

Chapter 2

TOWARD A THEORY OF ENVIRONMENTAL LAW

Not until the second half of this century was well under way was it generally recognized that individual and societal welfare requires attention be paid to the formulation of a distinct body of environmental law. Previously man's ravaging of the earth's natural resources and his blameful over-burdening of nature's life sustaining processes were regarded as having but little impact on the nation's bountiful resources and individual and group well-being. Most conduct which adversely affected the environment was allowed to pass unrestrained by the legal system. Many forms of debilitating behavior were simply seen as unavoidable if man's needs were to be met and socially satisfactory ambitions were to be satisfied. There was a working consensus which assumed that with few exceptions environmentally destructive behavior was tolerable since the damage wrought was outweighed by the benefits conferred.

As industrialization and advanced technology swept across the United States in the latter part of the nineteenth and early twentieth centuries they were greeted and buttressed by an amalgam of socio-economic teachings which decried governmental interference with business enterprise, held property rights sacrosanct, lauded rugged individualism, applauded material success, and envisioned the earth's offerings as without limit, to be gathered, molded, and used for personal gratification and gain. It was only when individual or entrepreneurial activities caused severe damage to the environment and in some way conflicted with the prevailing socio-economic gospel that the law stood ready to grant an injured party or enterprise relief. For example, persons might not use their property in ways which would deny others acceptable usage and enjoyment of theirs. Such behavior was classified as a nuisance and entitled the adversely affected property owner to successfully maintain a lawsuit to have the objectionable practice abated. The recognized owner of a supply of water, on or beneath the land's surface, could resort to the legal system to bar others from interfering with his use of this resource. Fear that the dumping of refuse into the nation's harbors, rivers, and streams would render them unusable led to passage of the Rivers and Harbors Act of 1899 which made it "unlawful to throw, discharge, or deposit * * * any refuse of any kind or description * * * [except for street and sewer refuse in liquid form] into any navigable water of the United States." These limited forms of environmental control recognized in a minor way the need to protect the environment. The deluge of recent unprecedented environmental rules of law which have appeared within the last decade and a half are of a different bent. They are predicated on a much broader array of con-

11

siderations. Early forms of environmental law were basically of an individual or commercial bent. The new directives are more society, less enterprise, oriented.

Far ranging programs of environmental research have been carried on since the end of World War II. From a broad assortment of vantage points, researchers have investigated the damage man has done to the vital biological and chemical processes which sustain life. The rate of appropriation of our natural resources has been examined in terms of the totality of availability and current and projected needs. Research continues. Those who research the very same phenomena may arrive at different conclusions as to the meaning of their findings and the type of responses called for. Specialists who study the environment do not always agree. Some are of the opinion that serious attention must be given to protect the environment but they do not favor the taking of prompt and stern defensive action. Others believe that immediate action is necessary. They rank adoption of stringent environmental protection policies at or near the very top of the nation's list of critical priorities. Many take a middle ground, classifying environmental control as a pressing, but not among the most pressing, of the country's problem areas.

Executive, legislative, judicial, and agency policies formulated to-date on the federal, state, and local levels indicate that in most instances governmental officials have opted for a middle ground approach to environmental regulation. The one-time indifference of law-makers and administrators to environmental issues is gone. There is a willingness on the part of most officials to include environmental considerations in their decision-making process. New procedural and substantive rules have been framed and old rules utilized to accommodate environmental factors. The unrestrained passion and fervor for immediacy, frequently sounded in the press, on radio, and on television, and voiced before executive officers, legislators, judges, and administrative agencies, while triggering the writing of new rules and the reinterpretation, modification, or rejection of old ones, have not so influenced the content of environmental law as to imbue it with the indicia of urgency insisted upon by the most stalwart of environmentalists.

In Chapter 7 the concepts of intervention, standing, and private attorney general will be considered. They place in the hands of persons who will suffer personal injury as a result of agency action which has a debilitating effect on the environment an opportunity to challenge such action. A number of state legislatures have enacted laws which expressly provide that an individual may maintain a lawsuit to protect the public's interest in the state of the environment. One who proceeds under such a statute is not in quest of a judgment which would vindicate a personal right, but a public one.

The class suit allows a person with even a small personal claim to prosecute within the context of a single lawsuit his claim as well as the like claims of others.   State statutes and court rules governing class suits vary.   Rule 23 of the Federal Rules of Civil Procedure which sets forth the conditions under which class actions may be maintained in the federal court system is typical of the present approach to such litigation.   Included in the stated prerequisites of such proceedings are the requirements that (1) the plaintiff be a member of the class he seeks to represent, (2) that the class "is so numerous that joinder of all members is impracticable," (3) involved "are questions of law or fact common to the class," and (4) it appears to the court that the plaintiff "will fairly and adequately protect the interests of the class."   In addition to these requirements, one of the following must be satisfied: (1) "prosecution of separate actions * * * would create a risk of (a) inconsistent or varying adjudications with respect to individual members of the class which would establish incompatible standards of conduct for the party opposing the class, or (b) adjudication with respect to individual members of the class * * * would as a practical matter be dispositive of the interests of the other members not parties to the adjudications or substantially impair or impede their ability to protect their interests," or (2) "the party opposing the class has acted or refused to act on grounds generally applicable to the class, * * * making appropriate final injunctive relief or corresponding declaratory relief with respect to the class as a whole;" or (3) "the court finds that the questions of law or fact common to the members of the class predominate over any questions affecting only individual members, and that a class action is superior to other available methods for the fair and efficient adjudication of the controversy."   To determine whether or not (3) is satisfied the court should regard as "pertinent . . . (A) the interest of members of the class individually controlling the prosecution . . .; (B) the extent and nature of any litigation concerning the controversy already commenced by or against members of the class; (C) the desirability or undesirability of concentrating the litigation of the claims in the particular forum; (D) the difficulties likely to be encountered in the management of a class action."   Rule 23 also specifies the circumstances under which one member of a class may be sued as a representative of a class allegedly liable to an individual plaintiff or a plaintiff who is suing on behalf of tens, hundreds, thousands, and perhaps even millions of persons.[1]   The class action is available to one who seeks relief under substantive environmental law principles.

Judicial enforcement of substantive rules of environmental law may involve use of such procedural tools as the temporary injunction, the permanent injunction, the filing of a bond, or the imposition of

1. Eisen v. Carlisle & Jacquelin (2d Cir. 1968) 391 F.2d 555.

an unconditional or conditional penalty. A temporary injunction may direct an immediate but temporary halt to the challenged conduct pending further action by the court. The permanent injunction, which follows a determination of the rights and duties of the parties, forever bars a particular form of behavior. A bond, a form of contractual agreement, sets forth circumstances under which the party signing the bond agrees to pay a sum of money to the designated person or persons or governmental entity. An unconditional penalty obliges one who has engaged in unlawful conduct to pay a sum of money. A conditional penalty requires one to pay a sum of money if he fails to comply with the stated conditions. The possibility of having to pay a sum of money may incite one to action or to refrain from engaging in some sort of action. For example, when an enterprise has failed to comply with an anti-pollution law, the imposition of a conditional penalty, providing that if compliance does not take place by a certain date the defendant must pay $25,000 to the state, may engender corrective action. In the absence of such a contingent liability the defendant may have decided to disregard the court's directive.

Legislators, viewing some types of conduct which injure the environment or interfere with the biological or chemical processes essential for life as a grave wrong to society, have enacted laws which make some types of such misconduct a crime. Persons found guilty of such conduct may be fined or imprisoned or be subject to both of these penalties. Should a corporate enterprise be guilty of such misconduct it may be fined. Its officers may be fined or imprisoned or be punished by both of these penalties.

Federal and state constitutions bar government from resorting to procedures which one, concerned exclusively with preservation of the environment, might desire to use. For example, the Fourth Amendment guarantees persons freedom from unreasonable searches and seizures. The Fifth Amendment shields persons from compulsory self-incrimination. The Eighth Amendment prohibits cruel and unusual punishment. The Fourteenth Amendment prohibits states from taking private property for public use without justly compensating the property owner for his loss. The Fifth Amendment places a like constraint on the federal government. These restrictions on governmental action, as well as others, will be examined in subsequent chapters.

Procedures are but tools and however cutting cannot protect or improve the environment. It is when, why, and how they are used which determine their true worth. The success or failure of environmental law will ultimately be dictated by the quality of its substantive rules. It is these principles which prescribe what must or must not be done vis-à-vis people or enterprise and the environment. They will afford a more accurate measure of the utility of law as a regulator of the environment. As is the case with procedural rules, substantive mandates cannot fulfill but a single objective. They must satisfy a catalog of constraints which emanate from other national, state, local, and individual needs, concerns, values, and goals. It is this multiplicity of demands which makes the task of the environmental law-maker, be he or she an executive officer, a legislator, jurist, or agency official, so difficult. Is it any wonder then why those who are charged with making and administering the law approach the question of environmental regulation with great care and at least some trepidation?

If substantive rules of environmental law are to be effective they must be keyed to the forms of activity they are intended to control. The dictates of each rule must be such that it insures that the interest sought to be protected or advanced will be protected or advanced and at the same time other than environmental-based constraints are not overlooked. The content of a substantive rule may be influenced by one or more of the following considerations.

Individual Liberty. Every substantive rule in some fashion denies some person the liberty to do something which in the absence of the rule he would or would not do. Substantive rules, if they are to respect individual liberty, should be as few in number as is consistent with environmental needs and should be no more restrictive than is absolutely necessary to protect the environment.

Humanism. Substantive rules of environmental law must not fail to make provision for distinctly human joys and desires. The opportunities to appreciate natural and man-made beauty, to view historical sites, and to take part in recreational activities add a significant positive dimension to human existence. They are entitled to protection.

Economics. The processes involved in supplying individuals with essential goods and services invariably affect some aspect of the environment. More often than not the impact on the environment is detrimental rather than beneficial. As the level of available and sought after amenities has risen, there has been a concomitant increase in the probability that further injury will be done to the environment. When deciding how to shield the environment from damage the law-maker must be mindful of the impact a new substantive rule will have on the flow of goods and services. Insuring the availability of goods and services is only part of the economic constraint. Keeping open and creating employment opportunities and making provision for the economically disadvantaged must be kept in mind. A process, somewhat harmful to the environment, but a viable source of employment or a critical factor in feeding, clothing, or housing the poor, might at first glance seem a candidate for immediate prohibition. Perhaps selective and limited regulation, rather than total prohibition, until an alternative means can be found would be the more responsible approach.

Politics. When most public officials are selected by an elective process in which a broad-based electorate takes part, environmental control must generally pass the test of public acceptability. Only in the short-run can lawmakers go their own way, disregarding commonly approved forms of behavior. When deciding what types of behavior should be outlawed or regulated and the nature of the constraints to be imposed, attention must be paid to the attitudes and beliefs of the populace. This does not mean that law-makers should simply be scorekeepers of popular will, doing only what a reliable count of yeas and nays indicates the public wants to be done. What is meant is that law-makers have a responsibility to seek out facts, responsibly inform the public of what action is necessary, do their work wisely and with dedication, and refrain from doing that which is certain to result in later rejection at the nation's polling places.

Societal Values. Every society treasures some values and abhors others. Environmental law must be generally compatible with those values which are highly prized by contemporary American society. But even popular values, if they constitute a danger to the environment, must be taken to task. When the law challenges a form of activity which is consistent with a cherished value the law-maker and the administrator must move with great caution, but move they must, if essential for the protection of the environment.

Biological and Life-Sustaining Processes. The law-maker and those charged with seeing to it that the law's directives are met must be ever alert and responsive to the danger various sorts of activity pose to human life and health. They must know what can and cannot be done to regulate or ban such activity. They must write, and when necessary rewrite, substantive rules designed to guard human life and health.

Scientific Knowledge and Technology. Environmental law, like all law, is not intended to exist in the abstract. Its mandates must be such that they can be operative in the everyday world. This means that if possible and compatible with other acceptable criteria, environmental law must impose demands which are consistent with the present state of scientific knowledge and technology. The failure to take these factors into account may result in either demanding too little or too much of persons or enterprises.

Problem-Solving. Our legal system is adversary in nature. Parties before a tribunal are viewed as contestants, each in quest of a victory. In many areas of the law it is assumed that it does not matter whether the plaintiff or the defendant is victorious since the law's focus is on the rights and duties of individuals who are pitted against one another. When a lawsuit or an agency proceeding pertains to the environment an exclusive adversary approach is untenable. Substantive rules which permit a result that would in turn injure the environment have no place in environmental law. Environmental law must be problem-solving in the societal sense. Its dictates must protect society's interest even when invoked in the context of a lawsuit between private persons. A result cannot be regarded as just unless it treats fairly society's interest in protecting and enhancing the environment.

Not all of the cited limiting factors are relevant to each decision having to do with environmental law. Even when one or more may be, the decision-maker may not expressly allude to them. At times they are neglected or intentionally disregarded. When recognized, the depth and breadth of their impact on the decision-making process varies with the individual jurist, legislator, executive, or agency official. One jurist, for example, may be greatly disturbed by what he views as a distasteful and unnecessary flurry of governmental intrusions on individual liberty. He may have but a passing interest in the adverse impact unrestrained individual action has on the environment. Another may place great emphasis on protecting job opportunities. He may be unwilling to place a restriction on an industry even though its processes constitute a danger to some aspect of the life-sustaining biological process. Even jurists who assign a high priority to the very same constraints may interpret their demands differently.

The eight identified counterveiling criteria to environmental considerations are not all of the possible considerations governmental officials may take into account as they go about the process of resolving environmental matters. As they carry on their tasks they may focus on one or more other categories of constraints. If the legal system is to be viable, if environmental needs are to be satisfied, if other critical values are to be accorded their due, it is essential that there be a constant re-evaluation of each of the principles of environmental law as well as the recognition of such new constraints as change makes necessary.

DIAMOND, COMMISSIONER OF ENVIRONMENTAL CONSERVATION OF THE STATE OF NEW YORK v. MOBIL OIL CORPORATION

Supreme Court, Erie County, New York, 1970.
316 N.Y.S.2d 734, 65 Misc.2d 75.

[After the State Commissioner of Health notified the defendant a hearing would be held to determine if it was unlawfully discharging effluents into the Buffalo River the parties agreed to an order dated March 31, 1967 which in part obliged the defendant on and after October 1, 1967 not to discharge wastes into the River in violation of law unless it (1) submitted to the Department of Health by October 1, 1967 final plans to halt discharges; (2) began to construct facilities by July 1, 1968 to treat wastes; and (3) completed by December 1, 1969 such facilities as would satisfy established antipollution standards. Defendant continued to discharge wastes into the River and failed to satisfy (1), (2), or (3). On July 17, 1970 plaintiff commenced an action to enforce the order, to restrain the defendant from discharging wastes in violation of established standards, and to recover penalties for defendant's violation of the order and the State's Public Health Law.]

CARMAN F. BALL, JUSTICE.   *   *   *

The Court finds, as a matter of law, upon all the proof and papers submitted, that there is no triable issue of fact, and that the plaintiff is entitled to summary judgment.

The defendant's violation of the order of the Commissioner of Health and the Public Health Law makes it liable for statutory civil penalties under the Public Health Law § 1250 as a matter of law.

The defendant is fined in the sum of $10,000.00 which is to be paid within ten (10) days and, if not paid within that time, a judgment may be entered without notice.

Air and water pollution have already inflicted a heavy toll on the quality of our environment. The Attorney General is to be complimented for his vigorous prosecution of this case. The defendant Mobil Oil Corporation owns and operates a long established oil refinery *   *   *   employing a large number of citizens of this community. Its products are needed and used by other businesses in this community and throughout the country. To grant an injunction closing down Mobil's operation would bring a large economic loss not only to the defendant but to its employees and would have an adverse economic effect on other businesses throughout the Buffalo community. This Court is not aware that any other business has been subjected to such drastic action in this community. This the Court would not hesitate to do if the Court felt there was any immediate danger to the health of this community. The papers before me do not disclose any such immediate threat to the health of the community.

The Court is well aware from personal observation that this defendant is only one of several industries contributing to the pollution of the Buffalo River, and the difficulties of implementing the pollution abatement and control law *   *   *.

          *   *   *

The Court must balance the interest represented by the right of the community to the immediate abatement of the discharge of industrial waste into the Buffalo River and the economic loss that would be suffered by the defendants, its employees and the community.

Although the defendant *   *   * has failed to comply with the commissioner's order of March 31, 1967 to clean up its effluent discharges and to prepare and submit plans for construction of pollution abatement facilities, it has since March 31, 1967 made an attempt to reduce pollution of the Buffalo River. The defendant has in the past made and installed water pollution abatement devices, * * * Part of the delay in installing water pollution abatement facilities was that in 1967, at the time of the commissioner's order, the defendant contemplated that it would close down its refinery and would only operate a marketing terminal from its plant. * * * The refinery was not closed and still is in operation and Mobil has submitted a number of plans to the state concerning the refinery which have not been approved.

The defendant is directed to undertake the water pollution abatement program * * *:

    * * *

4. After July 15, 1971, it shall operate said facilities in such manner that there is no violation * * * except in case of a mechanical failure, not due to any negligence on the part of the defendant, which is corrected within 24 hours.

This Court shall retain continuing jurisdiction of the parties in this action, and in the event of any default by defendant in complying with the terms and provisions of this decision, plaintiff may apply to the Court, upon five (5) days' written notice to the defendant, for such other or different relief as may be just and proper.

    * * *

DIAMOND, COMMISSIONER OF ENVIRONMENTAL CONSERVATION OF THE STATE OF NEW YORK v. PETER COOPER CORPORATION

Supreme Court, Cattaraugus County, New York, 1970.
317 N.Y.S.2d 40, 65 Misc.2d 82.

[On February 23, 1970 plaintiff instituted an action against the defendant to enforce the State's Law and Regulations governing air pollution. After plaintiff moved for summary judgment the defendant consented to the entry of a judgment on April 17, 1970 which decreed that (1) the defendant abate air pollution at its Gowanda plant by the installation of certain equipment and the conversion of other equipment in accordance with plans and specifications approved by the plaintiff; (2) the defendant by June 15, 1970 comply with § 191.-2 and Part 186 of the State's Rules for Air Pollution; and (3) if (1) and (2) were not satisfied the defendant would be required to comply with State Rules for Air Pollution, to install air-cleaning devices, convert equipment, and discontinue the operation of fuel burning equipment until it had been corrected to the satisfaction of the plaintiff. At the defendant's request the Court extended the deadline for compliance to July 19, 1970. On August 19, 1970 the plaintiff moved for an order (1) directing the defendant to immediately cease and abate emission of smoke and soot in violation of § 191.2 and Part 186 and

(2) assessing monetary penalties for defendant's violation of the April 17, 1970 judgment.]

JAMES O. MOORE, JUSTICE. * * *

The plaintiff's motion is * * * designed to show that since July 19, 1970, the defendant has violated Section 191.2 of the Rules * * * and * * * Part 186.1 of the Rules * * *.

The defendant counters the plaintiff's claims with respect to the violations of Section 191.2 * * * by a recitation of the steps taken by the defendant to install new equipment and convert combustion systems from coal to oil pursuant to plans approved by the plaintiff and at an expense of some $300,000 to the defendant. * * * it is clear that from July 19, 1970, through August 30, 1970, there occurred a series of violations of Section 191.2 * * *.

The defendant's opposing affidavits repeatedly advance the "in terrorem" argument that if full compliance with the decree (to which the defendant freely consented) is required, the result will be the termination of its operations and the consequent economic collapse of the Gowanda community. There is expressed, however, the hopeful prediction that the newly installed equipment will shortly bring about an operation which meets all the standards of the laws and regulations governing air pollution.

* * * Section 186.1 provides that no person shall cause any air contamination source to produce air pollution to the extent that it unreasonably interferes with the comfortable enjoyment of life and property in areas of the state affected thereby. The defendant argues that this standard is so vague and indefinite as to be unenforceable and that it is in conflict with the Ringelmann limits prescribed in Section 191.2. It is true that Section 186.2 provides that if there is a rule controlling a specific air contamination source Section 186.1 shall not be applied. On the other hand, the defendant freely consented to an order and judgment directing compliance with Part 186 of the Rules, and any doubts it may have entertained as to the meaning of the section or the validity of its application should have been raised at that time.

Be that as it may, the Court finds that during the period in question there were numerous violations of * * * Section 191.2 * * *. Therefore, the Court concludes that there have been violations of the judgment and order of June 12, 1970. The defendant's failure to operate its equipment in accordance with the applicable restrictions was not a sporadic technical violation but resulted in creating air pollution which unreasonably interfered with the comfortable enjoyment of the life and property of persons residing in the Armes Court area of Gowanda contrary to the provisions of Section 186.1.
* * *

There remains the problem of devising effectual remedies and meaningful sanctions to achieve future compliance with the judgment and order as well as the established public policy of the state.   This inevitably involves a balancing of the conflicting public interests represented, on the one hand, by the economic benefits that flow from the continued operation of industrial enterprises and, on the other, by the right of individual residents to enjoy the physical and esthetic benefits of an atmosphere relatively free from contamination and pollution.   The scales are no longer in any semblance of balance.   The lessons of the past decade have made all too clear that the great technological advances of this century have been purchased at the expense of creating a very clear and imminent danger to the environment.   It is no longer a question of the quality of life but, rather, one of survival.

The great technical expertise that has been responsible for these advances is surely capable of devising and installing equipment which will eliminate the fallout of oily, sooty particles over an area of a quarter of a mile.   It is the responsibility of industry to effect the necessary operational changes which will reduce air pollution to acceptable standards, and the expense of doing so must be deemed as a part of the cost of doing business.   There has been no showing in this proceeding that this is an impossible undertaking or that it involves prohibitive expenditures.   Indeed, both parties have implied that the applicable standards can be met by the equipment already installed provided it is properly adjusted and operated.

Under these circumstances, as the plaintiff conceded on the oral argument, there is no need for an order directing the discontinuance of the defendant's operations.   Sanctions must, however, be imposed to assure future compliance with the judgment and order of June 12, 1970.   Therefore, the Court imposes a fine in the amount of Five Thousand Dollars ($5,000) upon the defendant for the violations of the provisions of the decree through the period ending October 15, 1970, which direct compliance with Part 191, Section 191.2, of the New York State Rules for Air Pollution Control.   This fine shall be paid within ten (10) days of the entry of an order herein, and in the event of the failure to pay such fine judgment may be entered therefor.

* * *

PROBLEMS

1.   Four conservational groups, in a suit to enjoin the construction of a nuclear energy plant, moved for a temporary injunction barring the defendant from storing radioactive material on the projected plant site.   Defendant established that if it were obliged to store the materials elsewhere it would have to incur a $500,000 storage cost, a cost totally unrelated to the future operation of the plant.   The defendant insisted that if the court decided to grant the injunction, it

should do so on the condition that the plaintiffs post a $500,000 bond. What judgment?

2. Plaintiff corporation, the manufacturer of a pollution control device rejected by a state agency for state use, brought suit as a "private attorney general" challenging the agency's decision. He alleged that the agency's action was a product of "corruption" and that the approved device was inferior to his. The agency moved to dismiss the complaint on the ground that the defendant lacked standing, being "inherently antagonistic and unreliable." What judgment?

3. The defendant sold the plaintiff an air conditioner "guaranteed to filter out harmful substances." He brought a class action in a federal district court on behalf of all other persons who had bought one, alleging that the unit contained no filter equipment and the defendant, in violation of antitrust laws, had agreed with other manufacturers not to manufacture or market an air conditioner which contained an effective filtering device. Defendant, claiming it had sold 750,000 such units, moved to dismiss the class suit. What judgment?

4. "Defendant municipality asks the court to reject plaintiff's argument that cost must not be determinative of where to build a power plant. Defendant has approved a plan to reduce the size of the city's largest park from 350 acres to 250 acres. That portion of the park which fronts on the river will be the plant site. A large steel fence will separate the remaining parkland from the plant. This court is fully aware that this plan was overwhelmingly approved by the electorate. But in an age of affluence cost must be but a secondary factor. Injunction granted." What judgment on appeal?

5. "Plaintiffs ask this court to prevent the sale of state lands which lie beneath the lake to a purchaser who will fill in a portion of it and then erect luxury and middle income housing on the fill. The lake has been used as a recreational area for tens of thousands of people each year. While there may be a need for such housing the state owes an obligation to the citizenry to protect recreational areas from the ever grasping hands of enterprising builders. Injunction granted." What judgment on appeal?

Part Two

CONSTITUTIONAL CONSTRAINTS, THE ADMINISTRATIVE PROCESS, AND JUDICIAL REVIEW

Chapter 3

CONSTITUTIONAL LIBERTIES

The full range of powers of our federal and state governments are nowhere formally enumerated. They need not be. Courts, the ultimate arbiter in questions having to do with the powers of government, acknowledge that the national and state governments each inherently possess those powers which are vital for their own survival and to allow them to take such steps as may be reasonably necessary to protect the life, health, and safety of their constituents. Each possess power to protect and improve the environment. But this authority, like all authority vested in government, may not be used in such a fashion as to deprive individuals, associations of individuals, or corporations of their constitutionally guaranteed liberties.

Article I, § 9 of the Constitution prohibits the federal government from passing bills of attainder. Article I, § 10 imposes the same restriction on state governments.

The Supreme Court has defined a bill of attainder as "a legislative act, which inflicts punishment without a judicial trial." Commenting on such bills, the Court has noted that when passing a bill of attainder the legislature acts as a court, pronouncing the guilt of a party without affording him the usual safeguards which distinguish a trial from the legislative process. The "sufficiency of the proofs adduced, whether conformable to the rules of evidence" or not is determined by the legislature which also sets the "punishment in accordance with its own notions of the enormity of the offence." [1] Such bills were used "in sixteenth, seventeenth and eighteenth century England for dealing with persons who had attempted, or threatened to attempt to overthrow the government * * *. Most * * * named the parties to whom they were to apply; a few, however, simply described them * * *. During the American Revolution, the legislatures of all thirteen States passed statutes directed against the Tories; among these statutes were a large number of bills

---

1. Cummings v. Missouri, 71 U.S. (4 Wall.) 277, 18 L.Ed. 356 (1867).

ficials, and oppressive governmental action. It does not fall within any of the three traditionally recognized branches of government, the executive, legislative, or judicial. A grand jury is independent of, although it usually works with, a prosecuting agency. It is an "investigative" and an "inquisitorial" body. Its function is to probe "probabilities." Has a crime probably been committed? If one probably has been, who is probably guilty? Because of its role it may proceed to investigate and inquire in the absence of any evidence that a crime has taken place and without any evidence as to who committed a crime. Witnesses as well as potential defendants may be directed to appear before a grand jury.

Rule 6(a) of the Federal Rules of Criminal Procedure sets the size of a grand jury at "not less than 16 nor more than 23 members." Rule 6(f) directs that "[a]n indictment may be found only upon the concurrence of 12 or more jurors." This means that a grand jury may not hand up an indictment unless at least 12 of those serving on the jury conclude that they believe that the accused committed, or probably committed, the wrong with which he is being charged.

An indictment is labeled "A True Bill." It is signed by the Foreman of the grand jury and the United States Attorney for the Federal District in which the grand jury is sitting. It is a charging instrument, setting forth the time when and the place where the accused carried out the described wrongful act. It must apprise "the accused of the charges against him, so that he may adequately prepare his defense." It describes "the crime with which * * * [the defendant is charged] with sufficient specificity [so as] to enable him to protect [himself] against future jeopardy for the same offense."[7]

In cases in which the Constitutional directive or Rule 7(a) do not require an indictment, the government may proceed by way of indictment or information. An information is used when an accused, who may demand that an indictment precede his prosecution, waives this right. Grand juries play no part in the process when an information is used. An information contains the same material as an indictment. It must be signed by the United States Attorney for the Federal District in which it is filed. He may file it without permission of the court.

A state, if it wishes, may proceed by indictment or by way of information. The procedure it must follow will be found in either the state's constitution or statutory law. The Supreme Court of the United States has not found that the Federal Constitution requires states to make use of the indictment in those instances in which it must be employed by the Federal Government.

7. Gaither v. United States, 413 F.2d 1061, 134 U.S.App.D.C. 154 (1969).

The Fifth Amendment's mandate "nor shall any person be subject for the same offence to be twice put in jeopardy of life or limb" is commonly referred to as "The Double Jeopardy Clause." It restricts the national government. In 1969 the Clause was made "applicable to the States through the Fourteenth Amendment."[8]

One is placed in double jeopardy when the government is about to proceed against him or her in a criminal proceeding, which proceeding will place in issue an "ultimate fact [which] has once [before] been determined by a valid and final judgment." When an accused pleads double jeopardy as a defense, it is the court's obligation to scrutinize the prior proceeding to see if the previous judgment, taking into account every aspect of the proceeding, could have been grounded "upon an issue other than that which the defendant seeks to foreclose from consideration" by his plea. What is prohibited is forcing the accused to " 'run the gantlet' a second time" when his innocence or guilt has already been decided in a prior proceeding. The Supreme Court has depicted freedom from double jeopardy as a "fundamental" right, intended to prevent government, " 'with all its resources and power' " from " 'repeated attempts to convict an individual for an alleged offense, thereby subjecting him to embarrassment, expense and ordeal and compelling him to live in a continuing state of anxiety and insecurity, as well as enhancing the possibility that even though innocent he may be found guilty.' "[9]

The Fourth Amendment "protects individual privacy against certain kinds of [federal] governmental intrusion."[10] It reads: "The right of the people to be secure in their persons, houses, papers, and effects, against unreasonable searches and seizures, shall not be violated, and no Warrants shall issue, but upon probable cause, supported by Oath, or affirmation, and particularly describing the place to be searched, and the persons or things to be seized." This Amendment is made applicable to actions of state officials by the Fourteenth Amendment.

The Fifth Amendment, circumscribing the power of the federal government, directs that "[n]o person * * * shall be compelled in any criminal case to be a witness against himself, * * *." The Fourteenth Amendment's due process clause places the same limitation on state governments.

The Fourth and Fifth Amendments apply to all types of legal proceedings brought by the government against an accused, be they civil or criminal, administrative or judicial, investigatory or adjudicatory. They may be invoked before a grand jury as well as during a trial. They protect with equal force the guilty and the innocent.

8. Benton v. Maryland, 89 S.Ct. 2056, 395 U.S. 784, 23 L.Ed.2d 707 (1969).

9. Benton v. Maryland, 89 S.Ct. 2056, 395 U.S. 784, 23 L.Ed.2d 707 (1969).

10. Katz v. United States, 88 S.Ct. 507, 389 U.S. 347, 19 L.Ed.2d 576 (1967).

Their commands are consistent with the proposition that our legal system requires officials to proceed in an "investigative" rather than an "inquisitorial" fashion. To deter governmental officers from disobeying the admonitions found in these Amendments and to keep courts from being "made party to lawless invasions of the constitutional rights of citizens," tribunals ban the use by government of any incriminating evidence against an accused when such evidence was secured in violation of either of these Amendments.[11]

The "Fourth Amendment protects people, not places. What a person knowingly exposes to the public, even in his own home or office, is not a subject of Fourth Amendment protection * * *. But what he seeks to preserve as private, even in an area accessible to the public, may be constitutionally protected."[12] Because the Amendment protects "people and not places" from uninvited intrusion by government, it bars an unreasonable search or seizure "in a business office, in a friend's apartment, * * * in a taxicab, * * * [and] a person in a telephone booth may rely upon the protection of the Fourth Amendment * * * [when he] occupies it, [and] shuts the door behind him * * * [since] the public telephone [plays a "vital role"] in private communication."[13] The Amendment "governs not only the seizure of tangible items, but * * * [also the unauthorized] recording of oral statements, overheard" without consent or judicial authorization.[14]

Only *unreasonable* searches and seizures" are outlawed by the Fourth Amendment. Neither the Amendment, nor judicial decisions, prescribe a " 'ready test for determining reasonableness.' " What must be done in each case is to " 'balance the need to search [or seize] against the invasion which the search [or seizure] entails.' "[15] In every instance in which the constitutionality of a search or seizure is questioned, the court must decide whether, under the circumstances, the legitimate interest of society in a search or seizure being carried out was of sufficient magnitude to call for the denial of an individual's right to be free from governmental intrusion. If it concludes that society's interest does outweigh that of the individual, the search or seizure is reasonable; otherwise, it is not.

Officials "must, whenever practicable, obtain advance judicial approval of searches and seizures through the warrant procedure, * * * in most instances failure to comply with the warrant requirement can only be excused by exigent circumstances," such as when an officer is in "hot pursuit" of one he observed committing a

11. Terry v. Ohio, 88 S.Ct. 1868, 392 U.S. 1, 20 L.Ed.2d 889 (1968).

12. Katz v. United States, 88 S.Ct. 507, 389 U.S. 347, 19 L.Ed.2d 576 (1967).

13. Katz v. United States, 88 S.Ct. 507, 389 U.S. 347, 19 L.Ed.2d 576 (1967).

14. Katz v. United States, 88 S.Ct. 507, 389 U.S. 347, 19 L.Ed.2d 576 (1967).

15. Terry v. Ohio, 88 S.Ct. 1868, 392 U.S. 1, 20 L.Ed.2d 889 (1968).

crime.[16] To obtain a warrant the requesting official must persuade a magistrate who is authorized to issue one that there is "probable cause." A "mathematical formula" does not exist which courts may readily invoke to determine if "probable cause" is present. "Probable cause is a flexible, non-technical concept. It includes a conscious balancing of the governmental need for enforcement of the criminal law against the citizens' constitutionally protected right of privacy. It must be regarded as representing an effort to accommodate those often competing interests so as to serve them both in a practical fashion without unduly hampering the one or unreasonably impairing the significant content of the other * * *. Thus, although incapable of precise definition, the term has been construed to signify less evidence than would be required to establish guilt of the crime for which the warrant is sought * * *. It means something more than 'raw unsupported suspicion.' It is a suspicion of guilt that is well-grounded; a reasonable basis for a belief that a crime has been or is being committed. * * * A finding of probable cause may rest upon evidence not competent at a criminal trial * * *. Hearsay is an adequate basis for the finding and the issuance of a warrant, so long as there is something coupled with the hearsay to give it reasonable credit, something which gives it the appearance of trustworthiness." [17] Since "the true test is reasonableness, each case must necessarily turn on its own facts." [18]

The Fifth Amendment prohibits federal or state officials from compelling an individual to respond to inquiries which call for answers which may tend to incriminate him. One has a constitutional right to refuse to answer if the answers "would in themselves support a conviction" or "would furnish a link in the chain of evidence needed to prosecute." [19] A court must sustain one's right to refrain from answering when it is "evident from the implications of the question, in the setting in which it is asked, that a responsive answer to the question or an explanation of why it cannot be answered might be dangerous because injurious disclosure would result."[20] A judge may compel a witness who refuses to answer on the grounds that a response might tend to incriminate only when it is " *'perfectly clear, from a careful consideration of all the circumstances in the case, that the witness is mistaken, and that the answer cannot possibly have such tendency'* to incriminate." [21]

A statute that deprives one of his Fifth Amendment right to refuse to answer a question which calls for a response which may

16. Terry v. Ohio, 88 S.Ct. 1868, 392 U.S. 1, 20 L.Ed.2d 889 (1968).

17. State v. Kasabucki, 244 A.2d 101, 52 N.J. 110 (1968).

18. State v. Campbell, 250 A.2d 1, 53 N.J. 230 (1969).

19. Hoffman v. United States, 71 S.Ct. 814, 341 U.S. 479, 95 L.Ed. 1118 (1951).

20. Hoffman v. United States, 71 S.Ct. 814, 341 U.S. 479, 95 L.Ed. 1118 (1951).

21. Hoffman v. United States, 71 S.Ct. 814, 341 U.S. 479, 95 L.Ed. 1118 (1951).

tend to incriminate him is constitutional if it confers upon him immunity from future criminal prosecution. The breadth of the statutory immunity must be no less broad than the right guaranteed by the Fifth Amendment. The individual must in no wise be any more vulnerable to a criminal prosecution because he testifies under a cloak of statutory immunity than if he relied upon his right to refuse to answer. An immunity statute which provides that a witness may not be prosecuted for any crime about which he may testify or any transaction, matter, or thing concerning which he may testify, is constitutional.[22] One granted immunity by a governmental official, under the terms of such a statute, has no right to refuse to testify, even if his response may be embarrassing or cause him economic injury. The Fifth Amendment protects persons from the hazard of possible criminal prosecutions and nothing more.

Prosecutors, grand juries, and administrative agencies often make use of one's books and records to determine whether or not he is guilty of unlawful behavior. To obtain such records a *subpoena duces tecum* may be used. Such a *subpoena* commands the party to whom it is directed to produce the sought after documents. The power of governmental officials and bodies to obtain books and records by use of the *subpoena duces tecum* is limited by the Fourth and Fifth Amendments.

An individual upon whom a *subpoena duces tecum* has been served is obliged to appear at the specified place, on the stated date, at the prescribed time. At the time of his appearance, he may assert his Fifth Amendment right to refuse to submit the demanded documents on the ground that their contents might tend to incriminate him. Should the tribunal before which he makes his claim agree that to require him to display them would run counter to the Amendment he will be excused from having to do so.

Corporate records fall outside the pale of the Fifth Amendment but, to a limited degree, are protected by the Fourth. A court will strike down a *subpoena duces tecum* which calls for the production of corporate records unless it is convinced that "the records to be produced are relevant to the investigation being pursued" and that the "records are specified with reasonable particularity, * * * [and] cover a reasonable period of time. The Fourth Amendment requires that the subpoena be sufficiently limited in scope, relevant in purpose, and specific in directive."[23]

Corporate officers may not refuse to produce corporate books or records which contain material which may tend to incriminate them. Nor may they refuse to produce documents which contain information pertaining to corporate affairs simply because they paid for the books with their own funds, personally made the entries, or are the

22. Brown v. Walker, 16 S.Ct. 644, 161 U.S. 591, 40 L.Ed. 819 (1896).

23. Schultz v. Yeager (D.C.N.J.1967) 293 F.Supp. 794.

custodian of such writings. Members of unincorporated associations, such as labor unions, likewise may not refuse to produce association books on the ground that they contain incriminating material. Courts have generally recognized a partner's right to invoke the Fifth Amendment in regard to the production of partnership records only when the partnership to which he belongs has but few partners.

Courts have distinguished between requiring corporate officers to produce books and records and compelling them to give oral testimony. A corporate officer may not be compelled to give oral testimony in regard to corporate affairs if his answers might tend to incriminate him. Nor may a corporate officer be compelled to reveal the whereabouts of corporate books or records if he can persuade the court that their contents might tend to incriminate him. A corporate officer, however, can be required to orally testify as to the genuineness of documents which have already been produced pursuant to a *subpoena duces tecum* calling for corporate books and records.

The "required record" or "public record" doctrine is a significant exception to the Fifth Amendment right of individuals to refuse to display writings which might tend to incriminate them. This doctrine removes from the protection of the Amendment "records [which are] required by law to be kept in order that there may be suitable information of transactions which are the appropriate subjects of governmental regulation and the enforcement of restrictions validly established."[24] It recognizes that government "may require * * * [an individual] as a means of enforcing * * * [a] valid law, to keep a record showing whether he has in fact complied with it."[25] Such records, having a "public aspect," are not protected by the Fifth Amendment.

Fourth and Fifth Amendment rights, as well as other constitutional rights, can be waived. To find that one has consented to surrender a constitutional right the court must conclude that the consent was voluntarily, knowingly, and intelligently given.

Environmental statutes make various forms of behavior that are injurious to the environment a crime. Each of the constitutional rights examined in this chapter are relevant to proceedings in which one is charged with having committed an environmental crime or is involved in an agency proceeding. But the described rights are not the only constitutional rights enjoyed by persons who have been charged with the commission of a crime or are the subject of agency action. Several more of these rights are examined in the next chapter. Their content is examined in the context of the administrative process.

---

24. Shapiro v. United States, 68 S.Ct. 1375, 335 U.S. 1, 92 L.Ed. 1787 (1948).

25. Davis v. United States, 66 S.Ct. 1256, 328 U.S. 582, 90 L.Ed. 1453 (1946).

SEE v. CITY OF SEATTLE

Supreme Court of the United States, 1967.
87 S.Ct. 1737, 387 U.S. 541, 18 L.Ed.2d 943.

[Appellee's Code authorized firemen to enter and inspect buildings to determine if its fire prevention regulations were being violated. Appellant was convicted of refusing to permit a fireman engaged in a routine periodic city-wide inspection program to enter and inspect his locked commercial warehouse without a warrant and without probable cause to believe that a law was being violated. The State Supreme Court affirmed, distinguishing between an entry into and an inspection of a residence and a place of business. He appealed.]

MR. JUSTICE WHITE delivered the opinion of the Court.

* * *

In *Camara*, we held that the Fourth Amendment bars prosecution of a person who has refused to permit a warrantless code-enforcement inspection of his personal residence. The only question which this case presents is whether *Camara* applies to similar inspections of commercial structures which are not used as private residences. * * *

In Go-Bart Importing Co. v. United States, * * * this Court refused to uphold otherwise unreasonable criminal investigative searches merely because commercial rather than residential premises were the object of the police intrusions. Likewise, we see no justification for so relaxing Fourth Amendment safeguards where the official inspection is intended to aid enforcement of laws prescribing minimum physical standards for commercial premises. As we explained in *Camara*, a search of private houses is presumptively unreasonable if conducted without a warrant. The businessman, like the occupant of a residence, has a constitutional right to go about his business free from unreasonable official entries upon his private commercial property. The businessman, too, has that right placed in jeopardy if the decision to enter and inspect for violation of regulatory laws can be made and enforced by the inspector in the field without official authority evidenced by warrant.

* * *

It is now settled that, when an administrative agency subpoenas corporate books or records, the Fourth Amendment requires that the subpoena be sufficiently limited in scope, relevant in purpose, and specific in directive so that compliance will not be unreasonably burdensome. The agency has the right to conduct all reasonable inspections of such documents which are contemplated by statute, but it must delimit the confines of a search by designating the needed documents in a formal subpoena. In addition, while the demand to inspect may be issued by the agency, in the form of an administrative subpoena, it may not be made and enforced by the inspector in the field, and the subpoenaed party may obtain judicial review of the reasonableness of the demand prior to suffering penalties for refusing to comply.

It is these rather minimal limitations on administrative action which we think are constitutionally required in the case of investigative entry upon commercial establishments. The agency's particular demand for access will of course be measured, in terms of probable cause to issue a warrant, against a flexible standard of reasonableness that takes into account the public need for effective enforcement of the particular regulation involved. But the decision to enter and inspect will not be the product of the unreviewed discretion of the enforcement officer in the field. Given the analogous investigative functions performed by the administrative subpoena and the demand for entry, we find untenable the proposition that the subpoena, which has been termed a "constructive" search, * * * is subject to Fourth Amendment limitations which do not apply to actual searches and inspections of commercial premises.

We therefore conclude that administrative entry, without consent, upon the portions of commercial premises which are not open to the public may only be compelled through prosecution or physical force within the framework of a warrant procedure. We do not in any way imply that business premises may not reasonably be inspected in many more situations than private homes, nor do we question such accepted regulatory techniques as licensing programs which require inspections prior to operating a business or marketing a product. Any constitutional challenge to such programs can only be resolved, as many have been in the past, on a case-by-case basis under the general Fourth Amendment standard of reasonableness. We hold only that the basic component of a reasonable search under the Fourth Amendment—that it not be enforced without a suitable warrant procedure—is applicable in this context, as in others, to business as well as to residential premises. Therefore, appellant may not be prosecuted for exercising his constitutional right to insist that the fire inspector obtain a warrant authorizing entry upon appellant's locked warehouse.

Reversed.

MANCUSI v. DeFORTE

Supreme Court of the United States, 1968.
88 S.Ct. 2120, 392 U.S. 364, 20 L.Ed.2d 1154.

[The District Attorney issued a *subpoena duces tecum* to Local 266, directing it to produce certain books and records. When it refused, the officials who had served the subpoena at the Union's offices proceeded, without a warrant, to conduct a search. Over the protests of DeForte, a vice president of the Union, they seized Union records from an office he shared with other Union officers. In a state criminal proceeding in which he was convicted the seized materials, over his objection, were used to establish his guilt. The Federal District Court dismissed a writ of *habeas corpus*. The Court of Appeals reversed. Certiorari was granted.]

MR. JUSTICE HARLAN delivered the opinion of the Court.

* * *

* * * The decision below was based solely upon a finding that DeForte's Fourth and Fourteenth Amendment rights, * * * were violated by the search and seizure, and that the seized material was therefore inadmissible * * *. It is on this ground alone that DeForte argues for affirmance. * * * The questions for decision, then, are whether DeForte has Fourth Amendment standing to object to the seizure of the records and, if so, whether the search was one prohibited by the Fourth Amendment.

* * * The papers which were seized in this case belonged not to DeForte but to the Union. * * * DeForte can have personal standing only if, as to him, the search violated the "right of the people to be secure in their * * * houses * * *." This Court has held that the word "houses," as it appears in the Amendment, is not to be taken literally, and that the protection of the Amendment may extend to commercial premises. * * *

Furthermore, the Amendment does not shield only those who have title to the searched premises. * * * "anyone legitimately on premises where a search occurs may challenge its legality * * * when its fruits are proposed to be used against him." * * * capacity to claim the protection of the Amendment depends not upon a property right in the invaded place but upon whether the area was one in which there was a reasonable expectation of freedom from governmental intrusion. * * * The crucial issue, therefore, is whether, in light of all the circumstances, DeForte's office was such a place.

The record reveals that the office where DeForte worked consisted of one large room, which he shared with several other union officials. * * * DeForte spent "a considerable amount of time" in the office, and that he had custody of the papers at the moment of their seizure.

We hold that in these circumstances DeForte had Fourth Amendment standing to object to the admission of the papers at his trial. It has long been settled that one has standing to object to a search of his office, as well as of his home. * * * it seems clear that if DeForte had occupied a "private" office in the union headquarters, and union records had been seized from a desk or a filing cabinet in that office, he would have had standing. * * * It seems to us that the situation was not fundamentally changed because DeForte shared an office with other union officers. DeForte still could reasonably have expected that only those persons and their personal or business guests would enter the office, and that records would not be touched except with their permission or that of union higher-ups. * * * It is, of course, irrelevant that the Union or some of its officials might validly have consented to a search of the area where the records were kept, regardless of DeForte's wishes, for it is not claimed that any such consent was given, either expressly or by implication.

* * * it is settled for purposes of the [Fourth] Amendment that "except in certain carefully defined classes of cases, a search of private property without proper consent is 'unreasonable' unless it has been authorized by a valid search warrant." * * * the state officials' possession of a district attorney's subpoena of the kind involved here does not bring this case within one of those "carefully defined classes."

* * * the subpoena involved here could not in any event qualify as a valid search warrant under the Fourth Amendment, for it was issued by the District Attorney himself, and thus omitted the indispensable condition that "the inferences from the facts which lead to the complaint ' * * * be drawn by a neutral and detached magistrate instead of being judged by the officer engaged in the often competitive enterprise of ferreting out crime.' * * * the search of DeForte's office was "unreasonable" within the meaning of the Fourth Amendment.

* * * Affirmed.

PROBLEMS

1. For 52 years the defendant corporation dumped untreated sewage into a river adjacent to its plant. In 1970 the town in which the plant was located passed an ordinance making it a misdemeanor to dump raw sewage into a river, stream, lake or pond. Defendant moved to dismiss an information filed against it in which it was charged with dumping waste into the river between March 1 and April 1, 1971. The defendant's attorney argued that the ordinance was a bill of attainder and ex post facto legislation. In addition, he claimed that the town was barred from prohibiting the practice, having permitted it to continue for so long a period of time. What judgment?

2. A federal grand jury decided to "dig deep and long" into violations of environmental legislation by manufacturers. The defendant, a plastic container manufacturer, served with a *subpoena duces tecum* directing it to produce specified books and records, moved to vacate the *subpoena* on the ground that the grand jury had no evidence it was violating any law and that the jury's actions had been

inspired by the political ambitions of the United States Attorney. Should the motion be granted?

3.   Defendant was convicted of dumping sewage into the Tarton River between May 1 and May 20, 1971 in violation of federal law. An information was thereafter filed charging it with dumping sewage into the Tarton River between May 1 and May 20, 1971 in violation of state law.   Defendant moved to dismiss the information. What judgment?

4.   State law made it a crime to deal in goods made in whole or in part of alligator skin.   A police officer observed the defendant carry a long, narrow, and apparently heavy package into his garage and then close and lock the garage door.   The officer immediately forced the door open, ran into the garage, and seized and opened the package.   It contained 12 pairs of shoes, each made in part of alligator skin.   Charged with illegally making use of alligator skin, the defendant moved to suppress the evidence obtained by the officer.   What judgment?

5.   A *subpoena duces tecum* directed the defendant corporation to produce all of its income and liability reports for the calendar years 1960 through 1970.   Defendant moved that the *subpoena* be vacated.   What judgment?

Chapter 4

ADMINISTRATIVE PROCEDURE

Federal administrative agencies are the creatures of the Congress which dictates their spheres of competence and the manner in which they must go about their tasks. But, as is the case with their creator, they must comply with the restrictions the Constitution places on the exercise of their powers. State and local administrative agencies must comply with pertinent federal and state constitutional and statutory directives.

Theoretically, environmental policies adopted by Congress could be implemented exclusively by the courts or by Congress itself. The disadvantages inherent in each of these approaches renders them undesirable and impractical. If policies formulated by Congress are to be properly executed it is necessary that a myriad of complex general, specific, and atypical problems be responsibly probed and resolved. A special sort of expertise must be generated, upgraded, and utilized. A reasonably stable body of precedents and rules, not instantly responsive and totally tied to political exigencies, is essential. Administrative decisions and regulations should not be determined merely on the basis of the momentary wishes of the electorate. Persons charged with enforcing selected national policies should be more independent than those who must periodically stand for election. Men and women elected to Congress or serving as justices in the nation's courts more often than not lack the kind of expertise that is essential for the effective administration of established environmental programs. New legislative policies may be in conflict with previously announced judicial norms. Judges tend to look askance upon legislative mandates which are intended to undo court announced and enforced norms. Cumbersome and time consuming court procedures may hinder, rather than promote, the carrying out of congressional programs. Neither the Congress nor the courts are equipped to engage in the kind of extensive and continuous investigative and enforcement techniques necessary to carry out complicated legislative policies. Careful long-term planning and coordination generally do not neatly mesh with the day to day operations of either the Congress or the courts. While administrative agencies have neither completely nor satisfactorily overcome every one of the recited shortcomings which would mark either a strictly court or congressional arrangement, they have, for the most part, proved to be a viable alternative. The agency process is by no means problem-free. Administrative agencies have not proved to be a panacea. But they do hold promise of being of even greater service in the future as their procedures and practices are restructured and refined.

Article I, § 1 of the Constitution vests "[a]ll legislative Powers * * * in * * * Congress." This section has been interpreted as prohibiting Congress from delegating, in carte blanche fashion, its law-making power to some other branch of government. This does not mean that Congress must make every regulation on every aspect of every question with which it chooses to deal. To insure that legislative policy is complied with Congress may lodge in some other sector of government, such as an agency, a limited power to legislate. When delegating a portion of its legislative power, Congress must describe the function it delegates so that it "sufficiently marks the field within which * * * [the agency] is to act so that it may be known whether * * * [the agency] has kept within * * * the legislative will." [1] The factors Congress directs an agency to take into consideration when it exercises its power must be "sufficiently definite and precise to enable Congress, the courts and the public to ascertain whether the * * *, [agency] has conformed to those standards."[2] If the breadth of the power delegated to the agency is vaguely described rather than spelled out with reasonable certainty, the delegation is unconstitutional. Compare a delegation which reads "the Secretary may prescribe such regulations as he deems proper to effect pollution control" with the following delegation which is found in 42 U.S.C.A. § 1857f–1. Note the limiting factors which the Secretary is obliged to take into consideration as he goes about formulating regulations.

"(a) The Secretary shall by regulation, giving appropriate consideration to technological feasibility and economic costs, prescribe as soon as practicable standards, applicable to the emission of any kind of substance from any class or classes of new motor vehicles or new motor vehicle engines, which in his judgment cause or contribute to, or are likely to cause or to contribute to, air pollution which endangers the health or welfare of any persons, and such standards shall apply to such vehicles or engines whether they are designed as complete systems or incorporate other devices to prevent or control such pollution."

Agency rules, also referred to as regulations, have the effect of law. They are directed at an entire class of persons rather than any particular member of the class. An agency regulation dealing with thermal pollution, for example, may prohibit the discharge of fluids above a particular temperature level into lakes or streams. Since it is a rule it states what all persons and not a particular individual or enterprise may not do.

The process by which a rule is formulated is known as rule-making. It "is a legislative process. It is neither judicial, administrative, nor quasi-judicial. An agency performing a legislative function

---

1. Yakus v. United States, 64 S.Ct. 660, 321 U.S. 414, 88 L.Ed. 834 (1944).   2. Yakus v. United States, 64 S.Ct. 660, 321 U.S. 414, 88 L.Ed. 834 (1944).

need not proceed on evidence formally presented at hearings [even though by statute it is obliged to hold hearings prior to promulgating, amending, or abandoning a rule]. It may act on the basis of data contained in its own files, on information informally gained by members of the body, on its own expertise, or on its own views or opinions. It is not necessary for the * * * agency to cause to be submitted at hearings evidence that would support its rule-making decisions. The regulation ultimately promulgated need not be sustained by evidence. The purposes of rule-making hearings are to give an opportunity to interested parties to submit data and facts, and to present their views. Consequently, * * * [a] Court does not review a record of such hearings as it does records in judicial or quasi-judicial proceedings. Such hearings are analogous to hearings conducted by Congressional Committees. An Act of Congress need not be supported by formal evidence introduced at hearings."[3]

To be enforceable an agency rule must fall within the power Congress has conferred on the agency. When called upon to determine the validity of a challenged rule, a court must scrutinize "the statute [which authorizes the agency to act and to engage in rule-making] together with the underlying purpose of the act"[4] to see if the rule is consistent with the law and its purpose. It is the legislation and its purpose which must determine the content of agency rules and not the personal tastes, predilections, or ambitions of agency officials. An agency rule, having the effect of law, must be followed by the agency which promulgated it. Like a statute, it may not be disregarded or utilized at the whim of agency officials.

An agency engaged in the adjudication or order-making process is said to be acting in a quasi-judicial capacity. When so functioning it must proceed with its business in essentially the same fashion as a court since it is passing on the rights and duties of the parties to a controversy. The decision or order it hands down, unlike a rule or regulation, is binding only on the parties before the agency. The power to adjudicate, like the power to promulgate rules, must originate with legislative action. Absent congressional authority to undertake the order-making process, a federal agency has no power to do so.

The Fifth Amendment directs that "[n]o person shall be deprived of life, liberty, or property, without due process of law." While this limitation on governmental action is pertinent to all forms of agency proceedings, it is more often brought into play when agencies engage in adjudication than in rule-making proceedings.

Courts have refused to assign a precise meaning to the term "due process of law." They do not treat it as a technical concept. Jurists prefer to think of "due process" as a composite flexible stand-

3. Flying Tiger Line, Inc. v. Boyd (D.C. D.C.1965) 244 F.Supp. 889.

4. McMartin Industries v. Vinal (D.C. Neb.1969) 301 F.Supp. 749.

ard, ever in a state of flux, responsive to contemporary exigencies which confront individuals and society, in part molded by "history, reason, [and] the past course of decisions,"[5] in a large degree shaped by the nature of the particular proceeding in question and the consequences one may suffer should official action be taken against him.

When called upon to rule that "due process" requires a tribunal or an agency to abide by certain procedures prior to arriving at a decision adversely affecting one's life, liberty, or property, courts pose such queries as: Is the demanded procedure "among those 'fundamental principles of liberty and justice which lie at the base of all our civil and political institutions.' * * *; [is it] 'basic in our system of jurisprudence,' * * *; [is it] 'a fundamental right, essential to a fair trial,' * * *[?]"[6] If the response to any of these questions is yes, the Fifth Amendment requires a particular procedure be followed. Each of the following have been found to be an indispensable requisite of due process.

Notice. Should Congress wish to outlaw certain behavior or direct the performance of certain acts, it must so state in a statute which in a reasonable and meaningful fashion communicates to persons across the land what is and what is not demanded of them. When an agency promulgates a rule it must likewise inform within the context of its directive what must or must not be done. Copies of the acts of Congress are published and are available in law and public libraries. Federal agency regulations appear either in the Federal Register or the Code of Federal Regulations.

Persons who are parties to a court proceeding have a right to be notified as to its pendency and the matters before the tribunal. Prior to passing on the rights or duties or the guilt or innocence of an individual or enterprise, an agency, when acting in its quasi-judicial capacity, must reasonably and in a meaningful fashion advise one against whom it is proceeding as to the nature of the charges or issues to be adjudicated. The communication of such information is generally accomplished by the service of a complaint on the parties. The complaint must set forth the charges or issues that are to be decided.

A statute or regulation which is "so vague that men of common intelligence must necessarily guess at its meaning and differ as to its application * * *"[7] or which "leaves judges [or jurors or administrative officials] free to decide, without any legally fixed standards what is prohibited and what is not in each particular case"[8] violates the Fifth Amendment. A comparable test of reasonableness is used to

---

5. Joint Anti-Fascist Refugee Committee v. McGrath, 71 S.Ct. 624, 341 U.S. 123, 95 L.Ed. 817 (1951).

6. Duncan v. Louisiana, 88 S.Ct. 1444, 391 U.S. 145, 20 L.Ed.2d 491 (1968).

7. Baggett v. Bullitt, 84 S.Ct. 1316, 377 U.S. 360, 12 L.Ed.2d 377 (1964).

8. Giaccio v. Pennsylvania, 86 S.Ct. 518, 382 U.S. 399, 15 L.Ed.2d 447 (1966).

determine whether or not a complaint issued by an agency satisfies the Constitution.

Hearing. If arbitrary, capricious, or unreasonable adjudications by courts and agencies are to be avoided, it is essential that, except in those very rare instances when due to a dire emergency and the presence of an overwhelming compelling governmental interest immediate official action is required, that a hearing precede the taking of one's property; that the hearing be presided over by an impartial judge or hearing officer; that the affected person or enterprise have the opportunity to personally take part in the hearing, be permitted to introduce evidence and to confront and cross-examine those who give opposing evidence; that the prosecutor behave fairly; that the accused enjoy the opportunity to have the assistance of retained counsel; and that the judgment arrived at by the tribunal be supported by substantial evidence in the record.

Time of Hearing. In cases involving such things as the collection of taxes, the destruction of food unfit for human consumption, the seizure of mislabeled food, and the carrying out of anti-inflationary economic policy in time of war, it has been held that so long as there is available an "adequate opportunity * * * for a later judicial determination of the legal" [9] right of government to so act, government may proceed before the hearing is held. Official insistence that a hearing would slow down the speed with which government may take desirable action, would be burdensome and costly to the government, or would thwart the fulfillment of governmental policy does not excuse government from granting one a hearing prior to taking or destroying his or her property.

Impartial Hearing Officer. Hearing officers serve essentially the same function in an order-making proceeding as judges do in court proceedings. Each must treat fairly each party to the controversy, be impartial, disinterested, indifferent as to who wins and who loses, have no personal stake in the outcome, and be free from actual bias. A judge or hearing officer should recuse himself if there is present "a possible temptation to the average man as a judge * * * not to hold the balance nice, clear, and true." [10] Neither a judge nor a hearing officer should take part in a case in which he or she has aforehand decided upon the outcome.

Presence, Confrontation, and Cross-Examination. "Certain principles have remained relatively immutable in our jurisprudence. One of these is that where governmental action seriously injures an individual, and the reasonableness of the action depends on fact findings, the evidence used to prove the Government's case must be disclosed to the individual so that he has an opportunity to show that it is untrue. While this is important in the case of documentary evi-

9. Phillips v. Commissioner, 51 S.Ct. 608, 283 U.S. 589, 75 L.Ed. 1289 (1931).

10. Tumey v. Ohio, 47 S.Ct. 437, 273 U.S. 510, 71 L.Ed. 749 (1927).

dence, it is even more important where the evidence consists of the testimony of individuals whose memory might be faulty or who, in fact, might be perjurers or persons motivated by malice, vindictiveness, intolerance, prejudice, or jealousy. * * * [Courts] have formalized these protections in the requirements of confrontation and cross-examination. They have ancient roots. They find expression in the Sixth Amendment which provides that in all criminal cases the accused shall enjoy the right 'to be confronted with the witnesses against him.' * * * [Courts] have been zealous to protect these rights from erosion. * * * [They have] spoken out not only in criminal cases, * * *, but also in all types of cases where administrative and regulatory actions were under scrutiny * * *. Professor Wigmore, commenting on the importance of cross-examination, states in his treatise, * * *: 'For two centuries past, the policy of the Anglo-American system of Evidence has been to regard the necessity of testing by cross-examination as a vital feature of the law. The belief that no safeguard for testing the value of human statements is comparable to that furnished by cross-examination, and the conviction that no statement [unless by special exception] should be used as testimony until it has been probed and sublimated by that test, has found increasing strength in lengthening experience.' "[11] The Supreme Court has declared that "the right to confront and cross-examine witnesses is a fundamental aspect of procedural due process." [12]

Fair Prosecutor. An attorney, employed by the federal government as a prosecutor, must treat fairly one who is charged with the commission of an unlawful act. Speaking of the obligation of a United States Attorney, the Supreme Court has stated that he "is the representative not of an ordinary party to a controversy, but of a sovereignty whose obligation to govern impartially is as compelling as its obligation to govern at all; and whose interest, therefore, in a criminal prosecution is not that it shall win a case, but that justice shall be done. As such, he is in a peculiar and very definite sense the servant of the law, the twofold aim of which is that guilt shall not escape or innocence suffer. He may prosecute with earnestness and vigor—indeed, he should do so. But, while he may strike hard blows, he is not at liberty to strike foul ones. It is as much his duty to refrain from improper methods calculated to produce a wrongful conviction as it is to use every legitimate means to bring about a just one."[13]

One is denied due process if a federal or state prosecutor places in evidence in the course of a proceeding evidence he knows to be perjured in order to persuade the trier of fact of an accused's guilt.

11. Greene v. McElroy, 79 S.Ct. 1400, 360 U.S. 474, 3 L.Ed.2d 1377 (1959).

12. Jenkins v. McKeithen, 89 S.Ct. 1843, 395 U.S. 411, 23 L.Ed.2d 404 (1969).

13. Berger v. United States, 55 S.Ct. 629, 295 U.S. 78, 19 L.Ed. 1314 (1935).

Likewise, when a prosecutor deliberately suppresses evidence that is favorable to the accused, which evidence "is material either to guilt or to punishment, irrespective of the good faith or bad faith of the prosecution," the accused is denied due process.[14] The Supreme Court has pointed out that finding such behavior to be a denial of due process is not to punish "society for misdeeds of a prosecutor but avoidance of an unfair trial to the accused. Society wins not only when the guilty are convicted but when criminal trials are fair; our system of the administration of justice suffers when any accused is treated unfairly * * *. 'The United States wins its point whenever justice is done its citizens in the court.' "[15] Commenting on the prosecutor's role, it has been said that he "is an officer of the court, holding a quasi judicial position. '[H]is primary responsibility is essentially judicial—the prosecution of the guilty and the protection of the innocent.' "[16] Should it appear that a prosecutor has a personal stake in seeing to it that the accused is convicted rather than treated fairly, it is his duty to disqualify himself. His failure to do so constitutes a denial of due process.

Counsel. "What, then, does a hearing include? Historically and in practice, in our own country at least, it has always included the right to the aid of counsel when desired and provided by the party asserting the right. The right to be heard would be, in many cases, of little avail if it did not comprehend the right to be heard by counsel. Even the intelligent and educated layman has small and sometimes no skill in the science of law. * * * He is unfamiliar with the rules of evidence. Left without the aid of counsel he may be put on trial without a proper charge, and convicted upon incompetent evidence, or evidence irrelevant to the issue or otherwise inadmissible. He lacks both skill and knowledge adequately to prepare his defense, even though he has a perfect one. He requires the guiding hand of counsel at every step in the proceedings against him. Without it, though he be not guilty, he faces the danger of conviction because he does not known how to establish his innocence. If that be true of men of intelligence, how much more true is it of the ignorant and illiterate, or those of feeble intellect. If in any case, civil or criminal, a state or federal court were arbitrarily to refuse to hear a party by counsel, employed by and appearing for him, it reasonably may not be doubted that such a refusal would be a denial of a hearing, and, therefore, of due process in the constitutional sense."[17] Persons and enterprises have a right to enjoy the services of retained counsel in order-making procedures before almost all administrative agencies. If conviction of an indigent accused in a criminal case may result in his being confined to prison he has a constitutional right to have court assigned counsel

14. Brady v. Maryland, 83 S.Ct. 1194, 373 U.S. 83, 10 L.Ed.2d 215 (1963).

15. Brady v. Maryland, 83 S.Ct. 1194, 373 U.S. 83, 10 L.Ed.2d 215 (1963).

16. Ganger v. Peyton (4th Cir. 1967) 379 F.2d 709.

17. Chandler v. Fretag, 75 S.Ct. 1, 348 U.S. 3, 99 L.Ed. 4 (1954).

assist him. At present, unless an agency voluntarily undertakes to provide persons before it with an attorney, one has neither a constitutional nor a statutory right to compel the agency to provide counsel. One is denied due process if counsel, either assigned or retained, is incompetent. "[M]ere tactical or strategic errors in the handling of a * * * case, which become visible only in hindsight" do not raise a constitutional issue.[18] "In order to assume constitutional proportions, '[a] lack of effective assistance of counsel must be of such a kind as to shock the conscience of the Court and make the proceedings a farce and mockery of justice.' "[19]

Substantial Evidence in the Record. The decision handed down at the completion of a quasi-judicial administrative proceeding must be supported by substantial evidence in the record. The "record" consists of all of the testimony, documents, and other forms of proof presented to the trier of fact during the hearing. The requisite that the result be supported by evidence is intended to insure that there is a rational reasoned relationship between the evidence and the outcome. Absent such a relationship the ruling denies the unsuccessful party due process of law. Condemning a criminal proceeding in which a guilty verdict was not supported by the evidence, the Supreme Court said: "[I]t is as much a denial of due process to send an accused to prison following conviction for a charge that was never made as it is to convict him upon a charge for which there is no evidence to support that conviction."[20]

There is no mechanical scale nor electronic device nor litmus paper test which can be used to distinguish between substantial and less than substantial evidence. The weighing process is performed by the decision-maker's mental processes. He or she must make a qualitative and quantitative evaluation. The worth and the amount of the evidence must be determined. The outcome of the proceeding must be a reasonable product of the interaction of the evidence and the law.

"Substantial evidence has been defined innumerable times as more than a scintilla, but less than preponderance."[21] Scintilla has been defined as "[a] spark, a glimmer, a faint show of evidence." [22] Preponderance "means more than 'weight', it denotes a superiority of weight, or outweighing." [23] Substantial evidence may also be thought of as meaning that there was introduced "such relevant evidence as a

18. United States ex rel. Pugach v. Mancusi (S.D.N.Y.1970) 310 F.Supp. 691.

19. United States ex rel. Maselli v. Reincke (2d Cir. 1967) 383 F.2d 129.

20. Garner v. Louisiana, 82 S.Ct. 248, 368 U.S. 157, 7 L.Ed.2d 207 (1961).

21. Thomas v. Celebrezze (4th Cir. 1964) 331 F.2d 541.

22. Black's Law Dictionary.

23. Black's Law Dictionary.

reasonable mind might accept as adequate to support * * * [the] conclusion" arrived at by the trier of fact.[24]

The Fourteenth Amendment, which bars state and local governments from depriving persons of their life, liberty, or property without due process of law, requires that state and local courts and administrative agencies accord persons and enterprises the same sort of hearing and accompanying procedural safeguards as they are entitled to receive at the hands of federal courts and agencies under the Fifth Amendment.

SCHROEDER v. CITY OF NEW YORK

Supreme Court of the United States, 1962.
83 S.Ct. 279, 371 U.S. 208, 9 L.Ed.2d 255.

[Prior to commencing a condemnation proceeding to divert water from a river 25 miles upstream from where it crossed appellant's property the appellee published in the winter of 1952 once a week, for six weeks, a notice of the planned proceeding in the *City Record*, its official newspaper, and in two newspapers published in two small communities located in the general vicinity of appellant's property. In January 1953 it posted handbills containing like notice on trees and poles near her property. These steps satisfied the notice requirement set forth in the State's Water Supply Act.

Appellant used the property as a summer home, residing there only during the months of July and August. Neither the printed nor posted notices contained her name or address although this information could have been obtained from the deed records or tax rolls. The appellant did not learn of the appellee's action until the three year limitation the Act placed on the submission for damage claims expired. The trial court dismissed her action brought for money damages for the impairment of the river's value to her for bathing, swimming, fishing, and boating purposes, finding that the statute barred relief and due process had been satisfied. The state appellate courts affirmed. She appealed.]

Mr. Justice Stewart delivered the opinion of the Court.
 * * *

"An elementary and fundamental requirement of due process in any proceeding which is to be accorded finality is notice reasonably calculated, under all the circumstances, to apprise interested parties of the pendency of the action and afford them an opportunity to present their objections." * * *

24. Consolo v. Federal Maritime Commission, 86 S.Ct. 1018, 383 U.S. 607, 16 L.Ed.2d 131 (1966).

As was emphasized in Mullane the requirement that parties be notified of proceedings affecting their legally protected interests is obviously a vital corollary to one of the most fundamental requisites of due process—the right to be heard. "This right * * * has little reality or worth unless one is informed that the matter is pending and can choose for himself whether to appear or default, acquiesce or contest." The Court recognized the practical impossibility of giving personal notice in some cases, such as those involving missing or unknown persons. But the inadequacies of "notice" by publication were described in words that bear repeating here:

"Chance alone brings to the attention of even a local resident an advertisement in small type inserted in the back pages of a newspaper, and if he makes his home outside the area of the newspaper's normal circulation the odds that the information will never reach him are large indeed. The chance of actual notice is further reduced when as here the notice required does not even name those whose attention it is supposed to attract, and does not inform acquaintances who might call it to attention."

The general rule * * * is that notice by publication is not enough with respect to a person whose name and address are known or very easily ascertainable and whose legally protected interests are directly affected by the proceedings in question. * * *

* * * "[n]otice by publication is a poor and sometimes a hopeless substitute for actual service of notice," and that "[i]ts justification is difficult at best." * * *

* * * It is true that in addition to publishing in newspapers, the city in the present case did put some signs on trees and poles along the banks of the river. But no such sign was placed anywhere on the appellant's property, or ever seen by her. The posting of these signs, therefore, did not constitute the personal notice that the rule * * * requires.

The majority opinion in the New York Court of Appeals seems additionally to have drawn support from an assumption that the effect of the city's diversion of the river must have been apparent to the appellant before the expiration of the three-year period within which the statute required that her claim be filed. * * * But * * * knowledge of a change in the appearance of the river is far short of notice that the city had diverted it and that the appellant had a right to be heard on a claim for compensation for damages resulting from the diversion. That was the information which the city was constitutionally obliged to make at least a good faith effort to give personally to the appellant—an obligation which the mailing of a single letter would have discharged.

* * * reversed * * *.

CINDERELLA CAREER AND FINISHING SCHOOLS, INC. v. FEDERAL TRADE COMMISSION

United States Court of Appeals, District of Columbia Circuit, 1970.
425 F.2d 583.

[The respondent filed a complaint against the petitioner, charging it with violating the Federal Trade Commission Act because of its advertisements which offered a quick college education and airline hostess training. A hearing examiner held a lengthy series of hearings which consumed 16 days. He heard 52 witnesses and received 247 exhibits. The transcript was 1,810 pages in length. He ruled that the charges should be dismissed. Complaint counsel appealed and the full Commission reversed the examiner as to 6 of the original 13 charges and entered a cease and desist order. The petitioner appealed.]

TAMM, CIRCUIT JUDGE: * * * We are faced with two principal issues on this appeal: whether the action of the Commission in reversing the hearing examiner comports with standards of due process, and whether then Chairman Paul Rand Dixon should have recused himself from participation in the review of the initial decision due to public statements he had previously made which allegedly indicated pre-judgment of the case on his part.

* * *

In their final decision the Commissioners first criticized the hearing examiner for his handling of some of the testimony, stating that "[f]rom the initial decision it appears that the examiner ignored some of this testimony and some of it was given little or no weight because the examiner either questioned the credibility of the witness or considered their testimony hearsay." * * * The Commissioners themselves then proceeded to ignore all testimony completely: "[I]n view of our decision to independently analyze—and without assistance from consumer or other witnesses—the challenged advertisements and their impact * * * *it becomes unnecessary to review the testimony of these expert and consumer witnesses.*" (* * * emphasis added.) Later in the opinion they again noted that "for the reasons stated above *the Commission will rely on its own reading and study of the advertisements to determine whether the questioned representation has the capacity to deceive.*" (* * * emphasis added.) The hearing examiner in a Federal Trade Commission proceeding has both the right and duty to make determinations concerning the credibility of witnesses and the exclusion of hearsay evidence; while the Commissioners may review those determinations on appeal, in light of the record, they may not choose to ignore completely the testimony adduced at the hearing.

* * * Not only do we find this conduct on the part of the Commissioners a violation of their own rules and hence of due process, but we also seriously question their ability to make the determination called for without the aid of the testimony in the record. * * *

* * * We are unable to find any authority for their proposition—that a sixteen-day hearing may be completely ignored if the Commissioners are dissatisfied with the result reached by their hearing examiner. * * *

* * * We think it as preposterous for the Commission to claim a right to ignore that evidence and, with more daring than prudence, to decide a case de novo as it would be for this court to claim a right to ignore the findings of fact and conclusions of law of a district court in a proceeding here, substituting the judgment of this court on a cold record for that of the finder of the fact below.
* * *

Notice that the hearing examiner's dismissal of all charges would be appealed was filed by the Commission staff on February 1, 1968 * * *. On March 12, 1968, this court's decision was handed down in a prior appeal arising from this same complaint, in which we upheld the Commission's issuance of press releases which called attention to the pending proceedings. Then, on March 15, 1968, while the appeal from the examiner's decision was pending before him, Chairman Dixon made a speech * * * in which he stated:

What kind of vigor can a reputable newspaper exhibit? * * * How about ethics on the business side of running a paper? What standards are maintained on advertising acceptance? * * * *What about carrying ads that offer college educations in five weeks,* * * * *or becoming an airline's hostess by attending a charm school?* * * * *Granted that newspapers are not in the advertising policing business, their advertising managers are savvy enough to smell deception when the odor is strong enough.* And it is in the public interest, as well as their own, that their sensory organs become more discriminating. The Federal Trade Commission, even where it has jurisdiction, could not protect the public as quickly. (* * * emphasis added.) It requires no superior olfactory powers to recognize that the danger of unfairness through prejudgment is not diminished by a cloak of self-righteousness. We have no concern for or interest in the public statements of government officers, but we are charged with the responsibility of making certain that the image of the administrative process is not transformed from a Rubens to a Modigliani.

We indicated in our earlier opinion in this case that "there is in fact and law authority in the Commission, acting in the public interest, to alert the public to *suspected violations* of the law by *factual press releases* whenever the Commission shall have reason to believe that a respondent is engaged in activities made unlawful by the Act * * *." * * * This does not give individual Commissioners license to prejudge cases or to make speeches which give the appearance that the case has been prejudged. Conduct such as this may have the effect of entrenching a Commissioner in a position which he has publicly stated, making it difficult, if not impossible, for him to reach a different conclusion in the event he deems it necessary to do so after consideration of the record. There is a marked difference between the issuance of a press release which states that the Commission has filed a complaint because it has "reason to believe" that there have been violations, and statements by a Commissioner after an appeal has been filed which give the appearance that he has already prejudged the case and that the ultimate determination of the merits will move in predestined grooves. While these two situations —Commission press releases and a Commissioner's pre-decision public statements—are similar in appearance, they are obviously of a different order of merit.

* * *

The test for disqualification has been succinctly stated as being whether "a disinterested observer may conclude that [the agency] has in some measure adjudged the facts as well as the law of a particular case in advance of hearing it." * * *

* * * an administrative hearing "must be attended, not only with every element of fairness but with the very appearance of complete fairness," * * *

* * * the United States Court of Appeals for the Sixth Circuit was required to reverse a decision of the FTC because Chairman Dixon refused to recuse himself from the case *even though he had served as Chief Counsel and Staff Director* to the Senate Subcommittee which made the initial investigation into the production and sale of the "wonder drug" tetracycline. * * * Incredible though it may seem, the court was compelled to note in that case that:

[T]he Commission is a fact-finding body. As Chairman, Mr. Dixon sat with the other members as triers of the facts and *joined in making the factual determination* upon which the order of the Commission is based. *As counsel for the Senate Subcommittee, he had investigated and developed many of these same facts.*

* * *

The rationale for remanding the case despite the fact that former Chairman Dixon's vote was not necessary for a majority is well established:

Litigants are entitled to an impartial tribunal whether it consists of one man or twenty and there is no way which we know of whereby the influence of one upon the others can be quantitatively measured.

* * *

Vacated and remanded.

PROBLEMS

1. Would a federal statutory provision providing "the Administrator may issue such regulations as he deems necessary to carry out environmental policy as found in executive orders, legislation, and court decisions" constitute an improper delegation?

2. Would the following statute be constitutional? "In so far as environmental considerations are matters of public rather than private concern, and whereas adversary proceedings fail to adequately protect the public interest, a National Environmental Board composed of five environmental experts, appointed by the President, with the consent of the Senate, is hereby established. The Board is to make such rules as it deems necessary to protect the environment, with or without prior hearings. In all cases involving an alleged violation of a Board regulation, the Board may rely upon its expertise to arrive at a decision, whether or not the evidence presented to the Board supports the Board's conclusion."

3. An avid advocate of radical new approaches to environmental control and a recognized environmental activist was appointed state environmental administrator. His duties included rule-making and the review of determinations made by hearing officers. Defendant manufacturer objected to the administrator reviewing a decision handed down by a hearing officer in which he decided that a rule promulgated by the administrator violated the Fourteenth Amendment. From the administrator's reversal of the officer's decision, the defendant appealed. What judgment?

4. Defendant was sentenced to prison for illegally trafficking in radioactive material. In a *habeas corpus* proceeding he established that before his trial three federal officers had informed the prosecutor that they had "good reason to believe the defendant had been 'framed.'" The prosecutor had never informed the defendant or his attorney of what the officers had said. Opposing the petition, the prosecutor said he did not believe the officers and they were free to contact the defendant if they had wished to do so. What judgment?

5. Defendant was imprisoned after being found guilty of filing a false report about an oil spill. In a *habeas corpus* proceeding he alleged he had been denied due process because before sentence was imposed his court appointed attorney told the court: "This defendant should be dealt with severely. Otherwise others will be tempted to file false reports. Environmental legislation will be flouted." What judgment?

Chapter 5

JUDICIAL REVIEW

Administrative agencies functioning on all levels of government are entrusted with a crucial role in the planning, interpreting, policing, and application of diverse aspects of federal, state, and local environmental policies. Congress, state legislatures, and county and town councils establish environmental policy. Administrators and administrative agencies have the task of marshaling and supplying the requisite expertise; the making of rules; adjudicating the rights and duties of persons, enterprise, and government; and doing the sorts of things which must be done to effectively implement selected legislative policies.

Statutes prescribe the procedures agency officials must follow and the criteria they must employ in the performance of their duties. Consistent with legislative objectives, agencies may elaborate upon and refine legislatively designed procedures and criteria. So long as agency officials act in a constitutional fashion and in compliance with germane legislation, the rules and orders they make and the actions they may or may not take are enforceable within the framework of the legal system. Official behavior which violates the Constitution or fails to comply with pertinent legislative mandates is unlawful and so unenforceable within the framework of our legal system.

Legislatures seldom vest in an administrative agency exclusive, and perforce final, competence to serve as the ultimate arbiter of the propriety or impropriety of the behavior of an individual or an enterprise. By statute, under a variety of circumstances, and under stated conditions, persons, enterprises, or government, if dissatisfied with what an agency official has or has not done, may turn to the judicial system for relief. The process of a court passing upon the correctness of an official's or an agency's action is known as judicial review. When invoked, judicial review requires the judge or judges, sitting on the court which under law has jurisdiction to scrutinize the challenged behavior, to decide its lawfulness under constitutional, statutory, and decisional law, as well as agency rules.

The respective roles legislators assign to agencies and judges to facilitate the promotion and enforcement of legislative policies circumscribe the power of each of these actors within the framework of our legal system. Assumedly, administrative officials possess and continually enhance their expertise in those spheres of activity which have been entrusted to them by statute. Judges are most competent to rule on constitutional questions, various aspects of statutory construction, and decisional law. When problems call for answers which should be arrived at on the basis of unique information, when familiarity with a particular field can substantially contribute to the problem-solving process, or when an awareness of distinct demands and constraints can be helpful to the decision-maker, the judgment of non-judicial officers who are specially qualified to shed light on the questions at hand may be far superior to that of even the most learned of jurists. This variance of relative competence, in part the product of a legislative determination, in part founded on fact, severely circumscribes the extent to which courts may properly probe agency behavior when called upon to decide whether or not the complained of action should be affirmed or overruled.

When an environmental agency is involved in the adjudication process under federal, state, or local law it generally acts as an investigator, fact-finder, and decision-maker. Within the agency it is generally an examiner or hearing officer who initially hears and decides the controversy. His role resembles that of a trial judge who hears and decides a case in a non-jury proceeding. He deals with both law and fact. Like a trial judge, the hearing officer rules on the admissibility of oral, documentary, and other forms of evidence. Because of the nature of the duties assigned to agencies the rules governing the admissibility of evidence are not as technical or as restrictive as in criminal, quasi-criminal, or civil court cases. If a hearing officer were required to use the same standards as a trial judge, agency efforts directed at carrying out legislative policies frequently would be hampered. As the trier of fact, a hearing officer must pass on the credibility of witnesses and decide the value and the weight of the evidence. To arrive at his decision he may draw inferences from real and circumstantial evidence. His decision must be the product of a rational application of the law to the admissible evidence which he heard, read, or observed. Ideally, a hearing officer is free from agency influence. His duty is not to the agency as such, but to decide what did or did not happen and to then apply the law in a fair, impartial, and responsible manner.

Agency procedures ordinarily allow one who is dissatisfied with a hearing officer's decision to seek a reversal within the agency hierarchy. The person or enterprise may be permitted to appeal to either an official who has been designated as "Director" or "Administrator" of the agency or to a complement of top level agency officials, usually three or five persons, one of whom holds the title of "Chairman," the others each carrying the title of "Commissioner." In addition to their duty to serve as appeal officers, these persons may also be charged with the responsibility of making agency policy, promulgating agency rules, and overseeing the operation of the agency.

The power of a director or a body of commissioners, when acting as a reviewing panel, unless otherwise defined by statute, parallels that of an appellate court vis-à-vis a trial court. "Conclusions, interpretations, law, and policy * * * [are] open to full review [by the director or commissioners]. On the other hand, on matters which the hearing   *   *   *   [officer], having heard the evidence and seen the witnesses, is best qualified to decide, the   *   *   *   [reviewing body] should be reluctant to disturb his findings unless error is clearly shown.[1]

The decision arrived at by the director or commissioners may be challenged by the party in quest of a different result. If the statute governing appeals from the agency to an appellate court is satisfied, the case may now be removed from the domain of the agency and be transferred to the judicial arena. Statutes provide the nature of the review which may take place in the appellate court. Ordinarily, the court may not hear the case *de novo*. If it could, it would begin afresh and perform the very same tasks as the hearing officer. Such a procedure would probably be inconsistent with the reason why the agency was established and why the case was initially heard and decided within the agency. The appellate court does not accept any additional evidence. Commonly, the exclusive duty of the tribunal is to deal with the objections raised by the appealing party and to determine, on the basis of such objections, whether the Constitution, statutes, agency regulations, and other pertinent legal principles have been observed and whether the results arrived at by the agency are supported by "substantial evidence in the record." The hearing officer's findings of fact, in turn, must be predicated on the admissible evidence he received. The court must scrutinize the facts he found to see if they could be reasonably derived from the evidence presented. It must determine if the agency's conclusions are rational in light of the facts. If the court decides that there is in the record of agency proceedings " 'such relevant evidence as a reasonable mind might accept as adequate to support' " the conclusion arrived at by the agency, the agency's decision is said to be supported by "substantial evidence in the record" and is to be sustained.[2] In this regard it has been said that " '[t]he judicial function is exhausted when there is found to be a rational basis for the conclusion approved by the administrative body.' " [3]

To properly fulfill its function a reviewing court must have access to the evidence presented to the agency. This is generally done by requiring the appellant to supply the court with a record which contains in written form the testimony and copies of all of the documents presented before the agency. By probing the record the court can determine if the facts arrived at by the agency were supported by substantial evidence. The conclusions drawn by the agency are evaluated in light of the facts to see if they rationally follow from the

1. Universal Camera Corp. v. N. L. R. B., 71 S.Ct. 456, 340 U.S. 474, 95 L.Ed. 456 (1951).

2. Consolo v. Federal Maritime Commission, 86 S.Ct. 1018, 383 U.S. 607, 16 L.Ed.2d 131 (1966).

3. Rochester Telephone Corporation v. United States, 59 S.Ct. 754, 307 U.S. 125, 83 L.Ed. 1147 (1939).

facts found by the agency. To facilitate judicial review, statutes commonly provide that the hearing officer as well as other agency officials who took part in the fact-finding and decision-making process prepare findings of fact. In the absence of such a statute, should a court find that effective judicial review cannot take place without a statement by agency officials as to why they acted in the fashion they did, it "may require the administrative officials who participated in the decision to give testimony explaining their action" or allow them to prepare and deliver to the court written findings which "provide an adequate explanation for" their action.[4]

Questions that call for answers based on considerations about which an agency does not possess unique competence invite broader than usual judicial involvement. To resolve such questions courts may rely exclusively on their own judgment. When dealing with questions of law courts, not agencies, have paramount power. "On review the court may * * * correct errors of law and on remand the * * * [agency] is bound to act upon the correction."[5] When the meaning of a statute is in issue, a court may look to an agency for guidance, but it is the court which has the "ultimate responsibility to construe the language employed by" the legislature.[6]

Individuals or enterprises which are unsuccessful before an agency may be required to take such action, or refrain from taking such action, as the agency directs. If the directed behavior is reasonable and consistent with legislative policy, the appellate court will not disturb it. An agency may make its order sufficiently broad to insure that legislative policies are not violated. Courts generally defer to the expertise of the agency when an appellant objects to the action ordered by the agency. Judges do not substitute their judgment for that of the agency so long as the agency's directive is reasonably related to the facts as well as the legislative mandate.

When reviewing agency action, courts abide by the "judicial presumption of validity of administrative action, * * * the burden * * * [falling on the party who objects to what the agency has or has not done] to overcome that presumption."[7]

4. Citizens to Preserve Overton Park, Inc. v. Volpe, 91 S.Ct. 814, 401 U.S. 402, 28 L.Ed.2d 136 (1971).

5. Federal Communications Commission v. Pottsville Broadcasting Co., 60 S.Ct. 437, 309 U.S. 134, 84 L.Ed. 656 (1940).

6. Zuber v. Allen, 90 S.Ct. 314, 396 U.S. 168, 24 L.Ed.2d 345 (1969).

7. Udall v. Washington, Virginia and Maryland Coach Co., Inc., 398 F.2d 765, 130 U.S.App.D.C. 171 (1968).

GREAT LAKES SCREW CORPORATION v. NATIONAL LABOR RELATIONS BOARD

United States Court of Appeals, Seventh Circuit, 1969.
409 F.2d 375.

[On the 13th day of a 23 day hearing the trial examiner in a proceeding before the National Labor Relations Board excluded petitioner's chief counsel. The examiner found petitioner guilty of 56 violations of the National Labor Relations Act and recommended action be taken against it. The Board issued an order essentially adopting the examiner's findings and recommendations. Petitioner petitioned the Court to set aside the Board's order on the ground that the examiner's action constituted a denial of due process. The Board cross-petitioned for enforcement of the order.]

HASTINGS, SENIOR CIRCUIT JUDGE.   *   *   *

The Board's belated explanation for upholding the exclusion of counsel constitutes nothing more than mere conclusions unsupported by specific factual references to the record of the supposed contumacious and disruptive conduct of counsel.

     *   *   *

According to Board rule § 102.35, " *   *   *   no person will be precluded from being represented by the person of his choice, except in the case in which such representative has been contemptuous at a hearing *   *   *."

In reviewing judicial contempt orders, this circuit and others have espoused the view that mere conclusions of contempt, unsupported by specific facts or supporting citations to the record, carry no weight. *   *   *

     *   *   *   the Board has failed to render, with the required particularity its basis for finding propriety in the trial examiner's expulsion of counsel. Contemptuous behavior is the appropriate ground for excluding a person from the hearing. *   *   *   we conclude that counsel was wrongly excluded from the hearing.

The Administrative Procedure Act, *   *   *   provides:

"A person compelled to appear in person before an agency or representative thereof is entitled to be accompanied, represented, and advised by counsel *   *   *."

This right to counsel has been interpreted to mean the right to counsel of one's own choice. *   *   *

By excluding counsel without setting forth with sufficient particularity the basis for such action, the Board has substantially and prejudicially violated the Administrative Procedure Act. By denying petitioner his statutorily afforded right, administrative due process has been violated. *   *   *

    *   *   *   we are of the opinion that while counsel's conduct during the hearing was far from being the paragon of comportment, it did fall short of constituting contemptuous behavior. Consequently, we find counsel's expulsion to be unwarranted and therefore violative of petitioner's right to counsel as provided for by the Administrative Procedure Act.

    To constitute contemptuous conduct, there must be a clear showing that such conduct amounted to an obstruction of justice. We can not say from this record that counsel for the petitioner created such an obstacle here.

    *   *   *

    It would appear that in the heat of the proceedings the trial examiner mistook counsel's sometimes overzealous approach to the cause for contumacious behavior. This is an understandable error but is nevertheless prejudicial.

    *   *   *   the delay, expense and inconvenience inherent in setting aside the order of the Board and remanding the case to it for a new hearing is regrettable; however, the "avoidance of delay cannot justify a tolerance of violation of rights fundamental in the administration of justice." *   *   *

    Certainly the statutorily provided right to be represented by counsel of one's own choice is fundamental and has been violated by the unwarranted exclusion of counsel. It is impossible to soothsay what ill-effects this unwarranted exclusion may have had on the petitioner's case. Denying petitioner his chosen counsel may have had a prejudicially adverse effect on witnesses and inhibited succeeding counsel from fully advancing petitioner's position.

    It is axiomatic that if the order of the Board is found to be premised upon an unfair hearing then such order must be set aside and the case remanded to the Board for a new hearing. *   *   *

    Order Set Aside and Enforcement Denied. [Remanded for new hearing.]

BAUER v. REDWOOD COUNTY

Supreme Court of Minnesota, 1971.
185 N.W.2d 701, 290 Minn. 70.

[Appellants, along with other landowners, instituted a drainage proceeding under Minnesota Statute 106.081 by filing a petition with the county board requesting the establishment of a lateral ditch to drain lands specified in the petition. The board appointed an engineer who made a preliminary survey to determine the best route for the proposed ditch. His preliminary report included farm lands owned by petitioners but not specified in their petition. Later, when he determined that the tiling he had suggested in his report to protect petitioners' farm lands was inadequate he submitted a revised preliminary report which called for an extension of the proposed open ditch. Following a hearing, the board ordered a detailed survey. The engineer's final report, identical to his revised preliminary one, was adopted by the board. Appellants appealed to the district court, claiming that the engineer had made such substantial changes in the drainage plan proposed in their petition as to render the drainage proceedings invalid. The court affirmed the board's action. They appealed.]

PETERSON, JUSTICE. * * * It seems obvious that when landowners petition for the establishment of a drainage system, they do not know precisely what lands are within the watershed and should be drained, nor the most practicable course of the ditch, nor the most effective method of construction. The determination of these matters requires the special expertise and professional experience which the engineer has. Minn.St. 106.081 provides for it. To unduly restrict the engineer in making this determination would only frustrate the statutory purpose of the preliminary survey and report.

On the other hand, the statute does not give the engineer a roving commission to plan drainage improvements. Under the statute, the petition limits subsequent proceedings so that, while an engineer may modify the proposed plan for the purpose of providing the drainage requested, he may not substantially change the drainage plan. He clearly may not extend the survey to embrace lands not within the watershed of the lands described in the petition, "lest petitioners who may have intended and requested only a modest drainage project of a circumscribed marshy flat, awake to find themselves liable on their bond for the cost of an extensive survey of the hills and highlands of adjacent townships to be covered by tiled laterals."

State ex rel. Boetcher v. Nelson, and In re Judicial Ditch No. 9, although decided under earlier statutes governing drainage proceedings, are illustrative of the approach we have taken in these situations. In the former case, the petition proposed a main ditch of 11 miles in length, and the engineer extended this main ditch 7 miles in his report. The reason for the extension was to embrace all lands within the particular watershed; if this had not been done, the lands not within the project as petitioned would have cast their surplus waters down upon the drained land and thus have rendered the whole proceeding useless. We held that the extension was within the engineer's authority. In the latter case, the engineer included lands the drainage of which had no relation to the drainage of the lands in the petition other than that the water therefrom was to be discharged through the same outlet. We affirmed an order of the district court affirming the county board's refusal to establish the ditch.

The scope of judicial review, of course, is limited. * * * "in matters involving construction and improvement of drainage facilities a substantial amount of discretion must of necessity remain with the county board or other governmental body initially having jurisdiction over the matter." * * *

We cannot hold that the evidence, taken as a whole, furnishes no legal basis for the decision of the county board or that the engineer's preliminary survey and report constituted so substantial a change in the drainage plan proposed by the petitioners as to invalidate the drainage proceedings. The engineer merely modified the proposed plan to the extent necessary, in his expert opinion, to achieve the petitioners' drainage objective. It was deemed necessary to include other land within the watershed, although outside the area specified in the petition, to effect drainage from the land of petitioners, especially the lands of appellants. We must, in response to the stated principles relating to construction and improvement of drainage ditches, affirm the district court order.

Affirmed.

PROBLEMS

1. Four prosecution witnesses testified that the defendant had admitted to them that his plant was continuously discharging waste into the Rolo River. One of the four testified he had observed water being discharged into the river from the defendant's plant. Two of the defendant's witnesses stated they had observed the plant for a three week period and waste had not been discharged into the river during that time. Defendant testified likewise. The hearing officer dismissed the complaint, stating he did not believe the four witnesses, each being in the employ of one of the defendant's competitors. He said that the defendant's two witnesses, experts the defendant has specially employed to observe his plant, were "clearly reliable." On review, the administrator reversed, asserting that the testimony of the four witnesses "clearly outweighed" the evidence offered by the defendant. Defendant appealed. What judgment?

2. A statute provided that agency determinations "shall be reviewed by the superior court." On appeal, the appellant sought to submit to the court statistical data which, it insisted, established "beyond preadventure" that the agency determination was "clearly erroneous." The defendant had not offered to introduce the data in the proceedings before the agency. May the court take it into account?

3. The hearing officer, ruling against the defendant, stated: "One fact is certain. Someone was polluting the lake. There was no evidence that anyone other than the defendant was doing so. The defendant had every opportunity and reason to do so. The two expert witnesses called by the government stated that the pollutant 'probably emanated in the general area in which the defendant operated its plant.' It must be noted that the defendant failed to call any expert

witnesses on its behalf." Defendant appealed from the ruling. What judgment?

4. A court order dated April 1, 1972 directed the defendant to stop the emission of particles from its plant into the air no later than August 1, 1972. If the defendant wished to continue to operate the plant without halting the emission of particles between the date of the order and July 31, 1972 it was obliged to pay a $1,000 penalty for each day it did so. The order stated that the penalty was imposed to "incite a positive response." The relevant environmental control statute empowered a court to enter such orders as "may be necessary to carry out the act." The defendant appealed. What judgment?

Chapter 6

THRESHOLD OF JUDICIAL INVOLVEMENT

When a legislature establishes an environmental regulatory agency and endows that agency with rule-making power, or order-making power, or both, invariably it intends that the agency should, to the extent it is consistent with other vital considerations, be free from judicial intrusion until it has completed its delegated functions. Only after the agency has performed its duties may a court review its actions.

Legislatures usually express their intention to hold judicial review in abeyance pending culmination of agency action by providing that only "final" agency action may be reviewed. By barring judicial involvement until after the agency process had been completed full use can be made of agency expertise. Unwarranted delays in the administrative process can be averted when those who are parties to an administrative proceeding are required to await final agency action before they may resort to judicial review. If courts were permitted to intervene at any stage in agency proceedings at the behest of a dissatisfied party, the administrative process could unnecessarily be stalled and manipulated. An environmental control agency, for example, could be effectively stymied by a vigorous antagonist. Limitless opportunity to insist that a court evaluate each step in an agency proceeding could vitiate legislative environmental policy.

Courts, construing statutes governing their appellate jurisdiction, generally have held that agency determinations having to do with procedural matters are not "final orders" and therefore are usually non-reviewable. Illustrative of non-reviewable agency actions are the filing of a complaint by an agency or the holding of a hearing. Interlocutory determinations are generally not reviewable Such decisions are made in the course of an agency proceeding but do not mark the close of the proceeding. The fact that an agency labels an order interlocutory or final is not binding on a court. It is the court, rather than the agency, which has the power to ultimately decide whether or not agency action is final.

It has been said that "orders are ordinarily reviewable when 'they impose an obligation, deny a right or fix some legal relationship as a consummation of the administrative process.' Under this test, a final order need not necessarily be the very last order."[1] When convinced that in the case at bar an erroneous procedural or interlocutory order, if left standing, would cause an "irreparable" or "real, immediate, and incalculable" wrong that could not be rectified by judi-

1. Isbrandtsen Co., Inc. v. United States,
211 F.2d 51, 93 U.S.App.D.C. 293 (1954).

cial review and reversal following the close of the agency proceeding, a court will intervene and grant the complaining party relief.

Statutes generally provide that prior to seeking judicial review of an agency's actions one must first complete all of the available procedures open to him within the agency. Should the statute which governs an agency's procedures and judicial review not expressly impose such a requirement, a court will do so if it finds such an arrangement to be appropriate. The doctrine which treats as premature a request for judicial review when administrative procedures still remain open to one who is dissatisfied with what has already taken place before the agency, or is yet to take place, is known as exhaustion of administrative remedies. It serves to preserve the distinction between agency and judicial functions.

Legislation may provide that persons can seek relief before a specially constituted agency. It may be silent on the question of whether or not one desiring to bring legal action under such legislation can, if he wishes, by-pass the agency and proceed directly to the judicial forum. The possibility that a litigant may seek redress before one of two distinct bodies has given rise to the judicially created principle of primary jurisdiction. Under this principle a court is obliged to scrutinize the pertinent legislation to discern the intention of the legislature. If it concludes that the legislature intended that one seeking relief should initially institute action before the agency and only when the agency has completed its tasks might he seek judicial relief, then a litigant may not enter the judicial forum until he has first exhausted available agency procedures. The primary jurisdiction doctrine recognizes the desirability of making use of agency expertise and the probability that an agency is far better equipped than a court to evolve and apply a uniform body of pertinent legal norms in the furtherance of legislative policy.

WHITE LAKE IMPROVEMENT ASSOCIATION v. THE CITY OF WHITEHALL AND WHITEHALL LEATHER COMPANY

Court of Appeals of Michigan, 1970.
177 N.W.2d 473, 22 Mich.App. 262.

[Plaintiff, a non-profit corporation organized to represent the interests of its members, many of whom owned land abutting on White Lake, brought an action against the defendants to enjoin their discharging improperly treated wastes into the Lake. The trial court dismissed the complaint, finding that the plaintiff lacked standing to sue and, citing the State's Water Resources Commission Act, ruled that the doctrine of primary jurisdiction barred relief. The plaintiff appealed.]

LEVIN, JUDGE. The fight against pollution of natural resources has in recent times become a cause célèbre. Along with the increasing recognition of the importance of this effort, there has developed a feeling of futility when confronted with the overwhelming array of vested interests which are the often adventitious polluters.

* * *

Although we affirm the trial judge's dismissal of the complaint, we think that the plaintiff association is entitled to have its right to maintain this action clarified. The doctrine of primary jurisdiction does not preclude civil litigation; it merely suspends court action. The association may be entirely justified in proceeding with this litigation after it pursues its administrative remedy before the water resources commission.

"The doctrine of primary jurisdiction * * * governs only the question whether court or agency will *initially* decide a particular issue, not the question whether court or agency will *finally* decide the issue." * * *

"Court jurisdiction is not thereby ousted, but only postponed." * * *

* * * we are satisfied that the plaintiff association has an adequate interest to entitle it to maintain this action to the extent it seeks abatement of a private nuisance.

* * *

Section 7 of the act provides:

"Whenever in the opinion of the commission any person shall violate or is about to violate the provisions of this act, or fails to control the polluting content or substance discharged or to be discharged into any waters of the state, the commission may notify the alleged offender of such determination by the commission."

Section 7 then goes on to provide as to the form of the notice of a hearing, that "at such hearing any interested party may appear, present witnesses and submit evidence," and that the final order of determination of the commission shall be conclusive unless reviewed in accordance with the provisions of the administrative procedure act.

Section 8 of the act provides that "any person [who] shall feel himself aggrieved by the restriction of polluting content, waste or pollution, or any other order of the commission" has the right to petition the water resources commission for a public hearing with ultimate review through the courts under the administrative procedure act.

* * *

We agree with the defendant city that the association is an "aggrieved person" capable of challenging a commission order under section 8; it is likewise "interested" under section 7. * * *

The primary jurisdiction doctrine has been explained as follows:

"in cases raising issues of fact not within the conventional experience of judges or cases requiring the exercise of administrative discretion, agencies created by Congress for regulating the subject matter should not be passed over. This is so even though the facts after they have been appraised by specialized competence serve as a premise for legal consequences to be judicially defined. Uniformity and consistency in the regulation of business entrusted to a particular agency are secured, and the limited functions of review by the judiciary are more rationally exercised, by preliminary resort for ascertaining and interpreting the circumstances underlying legal issues to agencies that are better equipped than courts by specialization, by insight gained through experience, and by more flexible procedure."
* * *

To rule on the plaintiff's cause of action would require a court to duplicate the efforts of the water resources commission * * *. In order to achieve uniformity and consistency in this vital area, we think it would be wise for the courts to refrain from ruling on the merits of the association's claims at this time.

"The principal reason behind the doctrine of primary jurisdiction is not and never has been the idea that 'administrative expertise' requires a transfer of power from courts to agencies, although the idea of administrative expertise does to some extent contribute to the doctrine. *The principal reason behind the doctrine is recognition of the need for orderly and sensible coordination of the work of agencies and of courts.* Whether the agency happens to be expert or not, a court should not act upon subject matter that is peculiarly within the agency's specialized field without taking into account what the agency has to offer, for otherwise parties who are subject to the agency's continuous regulation may become the victims of uncoordinated and conflicting requirements." * * *

The association may administratively challenge the water resources commission's orders and then, if dissatisfied with the commission's disposition of its claim, it can obtain judicial review through the administrative procedure act. It may then again initiate an action in equity to abate the nuisance if it still feels itself aggrieved and entitled to equitable relief. * * * there does not appear to be a statute of limitations problem, there is no need to keep the present action pending in the interim.

* * *

In another case it might appear that immediate equitable intervention is necessary, that an administrative proceeding would not give the plaintiff the relief to which he is entitled. Or if the water resources commission refuses to act on a plaintiff's petition seeking relief, or if, before the applicability of the primary jurisdiction doctrine is asserted, judicial proceedings have advanced to a point where it would be unfair to remit the plaintiff to another and duplicative proceeding, a court of equity might well conclude that the proper administration of justice requires it to retain jurisdiction and itself to decide the matter. There are no absolutes, each case must be decided on its own facts.

We note the comprehensive powers of the water resources commission to regulate and prohibit pollution. The plaintiff association does not seek money damages; it expressly eschews a money recovery. It seeks only equitable relief and it may well obtain from the commission the relief which it seeks in this action and, perhaps, more complete and effective relief.

Affirmed. No costs.

McKART v. UNITED STATES

Supreme Court of the United States, 1969.
89 S.Ct. 1657, 395 U.S. 185, 23 L.Ed.2d 194.

[Petitioner, classified IV–A by Selective Service because he was "the sole surviving son of a family of which one or more sons or daughters were killed in action while serving in the Armed Forces of the United States" was reclassified I–A when his mother died. The local board decided that with the death of his mother the family unit had been terminated and he was no longer eligible for an exemption. When he refused to appear at a scheduled pre-induction physical he was declared a delinquent and was ordered to report for induction. He failed to report and was thereafter indicted for willfully and knowingly failing to report for induction. At his trial the petitioner's only defense was that he should have been exempted as a "sole surviving son." The District Court ruled that he could not raise the defense because he had failed to exhaust the administrative remedies provided for by the Selective Service System. He was convicted and sentenced to three years imprisonment. The Court of Appeals affirmed. Certiorari was granted.]

MR. JUSTICE MARSHALL, delivered the opinion of the Court.
* * *
We think it clear that petitioner was exempt from military service as a sole surviving son. * * *

The Government maintains, however, that petitioner cannot raise the invalidity of his I–A classification and subsequent induction order as a defense to a criminal prosecution for refusal to report for induction. According to the Government, petitioner's failure to appeal his reclassification after the death of his mother constitutes a failure to exhaust available administrative remedies and therefore should bar all judicial review. * * * we cannot agree.

The doctrine of exhaustion of administrative remedies is well established in the jurisprudence of administrative law. * * * The doctrine provides "that no one is entitled to judicial relief for a supposed or threatened injury until the prescribed administrative remedy has been exhausted." * * * The doctrine is applied in a number of different situations and is, like most judicial doctrines, subject to numerous exceptions. Application of the doctrine to specific cases requires an understanding of its purposes and of the particular administrative scheme involved.

* * * A primary purpose is, of course, the avoidance of premature interruption of the administrative process. The agency, like a trial court, is created for the purpose of applying a statute in the first instance. Accordingly, it is normally desirable to let the agency develop the necessary factual background upon which decisions should be based. And since agency decisions are frequently of a discretionary nature or frequently require expertise, the agency should be given the first chance to exercise that discretion or to apply that expertise. And of course it is generally more efficient for the administrative process to go forward without interruption than it is to permit the parties to seek aid from the courts at various intermediate stages. * * *

* * * The courts ordinarily should not interfere with an agency until it has completed its action, or else has clearly exceeded its jurisdiction. * * * This reason is particularly pertinent where the function of the agency and the particular decision sought to be reviewed involve exercise of discretionary powers granted the agency by Congress, or require application of special expertise.

Some of these reasons apply equally to cases like the present one, where the administrative process is at an end and a party seeks judicial review of a decision that was not appealed through the administrative process. Particularly, judicial review may be hindered by the failure of the litigant to allow the agency to make a factual record, or to exercise its discretion or apply its expertise. In addition, other justifications for requiring exhaustion in cases of this sort have nothing to do with the dangers of interruption of the administrative process. Certain very practical notions of judicial efficiency come into play as well. A complaining party may be successful in vindicating his rights in the administrative process. If he is required to pursue his administrative remedies, the courts may never have to intervene. And notions of administrative autonomy require that the agency be given a chance to discover and correct its own errors. Finally, it is possible that frequent and deliberate flouting of administrative processes could weaken the effectiveness of an agency by encouraging people to ignore its procedures.

In Selective Service cases, the exhaustion doctrine must be tailored to fit the peculiarities of the administrative system Congress has created. * * *

* * * We are not here faced with a premature resort to the courts—all administrative remedies are now closed to petitioner. * * * We cannot agree that application of the exhaustion doctrine would be proper in the circumstances of the present case.

* * * it is well to remember that use of the exhaustion doctrine in criminal cases can be exceedingly harsh. The defendant is often stripped of his only defense; he must go to jail without having any judicial review of an assertedly invalid order. * * * We must ask, then, whether there is in this case a governmental interest compelling enough to outweigh the severe burden placed on petitioner. * * *

The question of whether petitioner is entitled to exemption as a sole surviving son is, * * * solely one of statutory interpretation. The resolution of that issue does not require any particular expertise on the part of the appeal board; the proper interpretation is certainly not a matter of discretion. * * * the issue is different from many Selective Service classification questions which do involve expertise or the exercise of discretion, both by the local boards and the appeal boards. Petitioner's failure to take his claim through all available administrative appeals only deprived the Selective Service System of the opportunity of having its appellate boards resolve a question of statutory interpretation. Since judicial review would not be significantly aided by an additional administrative decision of this sort, we cannot see any compelling reason why petitioner's failure to appeal should bar his only defense to a criminal prosecution. There is simply no overwhelming need for the court to have the agency finally resolve this question in the first instance, at least not where the administrative process is at an end and the registrant is faced with criminal prosecution.

* * * in the present case, where there appears no significant interest to be served in having the System decide the issue before it reaches the courts, we do not believe that petitioner's failure to appeal his classification should foreclose all judicial review.

* * *

Reversed and remanded.

PROBLEMS

1. On June 1, 1971 defendant received a "notice of proceeding" informing it that the state environmental protection agency would hold a hearing at 9:00 a.m. on June 7, 1971 to determine if it was violating the state's wetlands control act. Defendant immediately made a written demand that the agency adjourn the hearing for three weeks so it could "adequately prepare a defense." The request was denied. At 9:00 a.m. on the 7th the defendant's attorney asked the

hearing officer for an adjournment on the ground that he had not had sufficient time to "adequately prepare" what he described as "a complete defense." His request was denied. If the attorney then left the hearing room, would a court sustain a ruling against the defendant based on evidence offered solely by witnesses called by the state? If after the hearing began over defendant's objection defendant's counsel promptly asked the superior court to enjoin the proceedings for three weeks so defendant could prepare its defense, would the request be granted?

2.   The defendant corporation asked a hearing officer to disqualify himself on the ground he owned stock of two of the defendant's competitors. He refused to do so, stating: "money cannot influence my decision. I am no man's man." Counsel for the defendant immediately petitioned the district court for an order enjoining the holding of the hearing. What judgment?

3.   Statute required that five days prior to a hearing the agency serve the defendant with a written statement detailing the charges against him. Two days before a scheduled hearing an agency official telephoned the defendant and told him he was prepared to read to him a statement of charges. He informed him that due to a shortage of personnel the agency had abandoned the use of written statements. The defendant refused to listen. He told the official that since the statute had not been complied with, he considered the hearing cancelled. When the defendant did not appear, the hearing officer proceeded to hear the government's witnesses. He entered an order revoking the defendant's permit to sell pesticides. The defendant appeals. What judgment?

Chapter 7

INTERVENTION AND STANDING

The question of who may and who may not demand to be heard by an agency or a tribunal is of critical importance in the formulation, alteration, evaluation, and application of environmental policy. A broad base of participation in the agency and judicial process permits a wide variety of conflicting points of view to be presented. A narrow base of participation curtails the spectrum of opinions which may be urged before an agency or a court. The scope of permissible participation is determined by the manner in which agencies and courts interpret the two closely related doctrines of intervention and standing.

The principle of intervention prescribes the circumstances under which an individual or an enterprise may present its position before an agency or a court when not initially joined as a party to the proceeding. Assume that the Federal Power Commission has under consideration a utility company's application requesting permission to build a nuclear power plant. An individual concerned with the preservation of natural scenic beauty and a conservationist group each desire to present evidence which, each insists, would establish that construction of the plant would entail inexcusable destruction of an area of great natural beauty. Whether or not the individual or the group has a right to be heard depends on whether or not each has a right to intervene. If each has such a right, then each may proceed to submit evidence to the agency and argue the merits of their respective positions.

Legislatures, in general terms, prescribe the class of persons who, although not initially included as parties to an agency order-making proceeding, may intervene. Such persons, classified as intervenors, have a right to be heard by the agency and to present evidence in support of their position. A statute may provide that an agency must hear "aggrieved parties" or persons "adversely affected" or "parties in interest." Courts interpret these terms in light of the purpose of the statute setting forth the agency's duties. If, for example, a statute directs that an agency (1) take into account environmental factors in the course of arriving at its decision and (2) hear "aggrieved parties," one who would personally suffer injury if such environmental considerations were not properly taken into account would have a right to be heard. He may intervene. A conservational group whose members would personally suffer injury could likewise intervene.[1]

---

1. Sierra Club v. Morton, 92 S.Ct. 1361,
405 U.S. 727, 31 L.Ed.2d 636 (1972).

One who wishes to make use of the judicial process may not do so unless the court is persuaded that he has "standing." Article III of the Federal Constitution enumerates the sorts of "cases" and "controversies" which may be heard by a federal court. This Article has been interpreted to mean that a federal court may not act as an advisory body. It may not respond to an inquiry in which the parties are simply seeking advice. The national judicial power may be used only when a court is asked to resolve a dispute between persons who have a personal stake in the outcome, have conflicting interests, and are each vying to convince the court of the superior merit of their own claim. A federal court will refuse to hear a case on the ground of lack of standing if it is persuaded that a party wishes nothing more than advice as to the state of the law, or has little or no interest in the outcome, or is engaged in a lawsuit with a party who nominally is at odds with him but in fact is not. Judges are fearful that in such cases the most desirable of the possible decisions may elude the court since the parties themselves will fail to adequately, forcefully, and concretely present their respective positions.

Persons or enterprises which may be deprived of property as a result of judicial action have standing. They are entitled to participate in the procedures which take place before the decision is made as to whether or not they will lose their property. Persons or enterprises which have a stake in the outcome of a proceeding pending before an agency have standing.

There was a time when courts narrowly defined standing. They equated it with the protection of one's life or liberty, or an economic interest. But a restrictive approach to standing ill serves today's society. There are groups, enterprises, and individuals who are concerned with priorities that are unrelated to traditional economic values. Environmental questions, for example, demand that standing have a flexible liberal meaning. The current approach views standing as a "practical and functional" concept "designed to insure that only those with a genuine and legitimate interest can participate in a proceeding." [2] Speaking of the sorts of things in which persons might have a genuine and legitimate interest, and therefore possess standing, the Supreme Court has said that in addition to economic values "interest, at times, may reflect 'aesthetic, conservational, and recreational' * * * values." [3]

The interest which gives rise to standing may have its source in the constitution, a statute, an agency regulation, or decisional law. Individuals have standing to challenge a denial of one of their constitutional rights. When a statute confers a right on a class of persons or enterprises those who fall within the protected class have standing

2. Office of Communications of United Church of Christ v. F. C. C., 359 F.2d 994, 123 U.S.App.D.C. 328 (1966).

3. Association of Data Processing Service Organization v. Camp, 90 S.Ct. 827, 397 U.S. 150, 25 L.Ed.2d 184 (1970).

to protect their statutory right. They may seek relief in the suitable forum, be it an agency or a court.

A complainant seeking judicial review may rely on a statute which he insists conferred upon him a statutory right which he is entitled to protect. To determine whether or not he arguably has a statutory right and therefore a right to invoke judicial review, a court must scrutinize the relevant statute to discern if the complainant falls "within the zone of interests protected by the [a]ct."[4] If the court concludes that it is *arguable* that he does have a statutory right it then must examine the law to decide if he does. Assume a portion of the Administrative Procedure Act is in question. The Act provides that "[a]ny person suffering legal wrong because of any agency action, or adversely affected or aggrieved by such action within the meaning of any relevant statute, shall be entitled to judicial review thereof."[5] If persuaded that the complainant *may* have a statutory right which he asserts was denied him, a court will grant him judicial review. Recognition of a possible right to judicial review is not synonymous with judicial vindication of the complainant's position. The granting of judicial review merely means that review will take place in accordance with the already discussed standards of judicial behavior. The court's ultimate decision might be to affirm, modify, or overrule what the agency has or has not done.

Indicative of the extent to which courts presently favor judicial review, the Supreme Court has said that "review of a final agency action by an aggrieved person will not be cut off unless there is a persuasive reason to believe that such was the purpose of Congress." Congressional intention to "restrict access to judicial review" is to be found "only upon a showing of 'clear and convincing evidence' of such an intent." Speaking of the judicial review provision embodied in the Administrative Procedure Act quoted above, the Court has asserted that the Act "manifests a congressional intention that it cover a broad spectrum of administrative action, and this Court has echoed that theme by noting that the * * * Act's 'generous review provisions' must be given a 'hospitable' interpretation."[6] This rubric requires "no explicit statutory provision * * * to confer standing."[7]

A number of courts have held that when an organization has manifested an "organizational interest" in protecting the environment it has standing.[8] For the present at least, the Supreme Court has rejected such an approach.[9] It has ruled that a group which has

4. Barlow v. Collins, 90 S.Ct. 832, 397 U.S. 159, 25 L.Ed.2d 192 (1970).

5. 5 U.S.C.A. § 702.

6. Abbott Laboratories v. Gardner, 87 S.Ct. 1507, 387 U.S. 136, 18 L.Ed.2d 681 (1967).

7. Hardin v. Kentucky Utilities Co., 88 S.Ct. 651, 390 U.S. 1, 19 L.Ed.2d 787 (1968).

8. Environmental Defense Fund, Inc. v. Hardin, 428 F.2d 1093, 138 U.S.App. D.C. 391 (1970).

9. Sierra Club v. Morton, 92 S.Ct. 1361, 405 U.S. 727, 31 L.Ed.2d 636 (1972).

manifested an interest in guarding the environment does not, *ipso facto*, enjoy standing. To satisfy the standing requirement a group must show that due to the challenged agency action its members will suffer personal injury. If the group simply takes the position that the public will suffer injury as a result of the agency action it does not qualify as an "aggrieved" as "adversely affected" person under the Administrative Procedure Act.

The Supreme Court has recognized that legislation may vest in individuals authority to commence a lawsuit to protect or promote a particular facet of national policy. When acting in this capacity the individual litigant is fulfilling a function ordinarily entrusted to the Attorney General. He is known as a private attorney general. The Supreme Court has ruled that to qualify as a private attorney general in a suit directed at agency action which supposedly has an unlawful adverse impact on the environment one must show that the action will cause him personal injury.[10] A private attorney general has standing only as a representative of the public interest. The only relief to which he is entitled is a judgment framed to protect or promote the public interest.[11]

Agency officials as well as others at times insist that a liberal approach to intervention and standing will impose so heavy a burden on agencies and courts that they will be unable to perform all of their essential duties. Courts have rejected this proposition. Judges insist that few persons are willing to bear the cost and endure the pain of litigation. They point to the fact that courts and agencies ordinarily possess sufficient power over their procedures so that they can formulate and enforce procedural rules which would allow interested persons to be heard and still permit agencies to adequately protect the public interest and carry out their tasks.

In general, state rules governing intervention and standing mirror those of the federal system.

––––––

SCENIC HUDSON PRESERVATION CONFERENCE, TOWN OF CORTLANDT, TOWN OF PUTNAM VALLEY AND TOWN OF YORKTOWN v. FEDERAL POWER COMMISSION AND CONSOLIDATED EDISON COMPANY OF NEW YORK, INC.

United States Court of Appeals, Second Circuit, 1965.
354 F.2d 608.

[Scenic Hudson, an unincorporated association composed of a number of non-profit, conservationist organizations, and the above named Towns, petitioned the Court to set aside three orders of the

10. Sierra Club v. Morton, 92 S.Ct. 1361, 405 U.S. 727, 31 L.Ed.2d 636 (1972).

11. Scripps-Howard Radio, Inc. v. F. C. C., 62 S.Ct. 875, 316 U.S. 4, 86 L.Ed. 1229 (1942).

Federal Power Commission, one of which granted a license to Consolidated Edison authorizing it to build a storage hydroelectric project known as Storm King. When completed the project would include a water storage reservoir fronting on the Hudson River, a powerhouse 800 feet long, and 25 miles of overhead transmission lines placed on towers 100 to 150 feet high located on a path up to 125 feet wide. The Commission contended petitioners lacked standing to obtain review.]

HAYS, CIRCUIT JUDGE: * * * The Storm King project is to be located in an area of unique beauty and major historical significance. The highlands and gorge of the Hudson offer one of the finest pieces of river scenery in the world. The great German traveler Baedeker called it "finer than the Rhine." Petitioners' contention that the Commission must take these factors into consideration in evaluating the Storm King project is justified by the history of the Federal Power Act.

The Federal Water Power Act * * * was the outgrowth of a widely supported effort on the part of conservationists to secure the enactment of a complete scheme of national regulation which would promote the comprehensive development of the nation's water resources. * * * It "was passed for the purpose of developing and preserving to the people the water power resources of the country."

* * *

"Recreational purposes" are expressly included among the beneficial public uses to which the statute refers. The phrase undoubtedly encompasses the conservation of natural resources, the maintenance of natural beauty, and the preservation of historic sites. * * * All of these "beneficial uses," the Supreme Court has observed, "while unregulated, might well be contradictory rather than harmonious." * * * In licensing a project, it is the duty of the Federal Power Commission properly to weigh each factor.

In recent years the Commission has placed increasing emphasis on the right of the public to "out-door recreational resources." * * * Regulations issued in 1963, for the first time, required the inclusion of a recreation plan as part of a license application. * * * The Commission has recognized generally that members of the public have rights in our recreational, historic and scenic resources under the Federal Power Act. * * *

Section 313(b) of the Federal Power Act, * * * reads:

"(b) Any party to a proceeding under this chapter aggrieved by an order issued by the Commission in such proceeding may obtain a review of such order in the United States Court of Appeals for any circuit wherein the licensee or public utility to which the order relates is located * * *."

The Commission takes a narrow view of the meaning of "aggrieved party" under the Act. The Supreme Court has observed that the law of standing is a "complicated specialty of federal jurisdiction, the solution of whose problems is in any event more or less determined by the specific circumstances of individual situations * * *." * * * The "case" or "controversy" requirement of Article III, § 2 of the Constitution does not require that an "aggrieved" or "adversely affected" party have a personal economic interest. * * * Even in cases involving original standing to sue, the Supreme Court has not made economic injury a prerequisite where the plaintiffs have shown a direct personal interest. * * *

* * * The Federal Power Act seeks to protect non-economic as well as economic interests. * * *

In order to insure that the Federal Power Commission will adequately protect the public interest in the aesthetic, conservational, and recreational aspects of power development, those who by their activities and conduct have exhibited a special interest in such areas, must be held to be included in the class of "aggrieved" parties under § 313(b). We hold that the Federal Power Act gives petitioners a legal right to protect their special interests. * * *

The * * * transmission lines are an integral part of the Storm King project. * * * The towns that are co-petitioners with Scenic Hudson have standing because the transmission lines would cause a decrease in the proprietary value of publicly held land, reduce tax revenues collected from privately held land, and significantly interfere with long-range community planning. * * * Yorktown, for example, fears that the transmission lines would run over municipal land selected for a school site, greatly decreasing its value and interfering with school construction. Putnam Valley faces similar interference with local planning and a substantial decrease in land tax revenues.

* * * case remanded for further proceedings.

OHIO v. WYANDOTTE CHEMICALS CORP.

Supreme Court of the United States, 1971.
91 S.Ct. 1005, 401 U.S. 493, 28 L.Ed.2d 256.

[The State of Ohio filed a motion for leave to file a complaint with the Supreme Court invoking the Court's original jurisdiction against three foreign corporations, incorporated respectively in Michigan, Delaware, and Canada. Ohio alleged that the defendants dumped mercury into streams whose courses ultimately reach Lake Erie, contaminating and polluting the Lake. It asked for a decree (1) declaring the dumping a public nuisance, (2) perpetually enjoining it, (3) requiring defendants to either remove the mercury from the Lake or to pay the costs of its removal, and (4) directing them to pay Ohio monetary damages for the harm done to the Lake, its fish, wildlife, and vegetation, and the citizens and inhabitants of Ohio.]

MR. JUSTICE HARLAN delivered the opinion of the Court.

*   *   *

That we have jurisdiction seems clear enough. Beyond doubt, the complaint on its face reveals the existence of a genuine "case or controversy" between one State and citizens of another, as well as a foreign subject. Diversity of citizenship is absolute. Nor is the nature of the cause of action asserted a bar to the exercise of our jurisdiction. * * * This Court has often adjudicated controversies between States and between a State and citizens of another State seeking to abate a nuisance that exists in one State yet produces noxious consequences in another. * * * In short, precedent leads almost ineluctably to the conclusion that we are empowered to resolve this dispute in the first instance.

*   *   *

As our social system has grown more complex, the States have increasingly become enmeshed in a multitude of disputes with persons living outside their borders. * * * the evolution of this Court's responsibilities in the American legal system has brought matters to a point where much would be sacrificed, and little gained, by our exercising original jurisdiction over issues bottomed on local law. This Court's paramount responsibilities to the national system lie almost without exception in the domain of federal law. As the impact on the social structure of federal common, statutory, and constitutional law has expanded, our attention has necessarily been drawn more and more to such matters. We have no claim to special competence in dealing with the numerous conflicts between States and nonresident individuals that raise no serious issues of federal law.

This Court is, moreover, structured to perform as an appellate tribunal, ill-equipped for the task of factfinding and so forced, in original cases, awkwardly to play the role of factfinder without actually presiding over the introduction of evidence. * * *

Thus, we think it apparent that we must recognize "the need [for] the exercise of a sound discretion in order to protect this Court from an abuse of the opportunity to resort to its original jurisdiction in the enforcement by States of claims against citizens of other States." * * * What gives rise to the necessity for recognizing such discretion is preeminently the diminished societal concern in our function as a court of original jurisdiction and the enhanced importance of our role as the final federal appellate court. * * *

Two principles seem primarily to have underlain conferring upon this Court original jurisdiction over cases and controversies between a State and citizens of another State or country. The first was the belief that no State should be compelled to resort to the tribunals of other States for redress, since parochial factors might often lead to the appearance, if not the reality, of partiality to one's own. * * * The second was that a State, needing an alternative forum, of necessity had to resort to this Court in order to obtain a tribunal competent to exercise jurisdiction over the acts of nonresidents of the aggrieved State.

* * * we do not believe exercising our discretion to refuse to entertain this complaint would undermine any of the purposes for which Ohio was given the authority to bring it here.

* * * History reveals that the course of this Court's prior efforts to settle disputes regarding interstate air and water pollution has been anything but smooth. * * *

The difficulties that ordinarily beset such cases are severely compounded by the particular setting in which this controversy has reached us. For example, the parties have informed us without contradiction, that a number of official bodies are already actively involved in regulating the conduct complained of here. * * *

Additionally, Ohio and Michigan are both participants in the Lake Erie Enforcement Conference, * * * And the International Joint Commission, established by the Boundary Waters Treaty of 1909 between the United States and Canada, * * * issued on January 14, 1971, a comprehensive report, * * *. That document makes specific recommendations for joint programs to abate these environmental hazards * * *.

* * * It can fairly be said that what is in dispute is not so much the law as the facts. And the factfinding process we are asked to undertake is, to say the least, formidable.

* * * Indeed, Ohio is raising factual questions that are essentially ones of first impression to the scientists. * * *

* * * It is vitally important to stress that we are not called upon by this lawsuit to resolve difficult or important problems of federal law and that nothing in Ohio's complaint distinguishes it from any one of a host of such actions that might, with equal justification, be commenced in this Court. Thus, entertaining this complaint not only would fail to serve those responsibilities we are principally charged with, but could well pave the way for putting this Court into a quandary whereby we must opt either to pick and choose arbitrarily among similarly situated litigants or to devote truly enormous portions of our energies to such matters.

To sum up, this Court has found even the simplest sort of interstate pollution case an extremely awkward vehicle to manage. And this case is an extraordinarily complex one both because of the novel scientific issues of fact inherent in it and the multiplicity of governmental agencies already involved. * * *

What has been said here cannot, of course, be taken as denigrating in the slightest the public importance of the underlying problem Ohio would have us tackle. Reversing the increasing contamination of our environment is manifestly a matter of fundamental import and utmost urgency. What is dealt with above are only considerations respecting the appropriate role this Court can assume in efforts to eradicate such environmental blights. We mean only to suggest that our competence is necessarily limited, not that our concern should be kept within narrow bounds.

Ohio's motion for leave to file its complaint is denied without prejudice to its right to commence other appropriate judicial proceedings.

Motion denied.

PROBLEMS

1. An association of married women petitioned for leave to intervene in a proceeding before the Atomic Energy Commission in which the safety of a proposed nuclear power plant was in issue. It wished to submit evidence that the plant would pose a danger to the life of persons yet to be born. What decision?

2. An association of women who believed in the nursing of infants demanded to be heard in a proceeding before the Environmental Protection Agency involving a proposed cancellation of a pesticide registration certificate. The association insisted that the pesticide in question constituted a threat to the survival of various species of wildlife. Does the association have a right to be heard?

3. A state's wetland control act provided that in instances in which the designated state agency decided it was in the public interest to protect a wetland area it could refuse to issue a permit authorizing the use of such land for home sites. The leading money lending institution in the community in which a large wetland area was located petitioned to intervene in a proceeding before the agency in which conservational groups were insisting that the wetland area should be left in its natural state. The institution predicated its right to be heard on the ground that the denial of use permits would keep out of the mortgage market at least 150 prospective home purchasers who would be in quest of mortgages if permitted to build a home. What judgment?

4. An air filter manufacturer submitted to a state agency a request for an award of state funds under a state program intended to underwrite the design of a new air filter. A competitor not interested in taking part in the state program petitioned the agency for permission to introduce evidence to establish that the manufacturer asking for state funds lacked sufficient expertise to develop a new filter and due to severe financial losses was destined to shortly go out of business. What judgment?

5. An association organized to protect consumers from fraudulent and misleading advertising asked for leave to be heard in a proceeding pending before the Federal Communications Commission in which the Commission was to decide whether or not the license of a television broadcaster was to be renewed. What judgment?

Part Three

AREAS AND MODES OF REGULATION

Chapter 8

NATIONAL ENVIRONMENTAL POLICY ACT

The stated purposes of the National Environmental Policy Act of 1969 [1] are: "[t]o declare a national policy which will encourage productive and enjoyable harmony between man and his environment; to promote efforts which will prevent or eliminate damage to the environment and biosphere and stimulate the health and welfare of man; to enrich the understanding of the ecological systems and natural resources to the Nation; and to establish a Council on Environmental Quality."[2] Addressing itself to the reasons why it passed the Act, Congress asserted that it had reacted to recognition of "the profound impact of man's activity on the interrelations of all components of the natural environment, particularly the profound influences of population growth, high-density urbanization, industrial expansion, resource exploitation, and new and expanding technological advances and * * * the critical importance of restoring and maintaining environmental quality to the overall welfare and development of man." Expressly, the national legislature declared "that it is the continuing policy of the Federal Government, in cooperation with State and local governments, and other concerned public and private organizations, to use all practicable means and measures, including financial and technical assistance, in a manner calculated to foster and promote the general welfare, to create and maintain conditions under which man and nature can exist in productive harmony, and fulfill the social, economic, and other requirements of present and future generations of Americans."[3]

"[T]o carry out the [stated] policy" Congress announced "that it is the continuing responsibility of the Federal Government to use all practicable means, consistent with other essential considerations of national policy, to improve and coordinate Federal plans, functions, programs, and resources to the end that the Nation may— (1) fulfill the responsibilities to each generation as trustee of the environment for succeeding generations; (2) assure for all Americans

1. Pub.L. 91–190, 83 Stat. 852.

2. 42 U.S.C.A. § 4321.

3. 42 U.S.C.A. § 4331(a).

safe, healthful, productive, and esthetically and culturally pleasing surroundings; (3) attain the widest range of beneficial uses of the environment without degradation, risk to health or safety, or other undesirable and unintended consequences; (4) preserve important historic, cultural, and natural aspects of our national heritage, and maintain, wherever possible, an environment which supports diversity and variety of individual choice; (5) achieve a balance between population and resource use which will permit high standards of living and a wide sharing of life's amenities; and (6) enhance the quality of renewable resources and approach the maximum attainable recycling of depletable resources." Congress further stated that it recognized "that each person should enjoy a healthful environment and that each person has a responsibility to contribute to the preservation and enhancement of the environment."[4]

Appreciative of the need that all segments of the national government pay attention to environmental considerations Congress authorized and directed "that, to the fullest extent possible: (1) the policies, regulations, and public laws of the United States * * * [be] interpreted and administered in accordance with the policies set forth in * * * [the Act], and (2) all agencies of the Federal Government * * * [should]—(A) utilize a systematic, interdisciplinary approach which will insure the integrated use of the natural and social sciences and the environmental design arts in planning and in decisionmaking which may have a[n] impact on man's environment; (B) identify and develop methods and procedures, in consultation with the Council on Environmental Quality * * *, which will insure that presently unquantified environmental amenities and values may be given appropriate consideration in decisionmaking along with economic and technical considerations; (C) include in every recommendation or report on proposals for legislation and other major Federal actions significantly affecting the quality of the human environment, a detailed statement by the responsible official on (i) the environmental impact of the proposed action, (ii) any adverse environmental effects which cannot be avoided should the proposal be implemented, (iii) alternatives to the proposed action, (iv) the relationship between local short-term uses of man's environment and the maintenance and enhancement of long-term productivity, and (v) any irreversible and irretrievable commitments of resources which would be involved in the proposed action should it be implemented." Before preparing the required statement the "responsible Federal official" is required to "consult with and obtain the comments of any Federal agency which has jurisdiction by law or special expertise with respect to any environmental impact involved. Copies of" statements together with "the comments and views of the appro-

4. 42 U.S.C.A. § 4331(b).

priate Federal, State, and local agencies, which are authorized to develop and enforce environmental standards," must "be made available to the President, the Council on Environmental Quality and to the public * * *, and * * * [must] accompany the proposal through the existing agency review process."   In those cases in which an agency proposal "involves unresolved conflicts concerning alternative uses of available resources" the agency is required to "study, develop, and describe appropriate alternatives to [its] recommended courses of action."[5]

Seeking to insure that Federal agencies view environmental considerations in the broadest possible perspective, Congress directed that they "recognize the worldwide and long-range character of environmental problems and, where consistent with the foreign policy of the United States, lend appropriate support to initiatives, resolutions, and programs designed to maximize international cooperation in anticipating and preventing a decline in the quality of mankind's world environment; * * * make available to States, counties, municipalities, institutions, and individuals, advice and information useful in restoring, maintaining, and enhancing the quality of the environment; * * * initiate and utilize ecological information in the planning and development of resource-oriented projects; and * * * assist the Council on Environmental Quality * * * [to carry out its assigned duties.]"[6]   Federal agencies are directed to review "their * * * statutory authority, * * * regulations, and current policies and procedures * * * [to determine] whether there are any deficiencies or inconsistencies therein which prohibit full compliance with the purposes and provisions of * * * [the Act] and * * * [they must] propose to the President * * * [by July 1, 1971], such measures as may be necessary to bring their authority and policies into conformity with the intent, purpose, and procedures" of the Act.[7]   Congress expressly made "[t]he policies and goals" of the Act "supplementary to those set forth in existing authorizations of Federal agencies."[8]

The President is required to "transmit to the Congress annually beginning July 1, 1970, an Environmental Quality Report * * * [setting] forth (1) the status and condition of the major natural, manmade, or altered environmental classes of the Nation, including, but not limited to, the air, the aquatic, including marine, estuarine, and fresh water, and the terrestial environment, including but not limited to, the forest, dryland, wetland, range, urban, suburban, and rural environment; (2) current and foreseeable trends in the quality, management and utilization of such environments and the effects of

5. 42 U.S.C.A. § 4332.   7. 42 U.S.C.A. § 4333.

6. 42 U.S.C.A. § 4332.   8. 42 U.S.C.A. § 4335.

those trends on the social, economic, and other requirements of the Nation; (3) the adequacy of available natural resources for fulfilling human and economic requirements of the Nation in the light of expected population pressures; (4) a review of the programs and activities (including regulatory activities) of the Federal Government, the State and local governments, and nongovernmental entities or individuals, with particular reference to their effect on the environment and on the conservation, development and utilization of natural resources; and (5) a program for remedying the deficiencies of existing programs and activities, together with recommendations for legislation."[9]

The Act establishes a three member Council on Environmental Quality. "Each member * * * [must] be a person who, as a result of his training, experience, and attainments, is exceptionally well qualified to analyze and interpret environmental trends and information of all kinds; to appraise programs and activities of the Federal Government in the light of the [Act's] policy * * *; to be conscious of and responsive to the scientific, economic, social, esthetic, and cultural needs and interests of the Nation; and to formulate and recommend national policies to promote the improvement of the quality of the environment."[10] The Council's duties and functions are: "(1) to assist and advise the President in the preparation of * * * [his annual] Environmental Quality Report; (2) to gather timely and authoritative information concerning the conditions and trends in the quality of the environment both current and prospective, to analyze and interpret such information for the purpose of determining whether such conditions and trends are interfering, or are likely to interfere, with the achievement of the * * * [Act's policy]; and to compile and submit to the President studies relating to such conditions and trends; (3) to review and appraise the various programs and activities of the Federal Government in the light of the policy set forth in [the Act] * * * for the purpose of determining the extent to which such programs and activities are contributing to the achievement of such policy, and to make recommendations to the President with respect thereto; (4) to develop and recommend to the President national policies to foster and promote the improvement of environmental quality to meet the conservation, social, economic, health, and other requirements and goals of the Nation; (5) to conduct investigations, studies, surveys, research, and analyses relating to ecological systems and environmental quality; (6) to document and define changes in the natural environment, including the plant and animal systems, and to accumulate necessary data and other information for a continuing analysis of these changes or trends

9. 42 U.S.C.A. § 4341.   10. 42 U.S.C.A. § 4342.

and an interpretation of their underlying causes; (7) to report at least once each year to the President on the state and condition of the environment; and (8) to make and furnish such studies, reports thereon, and recommendations with respect to matters of policy and legislation as the President may request."[11]

Executive Order 11472, dated May 29, 1969, established a fifteen member Citizen's Advisory Committee on Environmental Quality to advise the President and the Council on a variety of environmental problems. The Council is obliged to "consult with the" Committee and "with such representatives of science, industry, agriculture, labor, conservation organizations, State and local governments and other groups, as it deems advisable."

On July 9, 1970 the President submitted to Congress Reorganization Plan No. 3 of 1970.[12] The plan took effect on December 2, 1970. It established the Environmental Protection Agency. The title of the Agency's director is "Administrator." In the President's message which accompanied the Plan the President pointed out that "[t]he Government's environmentally-related activities * * * [had] grown up piecemeal over the years. [He believed that it was time] * * * to organize them rationally and systematically. As a major step in this direction," he said, he was using the power conferred upon him to create the new Agency and to vest in it a variety of powers until then held by several different agencies. The Plan enumerated the powers transferred from other agencies to the new agency. Included in the areas of Agency competence are protection of water quality, studying and registering pesticides, air quality control, solid waste management, the carrying on of "studies relating to ecological systems," which prior to the message had been entrusted to the Council on Environmental Quality, and a number of "functions respecting radiation criteria and standards" theretofore "vested in the Atomic Energy Commission and the Federal Radiation Council." The President declared that "[w]ith its broad mandate * * * [the Agency] would also develop competence in areas of environmental protection that * * * [had] not previously been given enough attention, such, for example, as the problem of noise, and it would provide an organization to which new programs in these areas could be added."[13]

The following is the Table of Organization of the Environmental Protection Agency. It should be noted that distinct offices exist within the Agency to handle those environmental problems which are

11. 42 U.S.C.A. § 4344.

12. 35 Fed.Reg. 15623.

13. Congressional and Administrative News, 91st Congress, 2d Session (1970) Volume 3, p. 6330.

its prime concern. In succeeding chapters the Agency's role in each of these areas will be examined.

ENVIRONMENTAL PROTECTION AGENCY

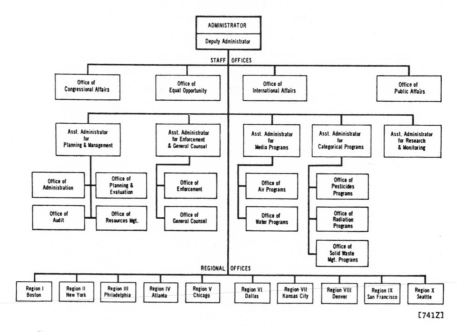

[741Z]

Source:
U. S. Government Organization Manual 1971/72

PENNSYLVANIA ENVIRONMENTAL COUNCIL, INC. v. BARTLETT

United States District Court, M.D. Pennsylvania, 1970.
315 F.Supp. 238.

[In the mid-1960's the Pennsylvania Highway Commission approved a proposal to improve a 5.1 mile stretch of Route 872. In May 1967 advertisements were placed in a local newspaper advising interested persons of the plan and informing readers that a hearing could be requested. No requests were made. Thereafter the State Highway Department consulted with other interested State agencies, most approving the plan by January 1969. In February 1969 one of the plaintiffs advised the Highway Commission that he opposed the plan. Later other plaintiffs did likewise. In October 1969 the Highway Department filed an application with the Secretary of Transportation of the United States for his approval of the plan. On November 20, 1969, with all interested State agencies now approving the construction, he approved the plan. The defendant awarded construction contracts on December 29, 1969. Work began in February 1970. On March 31, 1970 the plaintiffs brought an action to enjoin the construction.]

NEALON, DISTRICT JUDGE. * * * The Pennsylvania Secretary of Highways and the United States Secretary of Transportation have raised the equitable defense of laches in asserting that plaintiffs are not entitled to the injunctive relief sought. * * *

Laches is determined in the light of all the existing circumstances and requires that the delay be unreasonable and cause prejudice to the adversary. * * * The mere lapse of time is not sufficient to constitute laches. * * * In the circumstances of this case, I cannot find with absolute certainty that the plaintiffs knowingly slept on their rights. Granted that suit was not begun by plaintiffs until ninety days after the awarding of the construction contracts, but this is not the kind of deliberate delay with which we are normally confronted in laches situations. * * * there is simply no evidence of prejudice to the United States Secretary of Transportation or to the Secretary of Highways by whatever delay may have occurred in the filing of this suit. * * * I conclude that the defense of laches cannot be sustained on the present record.

* * *

The National Environmental Policy Act of 1969 was passed by the United States Senate on December 20, 1969, and the House of Representatives on December 22, 1969, and became effective on January 1, 1970. All of the planning for the improvement of Route 872 occurred prior to this time. The contract, in fact, was awarded on December 29, 1969. Thus, all that remained on January 1, 1970, was the actual construction of the improved Route 872. Should the National Environmental Policy Act of 1969 now be applied in a retroactive manner so as to hold the United States Secretary of Transportation to the principles enunciated therein?

* * * " 'the first rule of construction is that legislation must be considered as addressed to the future, not to the past * * * [and] a retrospective operation will not be given to a statute which interferes with antecedent rights * * * unless such be "the unequivocal and inflexible import of the terms, and the manifest intention of the legislature." ' " * * *

In my opinion, the most reasonable interpretation that can be given to the legislative history of the Act is that there is no manifest Congressional intention or unequivocal and inflexible import in the language used to indicate that the Act should be applied retroactively. * * * I conclude that the National Environmental Policy Act of 1969 was not designed by Congress to be given retroactive application. Since the contract here in question was awarded and finalized prior to the Act's passage no violation of the Act occurred on the part of the Secretary of Transportation.

Assuming arguendo, that retroactive application of the National Environmental Policy Act of 1969 is necessary   *   *   *   we will proceed to discuss this case on its merits. The Act, made effective January 1, 1970, declared:

"a national policy which will encourage productive and enjoyable harmony between man and his environment; to promote efforts which will prevent or eliminate damage to the environment and biosphere" * * *

This Statute properly demonstrates Governmental concern over the damage that man has inflicted, and continues to inflict, on the environment.   *   *   *   the Act proclaimed it to be "the continuing responsibility of the Federal Government to use all practicable means, consistent with other essential considerations of national policy, *   *   *.

   *   *   *   plaintiffs assert that the Secretary of Transportation approved the Pennsylvania Highways Department application *   *   *   relying on various certificates which were submitted to him, and did not make an independent and affirmative determination of the effect of this project on the environment. According to plaintiffs, the Secretary, in failing to make such a determination, violated his statutory responsibility "to use all practicable means" to protect the environment. The evidence in this case indicates that the Secretary of Transportation does not make an independent study of plans for secondary highways, but delegates that responsibility to the State Highways Department pursuant to 23 U.S.C. § 117(a),   *   *   *.

   *   *   *   A requirement that the Secretary of Transportation must make independent and affirmative evaluations of all phases of the multitude of State secondary highway projects relative to their impact on the environment not only would place a staggering burden on the Secretary, but also would cause him to duplicate State investigations and determinations. The purpose of the National Environmental Policy Act of 1969 is laudatory and urgently necessary, but I am satisfied that Congress did not intend it to necessitate Secretarial action of the import urged by plaintiffs.

   *   *   *

Plaintiffs are not entitled to injunctive relief.

Plaintiffs' complaint is dismissed.

PROBLEMS

1. NEPA [14] requires federal agencies to "utilize a systematic interdisciplinary approach   *   *   *   in planning and decision-making which may have a[n] impact on man's environment." Under this

14. NEPA is the acronym for The National Environmental Policy Act.

directive, would it be appropriate for an agency to establish regulations exclusively on the basis of the opinion of a small number of environmental experts of the agency's choosing without first hearing experts who vehemently oppose such regulations?

2.   NEPA calls upon federal agencies to "balance between population and resource use which will permit high standards of living and a wide sharing of life's amenities." Would the Department of Housing and Urban Development violate NEPA if it conditioned the granting of funds to a recipient on his constructing dwellings solely for childless married persons? The agency explained its action as a benign response to the need to cope with a burgeoning population which, if not controlled, would be detrimental to "high standards of living and a wide sharing of life's amenities."

3.   NEPA does not assign stated weights to any of the considerations it directs agency officials to take into account in their decision-making. Would it be consistent with the Act's purposes if an agency established a schedule of assigned weights for each factor found in the Act? Would *ad hocacy* or an established schedule best promote effective judicial enforcement of NEPA?

4.   How can a court determine whether or not an agency has satisfied NEPA's requirements that proper attention has been paid to environmental factors without proceeding *de novo*? Is the "substantial evidence" test adequate?

5.   The "fairness doctrine" enforced by the Federal Communications Commission requires a holder of a television or radio license who has aired a sponsor's point of view on one side of a controversial issue of public concern to allow, without charge, responsible persons to present an opposing point of view. An environmental group requested a television broadcaster to make free time available for announcements calling attention to the air pollution caused by automobiles and the combustion of gasoline after the licensee had aired automobile and gasoline commercials. Must the request be honored? An environmental group demanded free time to present its point of view as to the damage a proposed oil pipeline in Alaska would cause after the licensee had aired an advertisement which asserted that the pipeline would do little environmental damage. Should the request be granted? Does a licensee have a constitutional duty to accept paid one sided announcements on a controversial issue of public concern?

Chapter 9

AIR

Scientists long ago made man aware of the fact that if life is to continue the envelope of air which surrounds our planet must be composed of a biologically suitable mix. If the critical balance of the air's gases were upset or the air were to become so filled with deleterious substances as to either disrupt the conditions essential for life or put an end to critical life sustaining processes, *homo sapiens* as we know this species could no longer inhabit the earth. During the 1960's law-makers generally grew leery of the law's effectiveness as a protector of the air. Voluntary individual and enterprise behavior fell short of the sort of things they believed had to be done to preserve the air's critical mix. They opted for a new approach. By the end of the 1960's a plethora of federal, state, and local air control laws had been passed. They were designed to compel action necessary to shield the air from future damage. These laws do not constitute the last word from the nation's legislators. They are but guideposts along a long yet to be tread path of governmental regulation keyed to protecting the earth's atmosphere from destruction. A great deal more remains to be done. In the Clean Air Act [1] Congress asserted that it found "(1) that the predominant part of the Nation's population is located in its rapidly expanding metropolitan and other urban areas, which generally cross the boundary lines of local jurisdictions and often extend into two or more States; (2) that the growth in the amount and complexity of air pollution brought about by urbanization, industrial development, and the increasing use of motor vehicles, has resulted in mounting dangers to the public health and welfare, including injury to agricultural crops and livestock, damage to and the deterioration of property, and hazards to air and ground transportation; (3) that the prevention and control of air pollution at its sources is the primary responsibility of States and local governments; and (4) that Federal financial assistance and leadership is essential for the development of cooperative Federal, State, regional, and local programs to prevent and control air pollution."[2]

Congress enumerated the following reasons for passing the Act: "(1) to protect and enhance the quality of the Nation's air resources so as to promote the public health and welfare and the productive capacity of its population; (2) to initiate and accelerate a national research and development program to achieve the prevention and con-

---

1. Pub.L. 88–206, 77 Stat. 392 (1963), amended by Pub.L. 89–272, 79 Stat. 992 (1965), Pub.L. 89–675, 80 Stat. 954 (1966), Pub.L. 90–148, 81 Stat. 485 (1967), Pub.L. 91–137, 83 Stat. 283 (1969), Pub.L. 91–604, 84 Stat. 1676 (1970).

2. 42 U.S.C.A. § 1857(a).

trol of air pollution; (3) to provide technical and financial assistance to State and local governments in connection with the development and execution of their air pollution prevention and control programs; and (4) to encourage and assist the development and operation of regional air pollution control programs."[3]

Desiring state and local governments to play a productive role, Congress directed that the Administrator of the Environmental Protection Agency "encourage cooperative activities by the States and local governments for the prevention and control of air pollution; encourage the enactment of improved and, so far as practicable in the light of varying conditions and needs, uniform State and local laws, relating to the prevention and control of air pollution; and encourage the making of agreements and compacts between States for the prevention and control of air pollution."[4] Congress expressly granted its consent "to two or more States" negotiating and entering into "agreements or compacts, not in conflict with any law or treaty of the United States, for (1) cooperative effort and mutual assistance for the prevention and control of air pollution and the enforcement of their respective laws relating thereto, and (2) the establishment of such agencies, joint or otherwise, as they may deem desirable for making effective such agreements or compacts." However, "[n]o such agreement or compact * * * [may] be binding or obligatory upon any State a party thereto unless and until * * * approved by Congress." [5]

The Administrator is charged with the responsibility of establishing "a national research and development program for the prevention and control of air pollution."[6] Included among his tasks under this category of agency activity are the encouragement, cooperation with, and rendering of "technical services," providing "financial assistance to air pollution control agencies and other appropriate public or private agencies, institutions, and organizations, and individuals in the conduct of such activities."[7]

Under the Act each state has "the primary responsibility for assuring air quality within the entire geographic area comprising such State by submitting an implementation plan for such State which" specifies "the manner in which national * * * air quality standards will be achieved and maintained within each air quality control region in such State."[8] The Administrator is entrusted with the duty of designating "as an air quality control region any interstate area or major intrastate area which he deems necessary or appropriate for the attainment and maintenance of * * * quality standards."[9]

3.   42 U.S.C.A. § 1857(b).

4.   42 U.S.C.A. § 1857a(a).

5.   42 U.S.C.A. § 1857a(c).

6.   42 U.S.C.A. § 1857b(a).

7.   42 U.S.C.A. § 1857b(a) (2).

8.   Pub.L. 91–604 § 4.

9.   Pub.L. 91–604 § 4.

A comparatively small part of individual and enterprise activities account for most of our air pollution. Some industrial processes yield sulphur oxide which is discharged into the air. Some processes spew particulates into the air in the form of soot and smoke. The major sources of these two deleterious substances are electric power plants which burn high sulphur coal or oil, ore smelters, coke ovens which are used in conjunction with steel mill operations, and incinerators used to dispose of large volumes of garbage. Carbon monoxide, a by-product of less than complete oxidation of carbon containing fuels, makes its way into the air from automobile exhausts, factory chimneys, and heating units. Photochemical oxidants cause smog. Such oxidants are produced when hydrocarbons are exposed to sunlight. Common sources of such hydrocarbons are petroleum products and nitrogen oxides. Industrial processes, electric power plants, and automobiles are primarily responsible for this form of pollution. The Clean Air Act is intended to curb, and in time for the most part eliminate, the aforementioned forms of pollution.

The Act directs the Administrator of the Environmental Protection Agency to establish a "national primary ambient air quality standard and a national secondary ambient air quality standard for each air pollutant for which air quality criteria have been" established by law. The "national primary" standard must be based on criteria which, in the judgment of the Administrator, allow "an adequate margin of safety, * * * requisite to protect the public health."[10] The "national secondary" standard must be predicated on what the Administrator concludes, "is requisite to protect the public welfare from any known or anticipated adverse effects associated with the presence of such air pollutant in the * * * air."[11] States are asked to submit plans to implement the primary and secondary standards.[12] Primary standards are to be attained "as expeditiously as practicable but * * * [unless an exception is granted under the provisions of the Act] in no case later than three years from the date of approval of such [State] plan * * * in the case of a plan implementing a national secondary * * * air quality standard * * * [the standard should be attained in a] reasonable time."[13] Should a State fail to submit a plan implementing standards prescribed by the Administrator, then the Administrator may issue such regulations as may be necessary to effect the stated standards.[14]

The Administrator is empowered to prescribe minimum "standards of performance" covering emissions of air pollutants from "stationary sources."[15] The Act defines "standard of performance" as "a standard for emissions of air pollutants which reflects the degree of

---

10. 42 U.S.C.A. § 1857c–4(b) (1).

11. 42 U.S.C.A. § 1857c–4(b) (2).

12. 42 U.S.C.A. § 1857c–5(a) (1).

13. Pub.L. 91–604 § 4.

14. 42 U.S.C.A. § 1857c–5(c).

15. 42 U.S.C.A. § 1857c–6(b).

emission limitation achievable through the application of the best system of emission reduction which (taking into account the cost of achieving such reduction) the Administrator determines has been adequately demonstrated."[16] A "stationary source" is "any building, structure, facility, or installation which emits or may emit any air pollutant."[17] The Administrator may bar the introduction of new sources of hazardous air pollutants which in his judgment "may cause, or contribute to, an increase in mortality or an increase in serious irreversible, or incapacitating reversible, illness."[18] Already existing facilities found to produce such pollutants might, with the approval of the Administrator, continue to operate for up to two years after the Administrator finds that they constitute a source of one or more hazardous pollutants "if he finds that such period is necessary to the installation of controls and that steps will be taken during the period of the waiver to assure that the health of persons will be protected from imminent endangerment."[19] The President may authorize, for successive time periods of no more than two years each, the emission of hazardous pollutants "if he finds that the technology to implement * * * [the standard prescribed by the Administrator] is not available and the operation of such source is required for reasons of national security."[20] Congress must be informed of all such authorizations.[21]

The Administrator is empowered to establish "emission standards applicable to emissions of any air pollutant from any class or classes of aircraft or aircraft engines which in his judgment cause or contribute to or are likely to cause or contribute to air pollution which endanger the public health or welfare * * * after consultation with the Secretary of Transportation in order to assure appropriate consideration * * * [is paid to] aircraft safety."[22] He is also empowered to promulgate regulations which specify "standards applicable to the emission of any air pollutant from any class or classes of new motor vehicles or new motor vehicle engines, which in his judgment causes or contributes to, or is likely to cause or to contribute to air pollution which endangers the public health or welfare. Such standards * * * [are applicable] whether such vehicles and engines are designed as complete systems or incorporate devices to prevent or control such pollution."[23] Those regulations established by the Administrator to control "emissions of carbon monoxide and hydrocarbons from light duty vehicles and engines manufactured during or after model year 1975 * * * [must] require a reduction of at least 90 per centum from emissions of carbon monoxide and hydro-

16. 42 U.S.C.A. § 1857c–6(a) (1).   20. 42 U.S.C.A. § 1857c–7(c) (2).

17. 42 U.S.C.A. § 1857c–6(a) (3).   21. 42 U.S.C.A. § 1857c–7(c) (2).

18. 42 U.S.C.A. § 1857c–7.   22. Pub.L. 91–604 § 11.

19. 42 U.S.C.A. § 1857c–7(c) (1) (B) (ii).   23. 42 U.S.C.A. § 1857f–1(a) (1).

carbons allowable under the standards * * * applicable to light duty vehicles and engines manufactured in model year 1970 [24] * * * emissions of oxides of nitrogen from light duty vehicles and engines manufactured during or after model year 1976 * * * [must] contain standards which require a reduction of at least 90 per centum from the average of emissions of oxides actually measured from light duty vehicles manufactured during model year 1971 which are not subject to any Federal or State emission standards for oxides of nitrogen. Such average of emissions * * * [must] be determined by the Administrator on the basis of measurements made by him."[25] Beginning with July 1, 1971, and on July 1 "of each year thereafter, the Administrator * * * [must] report to the Congress with respect to the development of systems necessary to implement the [established] emission standards."[26] The Act allows the Administrator to grant up to a one year extension to manufacturers to satisfy specified emission standards.[27]

The Clean Air Act details a variety of procedures the Administrator of the Environmental Protection Agency may take to enforce the Act, Agency regulations, and State plans adopted pursuant to the Act. Upon finding that a State plan is being violated the Administrator may advise the wrongdoer of his finding. Should the violation continue for more than 30 days he may either order immediate compliance or begin a civil proceeding for appropriate relief which may or may not include a request for a temporary or permanent injunction.[28] If the Administrator finds that "violations of an applicable * * * [State] plan are so widespread that such violations appear to result from a failure of the State in which the plan applies to enforce the plan effectively," he must notify the State of his finding. Should the State fail to take corrective action within 30 days the Administrator must "give public notice of" his finding. Between the time he gives public notice and the "State satisfies the Adminis-

24. 42 U.S.C.A. § 1857f–1(b) (1) (A).

25. 42 U.S.C.A. § 1857f–1(b) (1) (B).

26. 42 U.S.C.A. § 1857f–1(b) (4).

27. 42 U.S.C.A. § 1857f–1(b) (5) (B).

28. Pub.L. 91–604 § 4. Title 42 U.S.C.A. § 1857h–2, entitled "Citizen suits" provides: "Except as provided in subsection (b) * * *, any person may commence a civil action on his own behalf—(1) against any person (including (i) the United States, and (ii) any other governmental instrumentality or agency to the extent permitted by the Eleventh Amendment to the Constitution) who is alleged to be in violation of (A) an emission standard or limitation under * * * [the Act] or (B) an order issued by the Administrator or a State with respect to such a standard or limitation, or (2) against the Administrator where there is alleged a failure of the Administrator to perform any act or duty under * * * [the Act] which is not discretionary with the Administrator. The district courts shall have jurisdiction, without regard to the amount in controversy or the citizenship of the parties, to enforce such an emission standard or limitation, or such an order, or to order the Administrator to perform such act or duty, as the case may be." Paragraph (b), entitled "Notice," sets forth the circumstances under which a suit may not be commenced until notice has been given to the Administrator, State and an alleged violator.

trator that it will enforce" the plan "the Administrator may enforce any requirement of such plan with respect to any person * * * by issuing an order to comply with such requirement, or * * * by bringing a civil action." The time during which the Administrator is authorized to act due to a State's failure to act is known as "a period of Federally assumed enforcement."[29]

When the Administrator issues an order it does "not take effect until the person to whom it is issued has had an opportunity to confer with the Administrator concerning the alleged violations." A copy of the order must be sent to the "State air pollution control agency of any State in which the violation occurs." The order must "state with reasonable specificity the nature of the violation, specify a time for compliance which the Administrator determines is reasonable, taking into account the seriousness of the violation and any good faith efforts to comply with applicable requirements." If the order is not obeyed, the Administrator may commence a civil proceeding "for appropriate relief."[30]

Civil actions commenced by the Environmental Protection Agency may be brought in the United States District Court "for the district in which the defendant is located or resides or is doing business, and such court * * * [has] jurisdiction to restrain such violation and to require compliance. Notice of the commencement of such action * * * must be given to the appropriate State air pollution control agency."[31]

"Any person who knowingly * * * violates any requirement of an applicable * * * [State] plan during any period of Federally assumed enforcement more than 30 days after having been notified by the Administrator * * * that * * * [he] is violating such requirement, or * * * violates or fails or refuses to comply with any order issued by the Administrator, or "violates the standards of performance promulgated by the Administrator for "stationary sources" of pollutants may "be punished by a fine of not more than $25,000 per day of violation, or by imprisonment for not more than one year, or by both. If the conviction is for a violation committed after the first conviction * * * [under the Act], punishment shall be by a fine of not more than $50,000 per day of violation, or by imprisonment for not more than two years, or by both."[32]

To facilitate the formulation of Agency regulations and state plans and the enforcement of the Act, regulations, and plans, "the Administrator may require the owner or operator of any emission source to (A) establish and maintain such records, (B) make such reports, (C) install, use, and maintain such monitoring equipment or methods, (D) sample such emissions (in accordance with such meth-

---

29. Pub.L. 91–604 § 4.   31. Pub.L. 91–604 § 4.

30. Pub.L. 91–604 § 4.   32. Pub.L. 91–604 § 4.

ods, at such locations, at such intervals, and in such manner as the Administrator shall prescribe) and (E) provide such other information, as he may reasonably require; and *   *   * the Administrator or his authorized representative, upon presentation of his credentials *   *   * shall have a right to entry to, upon, or through any premises in which an emission source is located or in which any records required to be maintained under *   *   * [the Act] are located, and *   *   * may at reasonable times have access to and copy any records, inspect any monitoring equipment or method required *   *   * [by the Administrator], and sample any emissions which the owner or operator of such source is required [by the Administrator] to sample."[33]

To assist state and local governments to abate out of state sources of air pollution which endanger the health or welfare of their citizens, the Act authorizes the Administrator, if requested by the Governor of the State subjected to harmful pollution, or such a State's air pollution control agency, or a municipality in whose request the Governor and State agency concur, to notify the local and State pollution control agencies of the State in which the air pollution originates, that he will hold a conference.[34]   Conference participants should include officials of the States in which the pollution originates as well as state and municipal air pollution control officials of those areas "adversely affected by such pollution."[35]   Following the conference the Administrator must "prepare and forward to all air pollution control agencies attending the conference a summary of conference discussions" together with his recommendations as to what measures should be taken to bring the emission of unlawful pollutants to an end.[36]   If six months after such recommendations are forwarded the Administrator concludes that action "reasonably calculated to secure abatement of such pollution has not been taken" he is to direct that a hearing be held.[37]   Should the evidence submitted at the hearing reveal that action is warranted the hearing board must recommend to the Administrator what action the board believes must be taken to "secure abatement of such pollution."[38]   In the event action ordered by the Administrator is not taken within the time he prescribes, he "may request the Attorney General to bring a suit on behalf of the United States *   *   * to secure abatement of the pollution."   In cases in which pollution "is endangering the health or welfare of persons only in the state in which the discharge or discharges (causing or contributing to such pollution) originate, at the request of the Governor of such State [the Administrator] shall request the

33. Pub.L. 91–604 § 4.

34. 42 U.S.C.A. § 1857d(b).

35. 42 U.S.C.A. § 1857d(b).

36. 42 U.S.C.A. § 1857d(d) (2).

37. 42 U.S.C.A. § 1857d(f) (1).

38. 42 U.S.C.A. § 1857d(f) (2).

Attorney General to bring suit on behalf of the United States * * * to secure abatement of the pollution."[39]

To permit prompt administrative action when such action is called for, the Act provides that "[n]otwithstanding any other provisions of * * * [the] Act, the Administrator, upon receipt of evidence that a pollution source or combination of sources (including moving sources) is presenting an imminent and substantial endangerment to the health of persons, and that appropriate State or local authorities have not acted to abate such sources, may bring suit on behalf of the United States in the appropriate United States district court to immediately restrain any person causing or contributing to the alleged pollution to stop the emission of air pollutants causing or contributing to such pollution or to take such other action as may be necessary."[40]

So that the efforts expended by Federal agencies dovetail rather than conflict Congress has directed that the Administrator of the Environmental Protection Agency should "cooperate with and encourage cooperative activities by all Federal departments and agencies having functions relating to the prevention and control of air pollution, so as to assure the utilization in the Federal air pollution control program of all appropriate and available facilities and resources within the Federal Government."[41] Recognizing that activities of the Federal Government, if left unregulated, could have an adverse impact on the quality of our air, Congress has further provided that "[e]ach department, agency, and instrumentality of the executive, legislative, and judicial branches of the Federal Government (1) having jurisdiction over any property or facility, or (2) engaged in any activity resulting, or which may result, in the discharge of air pollutants, shall comply with Federal, State, interstate, and local requirements respecting control and abatement of air pollution to the same extent that any person is subject to such requirements." [42] With some exceptions, "[t]he President may exempt any emission source of any department, agency, or instrumentality in the executive branch from compliance with such a requirement if he determines it to be in the paramount interest of the United States to do so * * *. No such exemption" is to "be granted due to lack of appropriation unless the President * * * specifically requested such appropriation as a part of the budgetary process and the Congress * * * failed to make available such requested appropriation. Any exemption" may not "be for a period * * * in excess of one year, but additional exemptions may be granted for periods not to exceed one year upon the President's making a new determination. The President" must "report each January to the Congress all exemptions from the re-

39.   42 U.S.C.A. § 1857d(g) (2).   **41.**   42 U.S.C.A. § 1857a(b).

40.   42 U.S.C.A. § 1857h–1.   **42.**   42 U.S.C.A. § 1857f.

quirements * * * granted during the preceding calendar year, together with his reason for granting each such exemption."[43]

To advise and assist the President and Administrator of the Environmental Protection Agency the Clear Air Act establishes within the Agency an Air Quality Advisory Board, with the Administrator or his designee, serving as Chairman together with "fifteen members appointed by the President, none of whom * * * [may] be Federal officers or employees."[44] Board members must "be selected from among representatives of various State, interstate, and local governmental agencies, of public or private interests contributing to, affected by, or concerned with air pollution, and of other public and private agencies, organizations, or groups demonstrating an active interest in the field of air pollution prevention and control, as well as other individuals who are expert in * * * [the] field."[45]

Illustrative of the regulations promulgated by the Environmental Protection Agency under the Clean Air Act are regulations appearing in the Code of Federal Regulations entitled "Control of Air Pollution from New Motor Vehicles and New Motor Vehicle Engines," Title 45, Part 1201; "Registration of Fuel Additives," Title 42, Part 479; and "Prevention, Control, and Abatement of Air Pollution from Federal Government Activities: Performance Standards and Techniques of Management," Title 42, Part 476.

The Clean Air Act invites state and local governments to play an active and critical role in the control of air pollution. The passage of federal and state legislation on the subject matter brings into play two intimately related constitutional doctrines: supremacy and preemption. Article VI, Clause 2 of the Constitution, commonly alluded to as the Supremacy Clause, provides that "[t]his Constitution, and the Laws of the United States which shall be made in Pursuance thereof; and all Treaties made, or which shall be made, under the Authority of the United States, shall be the supreme Law of the Land; and the Judges in every State shall be bound thereby, any Thing in the Constitution or Laws of any State to the Contrary notwithstanding." Speaking of the import of this Clause the Supreme Court has said that when Congress passes a valid law governing a particular sort of activity "it is of course the law of the land which no state law can modify or repeal * * * the States [are] devoid of power 'to retard, impede, burden or in any measure control, the operations of the constitutional laws enacted by Congress, to carry into execution the powers vested in the general government.' * * * a state law cannot stand that 'either frustrates the purpose of the national legislation, or impairs the efficiency of those agencies

43. 42 U.S.C.A. § 1857f.

44. 42 U.S.C.A. § 1857e(a) (1).

45. 42 U.S.C.A. § 1857e(a) (1).

of the Federal Government to discharge the duties for the performance of which they were created."[46]

If it wishes Congress, when constitutionally dealing with a particular subject, may preempt a field, that is, make its statute the sole source of governmental regulation. Consistent with the Supremacy Clause such legislative action would bar any state or local action designed to cover the same type of behavior. When Congress fails to specify within the context of a statute whether or not it intends that its pronouncement should preempt the field, a court, when asked to rule on the constitutionality of state or local action, must seek out its intention. To do so, the court scrutinizes the legislative plan. If it concludes that the statute reveals that Congress did intend to occupy the entire field, the state or local law will be condemned as unconstitutional, being "superceded [by federal law] regardless of whether it purports to supplement the federal law" or to simply cover a form of activity already embraced by federal legislation.[47]

Abiding by the premise that if air pollution is to be effectively dealt with action must be taken by all levels of government, Congress explicitly provided in the Clean Air Act that except where it expressly provided that States may not regulate particular forms of air pollution, "nothing in * * * [the] Act shall preclude or deny the right of any state or political subdivision thereof to adopt or enforce (1) any standard of limitation respecting emission of air pollutants or (2) any requirement respecting control or abatement of air pollution; except that if an emission standard or limitation is in effect under an applicable implementation plan or under * * * [those portions of the Act governing "standards of performance for new stationary sources" of pollution or "emission standards for hazardous air pollutants"], such State or political subdivision may not adopt or enforce any emission standard or limitation which is less stringent than the standard or limitation under such plan or * * * [portion of the Act]."[48] The Act also provides that "[n]o State or political subdivision thereof may adopt or attempt to enforce any standard respecting emissions of any air pollutant from any aircraft or engine thereof unless such standard is identical to a standard applicable to such aircraft under this * * * [Act]." [49]

State and local governments have enacted air pollution control laws which resemble the Clean Air Act. Such laws invariably make mention of the hazards posed by air pollution. They entrust an existing or new agency with the power to investigate the quality of the air and to promulgate regulations drawn to protect and upgrade air qual-

46. Nash v. Florida Industrial Commission, 88 S.Ct. 362, 389 U.S. 235, 19 L. Ed.2d 438 (1967).

47. Pennsylvania v. Nelson, 76 S.Ct. 477, 350 U.S. 497, 100 L.Ed. 640 (1956).

48. 42 U.S.C.A. § 1857d–1.

49. Pub.L. 91–604 § 11.

ity. The agency may also have the power to act in a quasi-judicial capacity. When vested with this function it may hold hearings and then enter suitable orders directing the curbing or elimination of a source of unlawful air pollution. Dissatisfied parties to order-making proceedings may secure judicial review. When warranted, a court will grant an agency's request for a temporary or permanent injunction. Fines may be imposed in civil proceedings upon one who violates antipollution laws or regulations. State law may make the unlawful emission of air pollutants a crime, subjecting a wrongdoer to possible fine and imprisonment. In both civil and criminal proceedings penalties may be imposed on a daily basis so as to incite prompt corrective action. Air control laws commonly provide that they are intended to be cumulative in nature, adding to, rather than replacing, already existing rights and duties. State legislation generally provides that while county, municipal, or town air pollution control laws may not supersede state legislation, they may supplement it. Where a state or municipality may suffer from a unique form of pollution because of the presence of a particular type of industry, legislation or regulations may be concocted with a view toward specifically bringing such pollution under control.

BISHOP PROCESSING COMPANY v. JOHN W. GARDNER, SECRETARY OF HEALTH, EDUCATION AND WELFARE OF THE UNITED STATES

United States District Court, District Maryland, 1967.
275 F.Supp. 780.

[Plaintiff operates a chicken processing plant in Maryland. The Delaware health authorities, contending that malodorous, noxious pollutants were being discharged from the plant and moving into Delaware, initiated a proceeding under the Clean Air Act, 42 U.S.C.A. § 1857 et seq. As provided for in the Act a conference was held of federal, state, and local officials. They recommended that Maryland take remedial action. As required by the Act the defendant convened a Hearing Board before which the plaintiff appeared and made 38 objections to evidence and other points. The Board made findings and recommendations and forwarded them to the defendant. On May 25, 1967 he forwarded the findings and recommendations to the plaintiff, together with a notice directing it to take corrective action no later than December 1, 1967 to end the discharge of malodorous pollutants. Plaintiff filed a petition for a declaratory judgment and judicial review of the Board's rulings. The defendant moved to dismiss the petition, claiming the plaintiff was not entitled to review at that juncture in the proceedings.]

THOMSEN, CHIEF JUDGE.

Section 10 of the Administrative Procedure Act * * * provides * * *:

"A person suffering legal wrong because of agency action, or adversely affected or aggrieved by agency action within the meaning of a relevant statute, is entitled to judicial review thereof."
 * * *

[The Act provides that actions may be brought for a declaratory judgment unless there is an "opportunity for judicial review * * * in civil or criminal proceedings for judicial enforcement." It also provides that] A preliminary, procedural, or intermediate agency action or ruling not directly reviewable is subject to review on the review of the final agency action. * * * "

The agency action in this case, i. e. the Notice of May 25, 1967, amplified by the Findings, Conclusions and Recommendations of the Hearing Board, are "subject to judicial review in civil or criminal proceedings for judicial enforcement", * * *

Undoubtedly, the court is given power to modify or refuse to enforce the recommendations made by the board. * * * But, asks Bishop, does the prospective defendant in such a suit have the right to challenge the constitutionality of the Clean Air Act, the composition of the hearing board, the "factual content" of the several resolutions, the adequacy of the proceedings before the board, procedural due process, and the admissibility of various items of evidence?

The principles of sound judicial administration indicate that the answer should be "yes". No case arising under the provisions of the Clean Air Act has been cited or found, so appropriate procedures * * * must be established. The Federal Rules of Civil Procedure permit Bishop to raise its points by preliminary motions or at the trial as fully and as satisfactorily as they could be raised in the present proceeding. Specifically, the Court may be asked to rule in advance of trial on the admissibility of items of evidence received by the board, so that the parties may know, e. g., whether a document offered before the board will be considered by the court, or whether the fact must be proved in some other way. If the Rules of Civil Procedure are applied flexibly to accomplish their purpose, there is no reason why the enforcement proceeding * * * should not afford an adequate opportunity for Bishop to raise any point it might be legally entitled to raise in the present proceeding. Moreover, if the Secretary does not ask the Attorney General to bring a suit * * * the many questions raised by Bishop need not be answered. It follows that the Administrative Procedure Act does not require or authorize the present petition for review.

 * * *

The motion to dismiss the petition is hereby granted and this action is hereby dismissed, with costs.

HOUSTON COMPRESSED STEEL CORP. v. STATE OF TEXAS

Court of Civil Appeals of Texas, Houston (1st Dist.) 1970.
456 S.W.2d 768.

[Appellants are a processer and a seller of scrap metal. To salvage metal from old box cars they burn the cars outdoors. A county agency and the State, intervening on behalf of the State Air Control Board, charged them with violating the Texas Clean Air Act and Regulation II adopted by the Board. Initially the trial court granted a temporary injunction limiting the hours during which outdoor burning could take place. It then enjoined outdoor burning *in toto pendente lite*. Appellants appealed.]

PEDEN, JUSTICE. * * * The outdoor burning of the boxcars was clearly prohibited by Regulation II, and the appellants had not been granted a variance by the Board as it was permitted to do under the provisions of the Act.

* * *

Appellants' assertion that the Texas Clean Air Act is an attempt to legislate in a field preempted by a federal statute, Title 42, § 1857, U.S.C.A., is without merit. Sec. 1857(a) (3) states that "The Congress finds * * * that the prevention and control of air pollution at its source is the primary responsibility of States and local governments; * * *." The federal Act is replete with evidence that cooperation between the states and the federal government in air pollution control is to be actively encouraged. See Sections 1857(b) (3), 1857a(a), 1857d(b) and 1857d(d) (1) (A).

* * *

Appellants complain that the Act is vague in that the definition of "air pollution" given in * * * the Act is inadequate, and that the flat prohibition against outdoor burning provided in Regulation II is also too vague to apply.

Until 1967 the basis of our laws regarding pollution was the nuisance doctrine, but the emphasis of our newer statutes is on regulatory standards. The science of air pollution control is new and inexact, and these standards are difficult to devise, but if they are to be effective they must be broad. If they are too precise they will provide easy escape for those who wish to circumvent the law. Air pollution is defined in * * * the Act: " 'air pollution' means the presence in the atmosphere of one or more air contaminants or combinations thereof, in such concentration and of such duration as are or may tend to be injurious to or to adversely affect human health or welfare, animal life, vegetation or property, as to interfere with the normal use and enjoyment of ainmal life, vegetation or property." This definition is clear and is easily capable of understanding. In fact, the appellants do not claim that they cannot determine whether their conduct fits within the defintion.

As to the appellants' challenge to Regulation II's almost blanket prohibition against outdoor burning, * * * the Act authorizes the Board to make regulations consistent with the intent of the Act, and * * * authorizes it to "adopt rules and regulations to control and prohibit the outdoor burning of waste and combustible material."

Regulation I was also adopted by the Board; it regulates, with great detail, indoor burning. The effect of the two Regulations is to hold that all burning, except that specifically allowed by Regulation II, will be done indoors. We consider this to be a reasonable governmental policy established in the interest of public health, safety and welfare. Outdoor burning is difficult, if not impossible, to regulate, because the amount of contaminants passing into the air cannot be accurately measured when the burning is not confined. When all the emissions must pass through a smoke stack or other exhaust system, the measure of the contaminants is much more readily subject to objective standards of control. An air polluter should not escape the consequences of his act merely because he is able to make his contaminants difficult to measure or control.

The Board is entitled to an injunction against outdoor burning under the Act without the necessity of proving toxicosity or injury or harm of any kind. Outdoor burning without a variance is all that need be proved.

Appellants next challenge the Act on the basis that they have been deprived of their property without due process of law. It is true that "a state cannot, under the guise of protecting the public, arbitrarily interfere with private business or prohibit lawful occupations, or impose unreasonable and unnecessary restrictions upon them." * * * However, the inherent right of a citizen to use and enjoy his property exists only so long as the use made of it does not interfere with the rights of others, and such right of enjoyment is subject to the police power. * * *

Laws vitally affecting the health of the people are within the legitimate police power. * * * "Legislation designed to free from pollution the very air that people breathe clearly falls within the exercise of the most traditional concept of what is compendiously known as the police power." * * * We consider that the Act's prohibiting of outdoor burning was not arbitrary.

It is appellants' position that Regulation II arbitrarily closes a previously lawful business. We believe that the Regulation was reasonable, not arbitrary, and it has not been shown that the enforcement of it will close the appellants' business. Their testimony was that they are building an incinerator but need to burn 48 boxcars to make room for it. When this suit was filed they had not applied for a variance even though the present Act and its predecessor have prohibited outdoor burning since 1967. The evidence does not conclusively establish that it would be impossible or even impractical to build the incinerator without first burning the 48 boxcars.

* * * affirmed.

PROBLEMS

1. The Administrator, having the requisite evidence of pollution and state and local inaction, brought suit to enjoin 23 companies from spewing pollutants into the air. Ordinarily the objectionable emissions from their plants did not present an imminent danger to health, but, due to a stagnant air mass which had remained over the area for several days, they did. What judgment?

2. May a state environmental control agency establish more stringent standards governing the emission of air pollutants from aircraft than those established by a federal agency when the aircraft make use of state operated airports and are engaged solely in intra-state flights?

3. In view of the present federal approach to air pollution control, how much weight should state legislators give to the argument that stringent state air pollution control standards would drive industry, which means jobs and tax dollars, from the state?

4. May the Administrator of the Environmental Protection Agency, when designing a timetable governing the elimination of emission of air pollutants from automobiles, use as a standard of acceptability the most effective devices made by foreign manufacturers when their devices surpass domestic ones?

5. Would a state penal statute which required an automobile owner to expend funds to comply with air pollution control standards be constitutional if it was made applicable to persons who purchased their vehicles prior to the passage of the law? Must one who lacks funds be excused from a statutory directive which requires the expenditure of money if it is to be complied with?

6. May a municipality, to control air pollution, outlaw the use of automobiles within city limits?

7. May one who operates a plant which emits particles which cause injury to a neighbor's property be required to pay punitive damages if he refused to cease operations after repeated requests that he do so?

Chapter 10

WATER

Primitive man was convinced that water was vital for earthly existence. He classified water as a basic element, hypothesizing that all things are composed of some combination of water, fire, and air. Today biologists can expound in great detail on the critical role water plays in the life processes of plants and animals. Aside from its direct biological function, water contributes to human existence in other ways. When used as a solvent it allows man to make beneficial use of a multitude of otherwise unusable or less attractive or unsatisfactory materials.

Waterways have traditionally served as a receptacle for sewage and refuse. Sewage and refuse deposited in streams or lakes may be decomposed or swept away, perhaps ultimately into the sea. The indiscriminate use of waterways as a depository for refuse may be acceptable in a sparsely populated heavily agrarian society. The debilitating effect may be of little or no consequence. On the other hand, the consequences of such a procedure in a densely inhabited geographic area can, even in the short-run, be disastrous. Federal, state, and local governments, since the latter part of the nineteenth century, have recognized the need to take action if the nation's waterways are to remain functional and the water supply wholesome. During the last decade and a half government has proceeded to impose more and more restraints on individuals and enterprises to insure that domestic, and to some extent the entire planet's waterways, are adequately and suitably protected from despoilation.

The Rivers and Harbors Act of 1899 makes it unlawful "to throw, discharge, or deposit, or cause, suffer, or procure to be thrown, discharged, or deposited either from or out of any ship, barge, or other floating craft of any kind, or from the shore, wharf, manufacturing establishment, or mill of any kind, any refuse matter of any kind or description whatever other than that flowing from streets and sewers and passing therefrom in a liquid state, into any navigable water of the United States, or into any tributary of any navigable water from which the same shall float or be washed into such navigable water; * * * or [to] deposit, or cause, suffer, or procure to be deposited material of any kind in any place on the bank of any navigable water where the same shall be liable to be washed into such navigable water, either by ordinary or high tides, or by storms or floods, or otherwise, whereby navigation shall or may be impeded or obstructed. * * * "[1] The Act provides "[t]hat the Secretary of the Army, whenever in the judgment of the Chief of En-

1. 33 U.S.C.A. § 407.

101

gineers anchorage or navigation will not be injured thereby, may permit the deposit of any * * * [of the mentioned materials] in navigable waters, within limits to be defined and under conditions to be prescribed by him, provided application is made to him prior to depositing such material: and whenever any permit is so granted the conditions thereof shall be strictly complied with, and any violation thereof * * * [is] unlawful."[2]

President Richard M. Nixon, by Executive Order No. 11574, directed that "[t]he executive branch of the Federal Government * * * implement * * * [the] permit program" in the following fashion: "The Secretary [of the Army] * * * after consultation with the Administrator [of the Environmental Protection Agency] respecting water quality matters * * * [may make] and amend regulations governing the issuance of permits * * * be responsible for granting, denying, conditioning, revoking or suspending * * * permits. In so doing: * * * He shall accept findings, determinations, and interpretations which the Administrator shall make respecting applicable water quality standards and compliance with those standards * * *. A permit shall be denied where the certification prescribed by the Federal Water Pollution Control Act [33 U.S.C.A. § 1171(b)] has been denied, or where issuance would be inconsistent with any finding, determination, or interpretation of the Administrator pertaining to applicable water quality standards and considerations. [The Secretary is directed to consider other factors as required by law. He is obliged to] consult with the [Secretaries of the Interior, Commerce, and Administrator], and with the head of the agency exercising administration over the wildlife resources of any affected state, regarding effects on fish and wildlife which are not reflected in water quality considerations, where the discharge for which a permit is sought impounds, diverts, deepens the channel, or otherwise controls or similarly modifies the stream or body of water into which the discharge is made. * * * [In the course of his consultations the Secretary must probe such] environmental amenities and values * * * [as required by the National Environmental Policy Act of 1969]. * * * The Attorney General * * * [is directed to] conduct the legal proceedings necessary to enforce the [Refuse] Act and permits issued pursuant to it. * * * The Council on Environmental Quality * * * [is directed to] coordinate the regulations, policies, and procedures of Federal agencies with respect to the * * * permit program. * * * and after [consulting with the Secretary, * * * Administrator, the Secretaries of the Interior, Commerce, Agriculture,] and the Attorney General, * * * from time to time or as directed by the President advise the President * * * [on] the implementation of the * * * permit program * * *."[3]

2. 33 U.S.C.A. § 407.   3. 35 Fed.Reg. 19627.

The Act directs the Department of Justice to "conduct the legal proceedings necessary to enforce" it. United States Attorneys are admonished "to vigorously prosecute all offenders" when "requested to do so by the Secretary of the Army" or other lawfully designated official.[4]

"Every person and every corporation" which unlawfully deposits refuse into navigable waters in violation of the Act is "guilty of a misdemeanor, and * * * [may] be punished by a fine not exceeding $2,500 nor less than $500 or by imprisonment * * * for not less than thirty days nor more than one year, or by both * * *, in the discretion of the court."[5]

To encourage persons to bring to the attention of governmental officials the sort of behavior outlawed by the 1899 Act, Congress has provided that "[o]ne half of the * * * [prescribed] fine * * * [to be paid by a person or enterprise convicted for having violated the Act is] to be paid to the person or persons giving information which shall lead to conviction."[6] This portion of the statute has raised the question of whether or not an informer may personally proceed against a supposed wrongdoer in a civil action to collect from him the sum of money he would have received if the government had made use of the supplied information and had successfully prosecuted the defendant. Such suits, labeled "qui tam" actions, have generally been unsuccessful. Courts have taken the position that a "qui tam" proceeding may not be maintained in the absence of either express or implied statutory authority. The 1899 Act is seen as establishing a criminal and not a civil fine. The right of action provided for by the law is treated as a right vested in government and not in individuals. Courts have also rejected actions in which an informer seeks a writ of mandamus directing federal officials to proceed to prosecute persons or enterprises which supposedly are violating the Act. Prosecution of one believed to be guilty of a crime is viewed as a discretionary rather than a ministerial duty of the Attorney General and his assistants and therefore is not subject to judicial directive.

Chapter 23 of Title 33 of the United States Code is entitled "Pollution Control of Navigable Waters." Section 1151 of the chapter, which Congress has stated "may be cited as the 'Water Quality Improvement Act of 1970'" provides that "[t]he purpose of * * * [the] chapter is to enhance the quality and value of our water resources and to establish a national policy for the prevention, control and abatement of water pollution.[7] In this Chapter Congress "declared [it] to be the policy of Congress to recognize, preserve, and protect the primary responsibilities and rights of the States in preventing and controlling water pollution, to support and aid technical

---

4. 33 U.S.C.A. § 413.

5. 33 U.S.C.A. § 411.

6. 33 U.S.C.A. § 411.

7. 33 U.S.C.A. § 1151(a).

research relating to the prevention and control of water pollution, and to provide Federal technical services and financial aid to State and interstate agencies and to municipalities in connection with the prevention and control of water pollution. * * * [Congress, speaking of the respective roles of the Federal and State governments asserted that n]othing in this chapter shall be construed as impairing or in any manner affecting any right or jurisdiction of the States with respect to the waters (including boundary waters) of such States." [8]

Administration of the Act is placed in the hands of the Administrator of the Environmental Protection Agency. [9]

"The Administrator * * * [is directed by Congress], after careful investigation, and in cooperation with other Federal agencies, with State water pollution control agencies and interstate agencies, and with the municipalities and industries involved, [to] prepare or develop comprehensive programs for eliminating or reducing the pollution of interstate waters and tributaries thereof and improving the sanitary condition of surface and underground waters. In the development of such comprehensive programs due regard * * * [should] be given to the improvements which are necessary to conserve such waters for public water supplies, propagation of fish and aquatic life and wildlife, recreational purposes, and agricultural, industrial and other legitimate use * * * [to fulfill his duties] the Administrator is authorized to make joint investigations with any such agencies of the condition of any waters in any State or States, and of the discharge of any sewage, industrial wastes, or substances which may adversely affect such waters." [10]

To encourage and assist States to undertake water planning programs, Congress has authorized the Administrator to fund up to fifty percent of the administrative expenses of a State's water planning agency for as long as three years if the conditions laid down by Congress are satisfied. [11] He is directed to "encourage cooperative activities by the States for the prevention and control of water pollution; encourage the enactment of improved and, so far as practicable, uniform State laws relating to the prevention and control of water pollution; and encourage compacts between States for the prevention and control of water pollution." [12] To make it possible for States to enter into compacts Congress has expressly granted its consent to States negotiating and entering "into agreements or compacts, not in conflict with any law or treaty of the United States, for (1) cooperative effort and mutual assistance for the prevention and control of water pollution and the enforcement of their respective laws relating there-

8.   33 U.S.C.A. § 1151(c).

9.   33 U.S.C.A. § 1151(b).

10.   33 U.S.C.A. § 1153(a).

11.   33 U.S.C.A. § 1153(c).

12.   33 U.S.C.A. § 1154(a).

to, and (2) the establishment of such agencies, joint or otherwise, as they may deem desirable for making effective such agreements and compacts. [However, n]o such agreement or compact * * * [is] binding or obligatory upon any State party thereto unless and until it has been approved by the Congress."[13]

The Administrator is directed to take part in "research, investigations, experiments, demonstrations, and studies relating to the causes, control, and prevention of water pollution."[14] To carry out this function he may "make grants-in-aid to public or private agencies and institutions and to individuals."[15] Congress has set forth in detail the sorts of grants and the size of grants which he may make.[16]

Individual states and interstate agencies wishing to receive federal funds to underwrite their water pollution prevention and control programs must submit their plans to the Administrator. If he finds that the criteria of eligibility prescribed by Congress are met he is to approve them.[17] Prior to disapproving a plan the Administrator must give "reasonable notice and opportunity for hearing to the State water pollution control agency or interstate agency which * * * submitted * * * such plan."[18] If "after reasonable notice and opportunity for hearing" the Administrator finds that a plan has been changed so that it no longer complies with the law[19] or the plan is not being administered as required by law he may notify the State or interstate agency that no "further payments will be made."[20]

"The Administrator is authorized to make grants to any State, municipality, or intermunicipal or interstate agency for the construction of necessary treatment works to prevent the discharge of untreated or inadequately treated sewage or other waste into any waters and for the purpose of reports, plans, and specifications in connection therewith." [21]

"Consistent with" its declaration that states should be involved with the prevention and control of water pollution,[22] Congress has made provision for states to take individual and "interstate action to abate pollution of interstate or navigable waters" located within their boundaries.[23] Only when a state has failed to take the requisite action and a court finds that proposed federal action "is in the public interest" and is equitable [24] is state action "displaced by Federal enforce-

13. 33 U.S.C.A. § 1154(b).

14. 33 U.S.C.A. § 1155(a).

15. 33 U.S.C.A. § 1155(a) (2).

16. 33 U.S.C.A. § 1156.

17. 33 U.S.C.A. § 1157(f).

18. 33 U.S.C.A. § 1157(g).

19. 33 U.S.C.A. § 1157(g) (A).

20. 33 U.S.C.A. § 1157(g) (B).

21. 33 U.S.C.A. § 1158(a).

22. 33 U.S.C.A. § 1160(b).

23. 33 U.S.C.A. § 1160(b).

24. 33 U.S.C.A. § 1160(h).

ment action."[25]   States may proceed to establish and enforce "water quality criteria" and plans "for the implementation and enforcement of" such criteria.[26]   If the criteria in the opinion of the Administrator are such that they "protect the public health or welfare, enhance the quality of water" and otherwise comply with federal law,[27] they then become "the water quality standards applicable to such interstate waters or portions thereof" within the state.[28]   Should a state fail to establish water quality criteria the Administrator may proceed to do so.[29]   If the Administrator concludes that a state has failed to take effective action to abate pollution he must arrange for an evidentiary hearing to be held before a five member Hearing Board selected by him.[30]   "If the * * * Board finds such pollution is occurring and effective progress toward abatement thereof is not being made, it * * * [is to] make recommendations to the Administrator concerning the measures, if any, which it finds to be reasonable and equitable to secure abatement of such pollution."[31]   The Administrator is authorized to specify "a reasonable time (not less than six months)" to accomplish abatement of the objectionable pollution.[32] "If action reasonably calculated to secure abatement * * * within the time specified * * * is not taken, the Administrator— * * * in the case of pollution * * * which is endangering the health or welfare of persons in a State other than that in which the discharge or discharges (causing or contributing to such pollution) originate, may request the Attorney General to bring suit on behalf of the United States to secure abatement * * * in cases [in which the objectionable effect and discharge occur in the same State he] may, with the written consent of the Governor of such State, request the Attorney General to bring suit on behalf of the United States to secure abatement of the pollution."[33]

"The Administrator is authorized to prescribe such regulations as are necessary to carry out his functions under * * * chapter [23]."[34]

The Administrator, "after consultation with the Secretary of the department in which the Coast Guard is operating, after giving appropriate consideration to the economic costs involved, and within the limits of available technology, * * * [is obliged to] promulgate Federal standards of performance for marine sanitation devices * * * which shall be designed to prevent the discharge of untreated or inadequately treated sewage into or upon the navigable waters

25.   33 U.S.C.A. § 1160(b).

26.   33 U.S.C.A. § 1160(c).

27.   33 U.S.C.A. § 1160(c) (3).

28.   33 U.S.C.A. § 1160(c) (1).

29.   33 U.S.C.A. § 1160(c) (2).

30.   33 U.S.C.A. § 1160(f) (1).

31.   33 U.S.C.A. § 1160(f) (1).

32.   33 U.S.C.A. § 1160(f) (1).

33.   33 U.S.C.A. § 1160(g).

34.   33 U.S.C.A. § 1172(a).

of the United States from new vessels and existing vessels, except vessels not equipped with installed toilet facilities. Such standards * * * [must be] consistent with maritime safety and the marine and navigation laws and regulations * * *. [They become] effective for new vessels two years after promulgation and for existing vessels five years after promulgation."[35] After the regulations become effective it is unlawful to manufacture a vessel subject to the standards unless the vessel meets such standards[36] and to operate a vessel in violation of the standards.[37] A noncomplying manufacturer is subject "to a civil penalty of not more than $5,000 for each violation" of the law[38] and a vessel operator who violates the law or any regulation is subject to a $2,000 civil penalty for each violation.[39]

In the Water Resources Planning Act[40] Congress declared that "[i]n order to meet the rapidly expanding demands for water throughout the Nation, it is * * * the policy of the Congress to encourage the conservation, development, and utilization of water and related land resources of the United States on a comprehensive and coordinated basis by the Federal Government, States, localities, and private enterprise with the cooperation of all affected Federal agencies, States, local governments, individuals, corporations, business enterprises, and others concerned."[41] The Act establishes a Water Resources Council[42] which is charged with studying and assessing "the adequacy of supplies of water necessary to meet the water requirements in each water resource region in the United States and the national interest therein[43] * * * and * * * [to] make recommendations to the President with respect to Federal policies and programs."[44] The Act states the circumstances under which States may receive Federal funds "to assist them in developing and participating in the development of comprehensive water and related land resource plans."[45]

Congress has conferred original jurisdiction on the "United States district courts * * * (concurrent with that of the Supreme Court * * * and * * * with that of any other court of the United States or of any State * * * [which] has original jurisdiction) of any case or controversy * * * which involves the construction or application of an interstate compact" pertaining "to the pollution of the waters of an interstate system or any portion thereof * * *, and [cases of] pollution * * * alleged to be in viola-

35. 33 U.S.C.A. § 1163(b) (1).

36. 33 U.S.C.A. § 1163(h) (1).

37. 33 U.S.C.A. § 1163(h) (1).

38. 33 U.S.C.A. § 1163(j).

39. 33 U.S.C.A. § 1163(j).

40. Pub.L. 89–80, 79 Stat. 244.

41. 42 U.S.C.A. § 1962.

42. 42 U.S.C.A. § 1962a.

43. 42 U.S.C.A. § 1962a–1(a).

44. 42 U.S.C.A. § 1962a–1(b).

45. 42 U.S.C.A. § 1962c.

tion of * * * [a] compact; and * * * in which one or
more of the States signatory * * * is a plaintiff or plaintiffs;
and * * * which is within the judicial power of the United
States as set forth in the Constitution of the United States."[46]

While federal legislation entrusts the states with a role in the
prevention and control of water pollution, the Supreme Court has
stated that Congress has made it "clear that it is federal, not state,
law that in the end controls the pollution of interstate or navigable
waters." In cases brought in federal courts to abate pollution of such
waters in which the desirable remedy "is not within the precise scope
of remedies prescribed by Congress," the Court has stated that "federal courts" may "fashion federal law." Federal courts can apply
"federal common law to abate a public nuisance in interstate or navigable waters" until that time when legislation "pre-empts the field of
federal common law of nuisance." Although "federal law governs,
consideration of state standards may be relevant. * * * There
are no fixed rules that govern * * * [actions to abate water pollution being] equity suits * * * the informed judgment of the
chancellor will largely govern."[47]

States have outlawed the discharge of garbage, various sorts of
refuse, industrial waste, untreated sewage, oil and oil products, and
gas into state waters. They have authorized agencies to implement
selected anti-pollution policies. A state agency may be empowered to
establish acceptable water quality standards for state waters. Established procedures may be comparable to those found in the 1899 Rivers and Harbors Act, authorizing the issuance of permits to pollute
under particular circumstances for a limited period of time. State
law may excuse compliance with established standards in instances in
which the authorized agency finds it is impossible, impracticable, or
financially not feasible for a polluter to expend the funds necessary
to abate the pollution, if the pollution is not of such a nature as to be
of grave immediate harm to the community. State law may detail
the procedures which must be employed to dispose of sewage.
Unique state concerns might find their way into legislation or administrative policies which do not have a counterpart in the laws or
agency criteria of other states. For example, a state bordering on an
ocean might expressly ban the discharge of ballast water from any
sea-going vessel or tank-cleaning waste water or other waste containing more than a minimum quantum of oil residue. Local pumping of
oil might militate legislation expressly banning the discharge of crude
oil into state waters. To be certain that the discharge of heated water—commonly known as thermal pollution—does not reach such a
level that it adversely affects fish which inhabit state waters, state
policy may set a maximum temperature at which heated water may

46. 33 U.S.C.A. § 466g–1(a).

47. Illinois v. City of Milwaukee, 92
S.Ct. 1385, —— U.S. ——, —— L.Ed.2d
—— (1972).

be dumped into state waters. Such legislation requires those who use water for cooling purposes to take such steps as may be necessary to reduce the temperature of heated water to a lawfully permissible level.

UNITED STATES v. STANDARD OIL COMPANY

Supreme Court of the United States, 1966.
86 S.Ct. 1427, 384 U.S. 224, 16 L.Ed.2d 492.

[Section 13 of the Rivers and Harbors Act of 1899 (33 U.S.C.A. § 407) provides "[i]t shall not be lawful to throw, discharge, or deposit * * * any refuse matter of any kind or description whatever other than that flowing from streets and sewers and passing therefrom in a liquid state into any navigable water of the United States * * *." Appellee was charged with violating § 13 by allowing to be discharged into the St. Johns River "refuse matter" consisting of 100-octane aviation gasoline. The District Court dismissed the indictment on the ground that "refuse matter" does not include commercially valuable oil. The United States appealed.]

MR. JUSTICE DOUGLAS delivered the opinion of the Court. * * *

This case comes to us at a time in the Nation's history when there is greater concern than ever over pollution—one of the main threats to our free-flowing rivers and to our lakes as well. The crisis that we face in this respect would not, of course, warrant us in manufacturing offenses where Congress has not acted nor in stretching statutory language in a criminal field to meet strange conditions. But whatever may be said of the rule of strict construction, it cannot provide a substitute for common sense, precedent, and legislative history. We cannot construe § 13 of the Rivers and Harbors Act in a vacuum. * * *

The statutory words are "any refuse matter of any kind or desscription." We said in United States v. Republic Steel Corp., that the history of this provision and of related legislation dealing with our free-flowing rivers "forbids a narrow, cramped reading" of § 13. * * *

Oil is oil and whether useable or not by industrial standards it has the same deleterious effect on waterways. In either case, its presence in our rivers and harbors is both a menace to navigation and a pollutant. This seems to be the administrative construction of § 13, the Solicitor General advising us that it is the basis of prosecution in approximately one-third of the oil pollution cases reported to the Department of Justice by the Office of the Chief of Engineers.

Section 13 codified pre-existing statutes:

* * *

From an examination of these statutes, several points are clear. *First*, the 1894 Act and its antecedent, the 1888 Act * * * drew on their face no distinction between valuable and valueless substances. *Second*, of the enumerated substances, some may well have had commercial or industrial value prior to discharge into the covered waterways. * * * *Third*, these Acts applied not only to the enumerated substances but also to the discharge of "any other matter of any kind." Since the enumerated substances included those with a pre-discharge value, the rule of *ejusdem generis* does not require limiting this latter category to substances lacking a pre-discharge value. *Fourth*, the coverage of these Acts was not diminished by the codification of 1899. The use of the term "refuse" in the codification serves in the place of the lengthy list of enumerated substances found in the earlier Acts and the catch-all provision found in the Act of 1890. The legislative history demonstrates without contradiction that Congress intended to codify without substantive change the earlier Acts.

* * * It is plain from its legislative history that the "serious injury" to our watercourses * * * sought to be remedied was caused in part by obstacles that impeded navigation and in part by pollution—* * *. The words of the Act are broad and inclusive: "any refuse matter of any kind or description whatever." Only one exception is stated: "other than that flowing from streets and sewers and passing therefrom in a liquid state, into any navigable water of the United States." More comprehensive language would be difficult to select. The word "refuse" does not stand alone; the "refuse" banned is "of any kind or description whatever," apart from the one exception noted. And, for the reasons already stated, the meaning we must give the term "refuse" must reflect the present codification's statutory antecedents.

The Court of Appeals for the Second Circuit in United States v. Ballard Oil Co., held that causing good oil to spill into a watercourse violated § 13. The word "refuse" in that setting, said the court, "is satisfied by anything which has become waste, however useful it may earlier have been." There is nothing more deserving of the label "refuse" than oil spilled into a river.

That seems to us to be the common sense of the matter. The word "refuse" includes all foreign substances and pollutants apart from those "flowing from streets and sewers and passing therefrom in a liquid state" into the watercourse.

That reading of § 13 is in keeping with the teaching of Mr. Justice Holmes that a "river is more than an amenity, it is a treasure." * * * It reads § 13 charitably as United States v. Republic Steel Corp., admonished.

* * *

Reversed.

* * *

ZABEL v. TABB

United States Court of Appeals, Fifth Circuit, 1970.
430 F.2d 199.

[Plaintiffs, owners of 11 acres of tidelands, applied to the Corps of Engineers pursuant to the Rivers and Harbors Act of 1899 for a permit to dredge and fill the area so it could be used as a commercial mobile trailer park. State and county bodies, 700 individuals, and the United States Fish and Wildlife Service opposed issuance on environmental grounds, the Service contending that dredging and filling "would have a distinctly harmful effect on fish and wildlife in the area." Following a public hearing, the District Engineer found that the "proposed work would have no material adverse effect on navigation," but recommended that a permit be denied, citing public interest, The Fish and Wildlife Coordination Act, and the opposition of the Service and state and county agencies. The Chief of Engineers concurred with the recommendation as did the Secretary of the Army. Plaintiffs brought an action in the District Court to review the Secretary's determination and for an order compelling him to issue a permit. From a summary judgment directing the issuance of the permit, the defendants appealed.]

JOHN R. BROWN, CHIEF JUDGE: * * *

The question presented to us is whether the Secretary of the Army can refuse to authorize a dredge and fill project in navigable waters for factually substantial ecological reasons even though the project would not interfere with navigation, flood control, or the production of power. To answer this question in the affirmative, we must answer two intermediate questions affirmatively. (1) Does Congress for ecological reasons have the power to prohibit a project on private riparian submerged land in navigable waters? (2) If it does, has Congress committed the power to prohibit to the Secretary of the Army?

The starting point here is the Commerce Clause and its expansive reach. The test for determining whether Congress has the power to protect wildlife in navigable waters and thereby to regulate the use of private property for this reason is whether there is a basis for the Congressional judgment that the activity regulated has a substantial effect on interstate commerce. * * * That this activity meets this test is hardly questioned. In this time of awakening to the reality that we cannot continue to despoil our environment and yet exist, the nation knows, if Courts do not, that the destruction of fish and wildlife in our estuarine waters does have a substantial, and in some areas a devastating, effect on interstate commerce. Landholders do not contend otherwise. Nor is it challenged that dredge and fill projects are activities which may tend to destroy the ecological balance and thereby affect commerce substantially. Because of these potential effects Congress has the power to regulate such projects.

* * *

The action of the Chief of Engineers and the Secretary of the Army under attack rests immediately on the Rivers and Harbors Act, 33 U.S.C.A. § 403, which declares that "the creation of any obstruction * * * to the navigable capacity of any of the waters of the United States is prohibited." * * * The Act itself does not put any restrictions on denial of a permit or the reasons why the Secretary may refuse to grant a permit to one seeking to build structures on or dredge and fill his own property. Although the Act has always been read as tempering the outright prohibition by the rule of reason against arbitrary action, the Act does flatly forbid the obstruction. The administrator may grant permission on conditions and conversely deny permission when the situation does not allow for those conditions.

But the statute does not prescribe either generally or specifically what those conditions may be. The question for us is whether under the Act the Secretary may include conservation considerations as conditions to be met to make the proposed project acceptable. * * * Governmental agencies in executing a particular statutory responsibility ordinarily are required to take heed of, sometimes effectuate and other times not thwart other valid statutory governmental policies. And here the government-wide policy of environmental conservation is spectacularly revealed in at least two statutes, The Fish and Wildlife Coordination Act and the National Environmental Policy Act of 1969.

The Fish and Wildlife Coordination Act clearly requires the dredging and filling agency (under a governmental permit), whether public or private, to consult with the Fish and Wildlife Service, with a view of conservation of wildlife resources. * * *

The second proof that the Secretary is directed and authorized by the Fish and Wildlife Coordination Act to consider conservation is found in the legislative history. * * *

* * * Congress intended the Chief of Engineers and Secretary of the Army to consult with the Fish and Wildlife Service before issuing a permit for a private dredge and fill operation.

* * *

The parallel of momentum as the three branches shape a national policy gets added impetus from the National Environmental Policy Act of 1969, * * *. This Act essentially states that every federal agency shall consider ecological factors when dealing with activities which may have an impact on man's environment.

Although this Congressional command was not in existence at the time the permit in question was denied, the correctness of that decision must be determined by the applicable standards of today.

The national policy is set forth in plain terms * * * we hold that while it is still the action of the Secretary of the Army on the recommendation of the Chief of Engineers, the Army must consult with, consider and receive, and then evaluate the recommendations of all of these other agencies articulately on all these environmental factors. * * *

* * * there is no doubt that the Secretary can refuse on conservation grounds to grant a permit under the Rivers and Harbors Act.

* * *

Landholders' * * * [contend] that their private submerged property was taken for public use without just compensation. They proceed this way: (i) the denial of a permit constitutes a taking since this is the only use to which the property could be put; (ii) the public use as a breeding ground for wildlife; and (iii) for that use just compensation is due.

Our discussion of this contention begins and ends with the idea that there is no taking. The waters and underlying land are subject to the paramount servitude in the Federal government which the Submerged Lands Act expressly reserved as an incident of [48] power incident to the Commerce Clause.

* * * reversed * * * judgment is rendered for the Government and the associated agent-defendants.

PROBLEMS

1. It is generally held that a "riparian land owner's title extends to the low-water mark, the state owning the bed of navigable waters below the low-water mark in trust for the people for public uses, which include commercial navigation, the drawing of water for various private and public uses, recreational activity, and similar water-connected uses * * * the owner's main right * * * is an exclusive right of access to the water in front of his land * * * he has a right to accretions and relictions in front of his land." Plaintiff filled in the lake on which his property abutted up to the point of navigability. Is he entitled to compensation when the state appropriated the artificially created dry land for use in a highway system?

2. In 1955 plaintiff and defendant had a dispute. The defendant insisted that he had a right to continue making use of spring water located on plaintiff's land by reason of a series of conveyances made to his predecessors in title. The plaintiff insisted that such conveyances were "worthless." The defendant continued to draw wa-

---

48. For a discussion of the Submerged Lands Act see Chapter 22, *infra.*

ter from the spring until May 1, 1970 when the plaintiff brought suit to bar defendant's future use of the spring. The trial court, relying on a five year statute of limitations governing property rights, ruled in favor of the defendant. What judgment on appeal?

3. Assume Congress outlaws the discharge of all pollutants into the nation's rivers and harbors by 1980. Does the Constitution require the federal government to compensate persons who would have to close their plants due to such legislation either because the available technology does not permit them to comply or they lack sufficient funds to make use of available technology?

4. Should it become necessary in order to shield the nation's harbors and rivers from pollution to severely limit the building of power generating plants, would it be constitutional for Congress to confer on an agency the authority to establish a quota system allotting quantities of power to individuals and enterprises?

5. State legislation banned the use of "any detergent, presoak, soap, enzyme, or other cleaning agent containing more than 8.7 per cent phosphorous by weight." Expressly exempted were "high phosphate detergents sold and used for cleaning dairy or industrial equipment." Plaintiff, an operator of a commercial laundry, brought an action challenging the constitutionality of the statute. What judgment?

6. Defendant, operator of 2 sightseeing vessels, was charged in a suit brought by the state with failing to install "on board" sewage treatment facilities as required by state law. In his defense, he argued, *inter alia*, that the challenged discharge was *de minimus* and the state was estopped from proceeding against him since it failed to seek relief against municipalities and municipally operated ferries which discharged tens of thousands of times more raw sewage into the very same river on which the defendant operated its vessels than was allegedly discharged from his vessels. What judgment?

Chapter 11

AESTHETICS AND HISTORICAL SITES

What one perceives when he gazes through a window, while walking, or seated in a moving automobile, affects his well-being. What he sees may distress him. He may wish he were somewhere else. He may be enraptured with the setting. Consciously he may seek to extend his feeling of euphora, hoping that the landscape would never be disturbed. Growing industrialization, various business marketing practices, tasteless designs, increased urbanization and suburbanization, and the continuous disruption of man's natural habitat have given rise to what has been described as visual pollution or uglification. Responding to public dissatisfaction, legislators have enacted laws directed at curbing various forms of individual and enterprise behavior which have an especially deleterious effect on the visual environment.

Some forms of outdoor advertising are garish, bizarre, and even grotesque. In the Highway Beautification Act of 1965 [1] Congress declared "that the erection and maintenance of outdoor advertising signs, displays, and devices in areas adjacent to the Interstate System and the primary system [of highways] should be controlled in order to protect the public investment in such highways, to promote the safety and recreational value of public travel, and to preserve natural beauty. * * * [2] Federal-aid highway funds apportioned on or after January 1, 1968, to any State which the Secretary [of the Department of Transportation] determines has not made provision for the effective control of the erection and maintenance along the Interstate [highway] System and the primary system of outdoor advertising signs, displays, and devices which are within six hundred and sixty feet of the nearest edge of the right-of-way and visible from the main traveled way of the system, shall be reduced by amount equal to 10 per centum of the amounts which would otherwise be apportioned to such State under * * * [federal law], until such time as such State shall provide for such effective control. Any amount which is withheld from apportionment to any State * * * [is to be] reapportioned to the other States. Whenever he determines it to be in the public interest, the Secretary may suspend, for such periods as he deems necessary, the application of this * * * [section] to a State." [3] Congress defined the term "effective control" as follows: "that after January 1, 1968, such signs, displays, and devices shall, pursuant to * * * [the Act], be limited to (1) directional and other official signs and notices, which signs and notices shall include,

---

1. Pub.L. 89–285, 79 Stat. 1028.

2. 23 U.S.C.A. § 131(a).

3. 23 U.S.C.A. § 131(b).

but not be limited to, signs and notices pertaining to natural wonders, scenic and historical attractions, which are required or authorized by law, which shall conform to national standards hereby authorized to be promulgated by the Secretary hereunder, which standards shall contain provisions concerning the lighting, size, number, and spacing of signs, and such other requirements as may be appropriate to implement this * * * [Act], (2) signs, displays, and devices advertising the sale or lease of property upon which they are located, and (3) signs, displays, and devices advertising activities conducted on the property on which they are located."[4]

Alert to the fact that in particular localities state, county, municipal or town governments may have followed a pattern of zoning or non-zoning practices which recognizes the existence of industrial or commercial areas, Congress provided that if the presence of outdoor advertising signs had become customary, then "signs, displays, and devices whose size, lighting, and spacing" consistent with customary use, may, if a state and the Secretary agree, "be erected and maintained within six hundred and sixty feet of the nearest edge of the right-of-way within areas adjacent to the Interstate and primary systems which are" within zoned or unzoned industrial or commercial areas.[5]

Signs, displays, or devices "lawfully in existence" on September 1, 1965, but violative of the Act, may not be required "to be removed until July 1, 1970. Any other sign, display, or device lawfully erected which does not conform to the * * * [Act may] not be required to be removed until the end of the fifth year after it becomes nonconforming."[6] The Act provides that "[j]ust compensation" should "be paid upon the removal of * * * advertising signs, displays, and devices * * * lawfully in existence on the date of the enactment of * * * [the Act or], lawfully on any highway made a part of the interstate or primary system on or after the date of enactment of * * * the Act or, * * * lawfully erected on or after January 1, 1968.[7] The Federal share of such compensation [is set at] 75 per centum."[8] Payment is to be made for "taking from the owner of such sign, display, or device of all right, title, leasehold, and interest in such sign, display, or device; and * * * taking from the owner of the real property on which the sign, display, or device is located, of the right to erect and maintain such signs, displays, and devices thereon."[9] In the event "the Federal share of the just compensation is not available to make any necessary payment, then "[n]o sign, display, or device * * * [may] be required to be removed under" the terms of the Act.[10]

4. 23 U.S.C.A. § 131(c).

5. 23 U.S.C.A. § 131(d).

6. 23 U.S.C.A. § 131(e).

7. 23 U.S.C.A. § 131(g).

8. 23 U.S.C.A. § 131(g).

9. 23 U.S.C.A. § 131(g).

10. 23 U.S.C.A. § 131(n).

To be certain that state and local governments would not be denied the opportunity to impose further restrictions on outdoor advertising Congress expressly provided that the Act should not be interpreted so as to "prohibit a State from establishing standards imposing stricter limitations with respect to signs, displays, and devices, on the Federal-aid highway systems than those established under * * * [the Act]."[11]

The Highway Beautification Act treats junkyards in essentially the same fashion as outdoor advertising. Congress asserted that it found and declared "that the establishment and use and maintenance of junkyards in areas adjacent to the Interstate System and the primary system [of highways] should be controlled in order to protect the public investment in such highways, to promote the safety and recreational values of public travel, and to preserve natural beauty."[12] A state's failure to provide "for effective control of the establishment and maintenance along the [highway systems] of outdoor junkyards, which are within one thousand feet of the nearest edge of the right-of-way and visible from the main traveled way of the system" would result in the state being denied ten percent of the federal-aid highway funds it had been scheduled to receive.[13] "Effective control" is said to mean "that by January 1, 1968, such junkyards shall be screened by natural objects, plantings, fences, or other appropriate means so as not to be visible from the main traveled way of the system, or shall be removed from sight."[14] Junk is defined as "old or scrap copper, brass, rope, rags, batteries, paper, trash, rubber debris, waste, or junked, dismantled, or wrecked automobiles, or parts thereof, iron, steel, and other old or scrap ferrous or nonferrous material."[15] For the purposes of the Act junkyard means "an establishment or place of business which is maintained, operated, or used for storing, keeping, buying, or selling junk, or for the maintenance or operation of an automobile graveyard, and * * * [includes] garbage dumps and sanitary fills."[16] Automobile graveyard is said to "mean any establishment or place of business which is maintained, used, or operated for storing, keeping, buying, or selling wrecked, scrapped, ruined, or dismantled motor vehicles or motor vehicle parts."[17] Similar to the exception provided for the maintenance of outdoor advertising, a junkyard may be operated within "one thousand feet" from a highway system if it is located in an area "used for industrial activities, as determined by the several States subject to approval by the Secretary [of Transportation]."[18] The time provisions pertaining to the

11.   23 U.S.C.A. § 131(k).

12.   23 U.S.C.A. § 136(a).

13.   23 U.S.C.A. § 136(b).

14.   23 U.S.C.A. § 136(c).

15.   23 U.S.C.A. § 136(d).

16.   23 U.S.C.A. § 136(f).

17.   23 U.S.C.A. § 136(e).

18.   23 U.S.C.A. § 136(g).

removal of a junkyard are the same as that specified for the termination of a prohibited form of outdoor advertising. The Federal government's share of the "just compensation" to "be paid the owner for the relocation, removal, or disposal of" a junkyard as provided for in the Act is "75 per centum." [19] When "landscaping and screening costs" are incurred by state government following the removal of a junkyard the "Federal share" is also "75 per centum." [20] States are accorded the right to establish "standards imposing stricter limitations with respect to outdoor junkyards."[21]

To restore, preserve, and enhance the "scenic beauty adjacent" to highways the Secretary of Transportation "may approve * * * [a]n amount equivalent to 3 per centum of the funds appropriated to a State for Federal-aid highways for any fiscal year * * * [to] be used for landscape and roadside developments within the highway right-of-way."[22]

Federal policy leaves most forms of visual pollution untouched, making it a matter primarily for state and local control. States have placed restrictions on outdoor advertising and junkyards which are located in close proximity to state roads. Zoning ordinances have been adopted to promote and protect visual aesthetics. Statutes may limit the amount of land space a builder may cover with a structure, requiring him to leave a portion of his property vacant.

A number of state legislatures have proclaimed it to be a matter of state policy that attention be paid to aesthetics. The New York State Legislature, for example, has declared that "[t]he state enjoys an abundance of natural and man-made beauty which greatly enriches the lives of the people of * * * [the state and announced that t]he preservation, enhancement and promotion of this beauty * * * [would] contribute significantly to the enjoyment of the people who live and work in the state, as well as the millions of visitors who come to the state each year."[23] It stated that [f]urther efforts by state government are needed to coordinate and promote programs contributing to the natural and man-made beauty, and to provide advice and assistance to local governments."[24] To carry out the declared policy the legislature created a "natural beauty commission." Among the powers and duties of the commission are the development of "policies and programs to preserve and enhance the natural and man-made beauty of the state," advising, encouraging, and assisting "local governments in the development and coordination of policies, programs and activities * * * to preserve and enhance the natural and man-made beauty of the state * * * [and to p]romote the application of aesthetic considerations in the location, design, con-

---

19. 23 U.S.C.A. § 136(j).

20. 23 U.S.C.A. § 136(i).

21. 23 U.S.C.A. § 136(l).

22. 23 U.S.C.A. § 319(b).

23. Executive Law § 620.

24. Executive Law § 620.

struction and maintenance of state lands, projects and buildings." [25] The New York State Legislature has also "declared" it "to be the policy of the state, in proper balance, with the prudent expenditure of public funds, to strive for architectural design of the highest quality in all state and other construction activities, and to make grants in aid to units of local government for the rehabilitation of public buildings which are of historic or architectural importance." [26] To implement this policy a Council on Architecture has been established. This body is charged with encouraging "excellence in architectural design in all public buildings and other structures constructed by the state or under the supervision of any state agency or authority" and stimulating "interest in architectural excellence in public and private construction throughout the state." [27]

Illustrative of judicial awareness of the need to protect the visual environment is judicial acceptance of the proposition that legislation may proscribe the erection of such structures as gasoline stations. Refusing to find such legislation unconstitutional, one court noted that unsuccessful stations tend to remain abandoned since such structures have no other commercial purpose. It asserted that often they become "magnets for junk cars and sometimes havens for mice, rats and insects. If there are several stations of this kind in one area, which there are likely to be in a commercial district, the neighborhood soon becomes a blighted eyesore and one greatly diminished in aesthetic and commercial appeal." Speaking of the deleterious aspects of abandoned stations the court asserted that it "recognized that the enhancement of the aesthetic appeal of a community is a proper exercise of police power. * * * For the value of scenic surroundings to tourists, prospective residents and commercial development cannot be overstated. But in an age in which the preservation of the quality of our environment has become such a national goal, a concern for aesthetics seems even more urgent. * * * Abandoned gas stations substantially detract from that environment * * *." [28]

The contemporary values, goals, and policies of a people are in part a product of their past. In search of perspective, looking for a sense of proportion, seeking to avoid alienation, in quest of identity, individuals may turn to the past for insights, guidance, support, and strength. Industrial, commercial, demographic, and a multitude of other factors incessantly press for the obliteration of historically significant sites. Making use of modern day technology and equipment one man, in a matter of moments, can despoil an irreplaceable landmark. A fervent desire to preserve historical sites has given rise to federal, state, and local governmental pronouncements aimed at preventing their destruction.

25. Executive Law § 622.

26. Executive Law § 670.

27. Executive Law § 672.

28. Stone v. City of Maitland (5th Cir. 1971) 446 F.2d 83.

On the national level Congress has recognized that "the major burdens of historic preservation have been borne and major efforts [have been] initiated by private agencies and individuals." Acknowledging that "both should continue to play a vital role" Congress has insisted that "it is nevertheless necessary and appropriate for the Federal government to accelerate its historic preservation programs and activities, to give maximum encouragement to agencies and individuals undertaking preservation by private means, and to assist State and local governments and the National Trust for Historic Preservation in the United States to expand and accelerate their historic preservation programs and activities." Congress stated that it "finds and declares — (a) that the spirit and direction of the Nation are founded upon and reflected in its historic past; (b) that the historical and cultural foundations of the Nation should be preserved as a living part of our community life and development in order to give a sense of orientation to the American people; and (c) that * * * the present governmental and nongovernmental historic preservation programs and activities are inadequate to insure future generations a genuine opportunity to appreciate and enjoy the rich heritage of our Nation * * *." [29]

To carry out the stated policy Congress has authorized the Secretary of the Interior "to expand and maintain a national register of districts, sites, buildings, structures, and objects significant in American history, architecture, archeology, and culture, * * * [to be known as the National Register], and to grant funds to States for the purpose of preparing comprehensive statewide historic surveys and plans, in accordance with criteria established by the Secretary, for the preservation, acquisition, and development of such properties; (2) to establish a program of matching grants-in-aid to States for projects having as their purpose the preservation for public benefit of properties that are significant in American history, architecture, archeology, and culture; and (3) to establish a program of matching grants-in-aid to the National Trust for Historic Preservation in the United States, chartered by act of Congress approved October 26, 1949 * * *, for the purpose of carrying out the responsibilities of the National Trust." States may obtain grants by complying with the conditions set forth by Congress and the "regulations and procedures prescribed by" the Secretary of the Interior.[30] The Secretary of Housing and Urban Development is empowered "to make grants to the National Trust for Historic Preservation, on such terms and conditions and in such amounts (not exceeding $90,000 with respect to any one structure) as he deems appropriate, to cover the costs incurred by such Trust in renovating or restoring structures which it considers to be of historic or architectual value and which it has ac-

29. 16 U.S.C.A. § 470.   30. 16 U.S.C.A. § 470b.

cepted and will maintain (after such renovation or restoration) for historic purposes."[31]

To effect the stated policy Congress has established an Advisory Council on Historic Preservation composed of twenty persons, including the Attorney General, the Secretaries of Interior, Housing and Urban Development, Commerce, Treasury, Agriculture, and the Smithsonian Institute, the Chairman of the National Trust for Historic Preservation, and ten persons "appointed by the President from outside of the Federal Government. In making these appointments, the President * * * [is to] give due consideration to the selection of officers of State and local governments and individuals who are significantly interested and experienced in the matters to be considered by the Council."[32]

The Council's duties include advising "the President and the Congress on matters relating to historic preservation;" recommending "measures to coordinate activities of Federal, State, and local agencies and private institutions and individuals relating to historic preservation;" encouraging, "in cooperation with the National Trust for Historic Preservation and appropriate private agencies, public interest and participation in historic preservation;" advising "as to guidelines for the assistance of State and local governments in drafting legislation relating to historic preservation;" and encouraging "in cooperation with appropriate public and private agencies and institutions, training and education in the field of historic preservation." [33] Annually, the Council must submit "a comprehensive report of its activities and the results of its studies to the President and the Congress.[34] Additional reports may be submitted whenever the Council "deems" it "advisable." [35]

To insure that Federal agencies take into account its declared policy, Congress has provided that "[t]he head of any Federal agency having direct or indirect jurisdiction over a proposed Federal or federally assisted undertaking in any State and the head of any Federal department or independent agency having authority to license any undertaking shall, prior to the approval of the expenditure of any Federal funds on the undertaking or prior to the issuance of any license, as the case may be, take into account the effect of the undertaking on any district, site, building, structure, or object that is included in the National Register. The head of any such Federal agency shall afford the Advisory Council on Historic Preservation * * * a reasonable opportunity to comment with regard to such undertaking."[36]

31. 16 U.S.C.A. § 470b–1.

32. 16 U.S.C.A. § 470i(a) (11).

33. 16 U.S.C.A. § 470(j) (a).

34. 16 U.S.C.A. § 470j(b).

35. 16 U.S.C.A. § 470j(b).

36. 16 U.S.C.A. § 470f.

States have displayed their interest in the preservation of historic sites by adopting legislation akin to that of Congress. For instance, Massachusetts has established a commission which has the authority "to examine * * * sites and structures * * * and to make recommendations concerning their historical significance. Any such site or structure deemed by the commission to be of substantial historical significance to the * * * state may, with the written consent of the person or persons claiming ownership, and * * * [others having] recorded interests * * * be certified by the commission as an historic landmark and a list of such certified historic landmarks * * * [is to be] maintained and published annually by the state secretary * * *. The commission may establish standards for the care and management of such certified landmarks, and may withdraw such certification for failure to maintain such standards * * *. No certified historic landmark * * * [may] be altered in such a manner as would seriously impair its historical values without permission of the commission, except that persons having recorded interests who have not given written consent to the certification and those claiming under them * * * [are] not * * * required to obtain such permission. Before granting such permission the commission * * * [must] hold a public hearing. The commission may grant such permission or may withhold permission for any period up to one year during which time the commission * * * [must] consult with civic groups, public agencies and interested citizens to ascertain what action, if any, ought to be taken to preserve such landmark, and * * * [is required to] make recommendations for its preservation to the * * * [state] or its political subdivisions, to historical societies or to other interested civic organizations."[37] The law vests in the state's court of general jurisdiction the authority to exercise its equity powers to enforce the law. "[O]n petition of any party in interest, [the court] may alter, amend, or revoke the order of the commission." State law provides that "[n]o historic landmark certified * * * [by the commission] and no property owned, preserved and maintained by any historical organization or society as an ancient landmark or as property of historical or antiquarian interest shall be taken without" the express consent of the legislature.[38]

The success of federal, state, and local governmental programs directed at preserving aesthetics and historical sites to a great extent will be determined by the level of funding adopted by legislative bodies. The police power may be employed to shield the public from blatant eyesores. When relying on this power government need not indemnify the property owner for the loss he incurs as a result of the restrictions placed on the use of his property. But the police power can not be invoked in every case in which the intended use of property will produce aesthetic blight or wreck a historic site. In instanc-

37. Chapter 9, § 27.   38. Chapter 79, § 5A.

es in which government denies one an opportunity to make some beneficial use of his property, government must rely upon its power of eminent domain and pay him just compensation. Without adequate funding progress toward protecting aesthetics and historical landmarks will be limited.

E. B. ELLIOTT ADV. CO. v. METROPOLITAN DADE COUNTY

United States Court of Appeals, Fifth Circuit, 1970.
425 F.2d 1141.

[Defendant's Ordinance No. 63–26 prohibits all commercial outdoor advertising signs oriented to and serving any expressway to be erected within 200 feet of an expressway except for (1) "temporary signs" such as those advertising the property on which they are located to be for sale or rent and (2) "point of sale signs" such as those advertising merchandise or products sold on the premises and then only if they are oriented to a street which provides access to the place of business and if visible from an expressway, only indirectly serving the expressway. Violations are punishable by fine or imprisonment and may be enjoined. Plaintiffs, engaged in the outdoor advertising business, brought a class declaratory judgment action challenging the constitutionality of the Ordinance. From a District Court judgment in favor of the defendant they appealed.]

Lewis R. Morgan, Circuit Judge: * * *

Ordinance No. 63–26 is apparently designed to accomplish two ends: to promote highway safety on the expressway system of Dade County and to improve the beauty of the land surrounding these expressways thus to maintain and increase the attractiveness of the area to tourists, and residents alike, and thus influence the economic prosperity of the county. There can be no doubt but that these objectives are constitutionally permissible under the police power of the State of Florida. Florida has long recognized that outdoor advertising can be regulated to promote highway safety. * * *

Once it be conceded that aesthetics is a valid subject of legislative concern, the conclusion seems inescapable that reasonable legislation designed to promote that end is a valid and permissible exercise of the police power.

The same can be said with equal vigor of highway safety.

* * *

The appellants argue that Ordinance No. 63–26 bears no reasonable relationship to highway safety, relying on the testimony of highway safety experts whose studies revealed no discernible correlation between the placement of outdoor advertising signs along limited access highways, as here involved, and the occurrence of automobile accidents. Even so, we are unable to say that the Board of County Commissioners of Dade County was unreasonable in basing the ordinance, at least partially, on highway safety. The essential purpose of an advertising sign placed adjacent to a highway is to attract the attention of the motoring public long enough to convey a commercial message. Conceding that the message presented by an average sign can be comprehended by a motorist of average intelligence in an insignificant amount of time, and that eye movement improves the alertness of an expressway driver, the speed and density of modern expressway traffic, coupled with the braking limitations of the modern automobile, can conceivably make even the most insignificant amount of time during which a driver's attention is diverted a matter of direst consequences.

It is also clear that the prohibition of outdoor advertising signs within 200 feet of an expressway bears a reasonable relationship to basic aesthetic considerations. Granting that "beauty is to the eye of the beholder," it cannot be denied that outdoor advertising signs tend to interrupt what would otherwise be the "natural" landscape as seen from the highway, something it is apparently more and more felt that the American public has a right to see unhindered by billboards, whether the view is untouched or ravished by man. See Highway Beautification Act of 1965, 23 U.S.C. § 131, as amended (1966). Moreover, the importance of the tourist industry to Dade County tends to make Ordinance No. 63–26 reasonable in an economic sense because of the commercial benefits hoped to be realized from beautification.

The fact that Ordinance No. 63–26 prohibits commercial advertising signs in industrial or commercial areas of little or no natural beauty, or that it prohibits 40 commercial signs while leaving undisturbed 82 "point of sale signs" visible from the expressways, does not destroy its reasonable relationship to constitutionally permissible objectives. * * *

The next issue to be decided is whether Ordinance No. 63–26 invidiously discriminates against the appellants and the class they represent so as to constitute a denial of the equal protection of the laws under the Fourteenth Amendment.

* * *

Simply stated, the requirements of the Equal Protection Clause are met if "the classifications drawn in a statute are reasonable in light of its purpose". * * *

The equal protection clause of the Fourteenth Amendment does not take from the State the power to classify in the adoption of police laws, but admits of the exercise of a wide scope of discretion in that regard, and avoids what is done only when it is without any reasonable basis and therefore is purely arbitrary." * * *

* * *   The legislature may select one phase of one field and apply a remedy there, neglecting the others.   * * *   The prohibition of the Equal Protection Clause goes no further than the invidious discrimination.

The classification between commercial advertising signs and point of sale signs which is challenged here has been upheld as reasonable by many state courts.   * * *

The business sign is in actuality a part of the business itself, just as the structure housing the business is a part of it, and the authority to conduct the business in a district carries with it the right to maintain a business sign on the premises subject to reasonable regulations in that regard as in the case of this ordinance.   * * *

* * *   Moreover, the classification is reasonable in light of the purpose of Ordinance No. 63–26: the promotion of highway safety and highway beautification, in that the removal of outdoor advertising signs which are not related to the operation of a business on the premises on which they are located will tend to reduce the overall number of outdoor advertising signs and thereby reduce the number of driver distractions and the number of aesthetic eyesores along the expressways of Dade County.   * * *

* * *   Ordinance No. 63–26 is directed to correcting an evil the Board of County Commissioners has found to exist on the County's expressway system and the Board is not required under the Equal Protection Clause to correct all similar evils wherever they may exist in the County or none at all.

Ordinance No. 63–26 was enacted on July 2, 1963, and provides that nonconforming signs may continue to be maintained until March 1, 1968, thus providing an amortization period of five years.   In Standard Oil Co. v. City of Tallahassee, * * * it was held a zoning ordinance requiring the discontinuance of a nonconforming use after the expiration of a five-year amortization period did not constitute a deprivation of property without due process of law. * * * Therefore, the requirement contained in the ordinance that all nonconforming signs be removed by March 1, 1968, does not constitute a taking of property for which compensation must be given under the Fourteenth Amendment.

* * *

Affirmed.

PROBLEMS

1. The federal agency charged with administering national monuments and parks authorized construction of an observation tower in close proximity to a Civil War battleground. An association devoted to the preservation of historical landmarks, claiming the structure marred the site and added a superficial dimension, brought an action challenging the action. What judgment?

2. A town situated a short distance from the outskirts of a large city enacted an ordinance which prohibited construction of more than one 2 family dwelling on a one acre lot on 75% of the town's remaining open land. The ordinance's preamble declared the law was necessary to "preserve the area's great natural beauty." Plaintiff, an association whose members were apartment dwellers, blacks, Puerto Ricans, and indigent persons brought an action to declare the ordinance unconstitutional, charging it denied them equal protection of the laws and that the town's concern with aesthetics was specious. Plaintiff insisted that a "cluster housing" approach, building multidwelling structures on only a part of the land devoted to residential use while leaving the remaining portion of the land in its natural state, was a viable alternative. What judgment?

3. A municipal ordinance barred alteration or destruction of any structure designated a landmark by the city council. Plaintiff owned several structures the council had designated a landmark. Desiring to erect apartment dwellings for low income persons, he brought an action to have the ordinance declared unconstitutional. What judgment?

4. To protect landmarks located in its expanding downtown area, a city enacted an ordinance which provided that an owner of property on which a landmark was located could request the city to deliver to him a "space certificate" which he could use or sell. Such a certificate set forth the maximum amount of floor space a new structure built on the property could contain under existing zoning legislation. A certificate holder could erect a structure elsewhere which, in addition to containing the maximum floor space authorized by existing law, could have part or all of the amount of space specified in the certificate. One who requested and received a certificate would be barred from altering or demolishing the landmark without the city's consent. Plaintiff, who did not own property on which a landmark was located, and unable to purchase a certificate at a price he regarded as reasonable, but desiring to construct an office building which contained more floor space than permitted by law, challenged the constitutionality of the ordinance. He claimed it placed him at a competitive disadvantage vis-à-vis builders who possessed a certificate since they would be permitted to build a larger office building than he on a parcel of property no larger than his. What judgment?

5. A federal agency charged with promoting law enforcement approved a state's request for federal funds to be used to construct a large, concrete-walled prison in a scenic area where there were many 18th and 19th century houses. The court was asked to reverse the agency's action on the ground that it had failed to comply with NEPA.[39] The agency stated that NEPA was not intended to apply to law enforcement activities. What judgment?

39. NEPA is the acronym for The National Environmental Policy Act.

Chapter 12

NOISE

Few persons enjoy total freedom from loud objectionable sounds. Some experience crescendos of raucous noises for only a small portion of the day. Others endure a cacophony of unwanted sounds throughout their waking hours. In some places an objectionable din plagues persons even during their sleeping hours.

Major discomforting noises emanate from subways, buses, trucks, automobiles, motorcycles, sirens, aircraft, industrial plants, and construction equipment. There are occupations in which disconcerting noises are always present. In the home refrigerators, air conditioners, washing machines, hair dryers, vacuum cleaners, exhaust fans, electric shavers, and blenders produce harsh sounds. Exposure to loud noise can result in physical injury and emotional upset. At particular levels under some circumstances noise can produce deafness, high blood pressure, a quickened pulse, a peptic ulcer, or heart damage. The emotional distress caused by noise can in turn trigger injury-causing accidents.

Federal, state and local governments have enacted laws designed to curb noise. Congress has undertaken to have the damage caused by noise studied. It has established within the Environmental Protection Agency an Office of Noise Abatement and Control. The task of this Office is to "carry out * * * a full and complete investigation and study of noise and its effect on the public health and welfare in order to (1) identify and classify causes and sources of noise and (2) determine—(A) effects at various levels; (B) projected growth of noise levels in urban areas through the year 2000; (C) the psychological and physiological effect on humans; (D) effects of sporadic extreme noise (such as jet noise near airports) as compared with constant noise; (E) effect on wildlife and property (including values); (F) effect of sonic booms on property (including values); and (G) such other matters as may be of interest in the public welfare."[1] Reports of the Office's studies and "recommendations for legislation or other action" are to be transmitted to the President and Congress. "In any case where any Federal department or agency is carrying out or sponsoring any activity resulting in noise which the Administrator [of the Environmental Protection Agency] determines amounts to a public nuisance or is otherwise objectionable, such department or agency * * * [is required to] consult with the Administrator, to determine possible means of abating such noise."[2]

The Secretary of Transportation is obliged, to "promulgate guidelines designed to assure that possible adverse economic, social,

---

1. 42 U.S.C.A. § 1858(a).   2. 42 U.S.C.A. § 1858(c).

and environmental effects relating to any proposed project on any Federal-aid [highway] system have been fully considered in developing such project, and that the final decisions on the project * * * [take] into consideration * * * such adverse effects * * * [as] noise."[3]

"In order to afford present and future relief and protection to the public from unnecessary aircraft noise and sonic boom, [Congress has provided that] the Administrator of the Federal Aviation Administration, after consultation with the Secretary of Transportation * * * [should] prescribe and amend standards for the measurement of aircraft noise and sonic boom * * * and * * * prescribe and amend such rules and regulations as he may find necessary to provide for the control and abatement of aircraft noise and sonic boom, including the application of such standards, rules, and regulations in the issuance, amendment, modification, suspension, or revocation of any certificate * * * [authorizing the operation and maintenance of an airport under 49 U.S.C.A. § 1432]."[4]

Congress has empowered the Secretary of Health, Education, and Welfare to "establish * * * mandatory * * * maximum noise exposure levels for all underground coal mines."[5]

Some states have set 90 decibels as the maximum noise an automobile may lawfully emit while in operation. Legislation has also been adopted prohibiting the use of snow vehicles which produce more than the prescribed decibel level. Cities and towns have passed ordinances barring activities which cause more than a stated maximum decibel level. Many state and local governments are in the process of setting decibel limits on such things as construction equipment, air conditioners, public address systems, garbage trucks, and emergency sirens.

GRIGGS v. COUNTY OF ALLEGHENY, PENNSYLVANIA

Supreme Court of the United States, 1962.
82 S.Ct. 531, 369 U.S. 84, 7 L.Ed.2d 585.

[Petitioner, whose home is located in close proximity to the airport owned and operated by the respondent, brought an action to recover compensatory damages claiming that the respondent had appropriated petitioner's property. The airport was designed for public use in conformity with the rules and regulations of the Civil Aeronautics Administration within the scope of the National Airport Plan. The approach area to the airport's northeast runway left a clearance of 11.36 feet between an approaching aircraft's glidepath and the top of the chimney of the petitioner's home. Following local practice,

3. 23 U.S.C.A. § 109(h) (1).   5. 30 U.S.C.A. § 846.

4. 49 U.S.C.A. § 1431(a).

the trial court appointed a Board of Viewers to determine if there had been a taking, and if so, the amount of compensation to be paid. The Board found that there had been a taking and that $12,690 was due the petitioner. The trial court approved the report. The Supreme Court of Pennsylvania, by a divided vote, decided that even if there had been a taking in the constitutional sense, the respondent was not liable. Certiorari was granted.]

MR. JUSTICE DOUGLAS delivered the opinion of the Court.

* * *   Judge Bell, dissenting below, accurately summarized the uncontroverted facts as follows:

"Regular and almost continuous daily flights, often several minutes apart, have been made by a number of airlines directly over and very, very close to plaintiff's residence. During these flights it was often impossible for people in the house to converse or to talk on the telephone. The plaintiff and the members of his household (depending on the flight which in turn sometimes depended on the wind) were frequently unable to sleep even with ear plugs and sleeping pills; they would frequently be awakened by the flight and the noise of the planes; the windows of their home would frequently rattle and at times plaster fell down from the walls and ceilings; their health was affected and impaired, and they sometimes were compelled to sleep elsewhere. Moreover, their house was so close to the runways or path of glide that as the spokesman for the members of the Airlines Pilot Association admitted 'If we had engine failure we would have no course but to plow into your house.' "

* * *

It is argued that though there was a "taking," someone other than respondent was the taker—the airlines or the C.A.A. acting as an authorized representative of the United States. We think, however, that respondent, which was the promoter, owner, and lessor of the airport, was in these circumstances the one who took the air easement in the constitutional sense. Respondent decided, subject to the approval of the C.A.A., where the airport would be built, what runways it would need, their direction and length, and what land and navigation easements would be needed. The Federal Government takes nothing; it is the local authority which decides to build an airport *vel non*, and where it is to be located. We see no difference between its responsibility for the air easements necessary for operation of the airport and its responsibility for the land on which the runways were built. Nor did the Congress when it designed the legislation for a National Airport Plan. * * * Congress provided * * * for the payment to the owners of airports, whose plans were approved by the Administrator, of a share of "the allowable project costs" including the "costs of acquiring land or interests therein or easements through or other interests in air space." * * * A county that designed and constructed a bridge would not have a usable facility unless it had at least an easement over the land necessary for the approaches to the bridge. Why should one who designs, constructs, and uses an airport be in a more favorable position so far as the Fourteenth Amendment is concerned? That the instant "taking" was "for public use" is not debatable. For respondent agreed with the C.A.A. that it would operate the airport "for the use and benefit of the public," that it would operate it "on fair and reasonable terms and without unjust discrimination," and that it would not allow any carrier to acquire "any exclusive right" to its use.

The glide path for the northeast runway is as necessary for the operation of the airport as is a surface right of way for operation of a bridge, or as is the land for the operation of a dam. * * * an adequate approach way is as necessary a part of an airport as is the ground on which the airstrip, itself, is constructed * * *." Without the "approach areas," an airport is indeed not operable. Respondent in designing it had to acquire some private property. Our conclusion is that by constitutional standards it did not acquire enough.

Reversed.

*   *   *

NAIR v. THAW

Supreme Court of Connecticut, 1968.
242 A.2d 757, 156 Conn. 445.

[To cool his $300,000 home in West Hartford located in an AA residence zone defendant built a semidetached commercial type cooling tower. The ordinary average-sized residence in the locality contained a 60,000 BTU unit. Defendant's tower had a 300,000 BTU unit. Plaintiff, occupying an adjoining residence, claiming that operation of the unit injuriously affected her health and made it impossible for her to occupy her home, brought an action for an injunction and $100,000 damages charging that the defendant's tower violated the zoning ordinance and constituted a nuisance. The trial court found that before the defendant had taken corrective steps the unit continually emitted noise which was "annoying and irritating to persons of average sensibilities." It awarded the plaintiff $3500 and enjoined operation of the unit between the hours of 10 p.m. and 8 a.m. until the sound level it produced was reduced. Both parties appealed.]

HOUSE, ASSOCIATE JUSTICE. * * * In an AA residence zone * * * no buildings are permitted other than single-family residences "together with such other buildings as are ordinarily appurtenant thereto." * * * The court found that the cooling tower "is reasonably suited to the air-conditioning needs of defendant's residence" and concluded that the installation and maintenance of the tower "does not violate the * * * zoning ordinance." * * * Although no similar air-conditioning unit exists in any other residence in West Hartford, the court found that there are approximately seven such units installed in residences throughout the country. We cannot say as a matter of law that the court could not reasonably conclude that the semidetached cooling tower which is reasonably suited to the air-conditioning needs of the particular residence is a building which is ordinarily appurtenant to such a residence.

* * *

"For over one hundred years in this state, we have recognized the general power of equity to afford relief by injunction and damages for injury caused by a nuisance created by the unreasonable conduct on one's own property of an otherwise lawful activity. * * *" "It is the duty of every person to make a reasonable use of his own property so as to occasion no unnecessary damage or annoyance to his neighbor. If the use is unreasonable the law will hold him responsible." * * * "Determining unreasonableness is essentially a weighing process, involving a comparative evaluation of conflicting interests in various situations according to objective legal standards."

* * * "[t]he issuance of an injunction and the scope and quantum of injunctive relief rests in the sound discretion of the trier." * * * There is nothing in the record in the present case which would justify us in holding on either the plaintiff's appeal or the defendant's appeal that the injunction as issued transcends the proper limits of the court's discretion exercised after a full hearing and after consideration of a mass of evidence and conflicting expert scientific opinion.

Nor do we find any error in the award of damages to the plaintiff in the amount of $3500. The plaintiff claims that the court erred in refusing to award exemplary damages. "Concerning this, it is enough to say that the plaintiff did not allege in * * * [her] complaint any wanton or malicious misconduct of the defendant, or negligence tantamount to such misconduct. Further, no facts have been found from which could be reached a reasonable conclusion that the acts of the defendant were of such a kind." The defendant in his appeal asserts that the award was excessive. The plaintiff was entitled to recover for the physical discomfort and annoyance caused by the defendant's unreasonable use of his air-conditioning equipment so far as it materially affected the comfortable enjoyment and occupancy of her home and interfered with her use and enjoyment of her property. "In the nature of things such damages are not susceptible of exact pecuniary computation and must be left largely to the sound judgment of the trier. * * * [W]e find nothing in the record which would justify us in concluding that the amount which the trial court has fixed is not reasonable compensation."

* * *

There is no error on either appeal.

* * *

———

PROBLEMS

1. The Federal Aviation Administration approved an engine for use in aircraft. The defendant's aircraft used two such engines. He was charged with violating a state anti-noise statute. The noise generated by each engine exceeded the state's prescribed maximum decibel level. In the Federal Aviation Act of 1958, Congress asserted that the United States possesses and exercises "complete and exclusive national sovereignty in the airspace of the United States." What judgment?

2. Plaintiff maintained and operated an elementary school. A portion of the land on which the school was located was condemned by the state highway commission for use in a new highway system. After the highway was constructed heavy traffic during school hours caused a high level of noise and air pollution. To permit students in classrooms fronting on the highway to hear their teachers and not suffer the anguish caused by the noxious odors and gases discharged from automobiles, the plaintiff sealed the classrooms and installed air conditioners. Prior to the construction of the highway, neither sealing nor the use of air conditioners was necessary. Is the plaintiff entitled to receive payment from the state for the reasonable cost of the alterations and installations?

3. The Federal Tort Claims Act, 28 U.S.C.A. § 1346(b) authorizes a suit against the government "for * * * loss of property * * * caused by the negligence or wrongful act or omission of any employee of the government while acting within the scope of his office or employment." Plaintiff's home was damaged by "sonic booms" caused by tests carried on by the Federal Aviation Administration. He brought suit under the Act. The government moved to dismiss, claiming that the agency's employees had not acted negligently or wrongfully. What judgment?

4. Sonic booms caused by United States Air Force planes damaged plaintiff's house beyond repair. In a suit brought under the Federal Tort Claims Act the government moved for summary judgment in its favor on the ground that the airmen had not acted negligently. The plaintiff relied upon the law of the state in which his home was located. It imposed a standard of strict liability with respect to concussion damage. He urged that supersonic flight was likewise an ultrahazardous activity and therefore imposed liability without fault. What judgment?

5.   Under the Tort Claims Act the government is not liable for damages resulting from "the exercise or performance or the failure to exercise or perform a discretionary function or duty."   A test firing of a Saturn rocket caused a concussion which severely damaged the plaintiff's home.   The government denied liability on the ground that the decision as to the time of the launch and the amount of the thrust was discretionary and hence did not subject the government to liability.   What judgment?

Chapter 13

STRIP-MINING

Coal is widely used for the production of electrical energy. It serves as a source for the manufacture of cleaner forms of fuel. Traditionally coal has been obtained by tunneling beneath the earth's surface. Within the last decade and a half strip mining has attracted the attention of coal operators. It is less expensive than the tunneling process. Instead of digging beneath the earth's surface, the land's surface is stripped of its overburden, that is, earth, vegetation and rock, and the underlying coal seams are then removed.

Strip-mining transforms what may have once been an aesthetically pleasing forested countryside into a barren ugly wasteland. When sides of mountains are strip-mined a cavity usually remains between the residue of the mountain and what was once the mountainside. The outermost edge is referred to as a highwall. On top of and alongside of the highwall, earth, rock, and remains of trees accumulate into a pile of debris known as a spoilbank. Spoilbanks may overhang streams, highways, or homes. They are a hazard to life, property, and the local water supply. Strip-mining commonly causes surrounding brooks and streams to become filled with silt and acid. After an area has been strip-mined, heavy rains are more likely to cause flooding than when the earth's surface was intact. Areas which have been strip-mined are more likely to have landslides than was the case before any mining was carried on. Following strip-mining, erosion occurs at a faster than ordinary rate. Strip-mining may put an end to what had been a sanctuary for wildlife.

There has been widespread clamor that legislative action be taken against strip-mining. Anti-strip-mining legislation may follow one of two patterns. It may totally ban it or prescribe the fashion in which it may be carried out and require that those who engage in it reclaim the land after they have stripped it of coal. It has been proposed that strip-mining be made a subject of federal regulation. Ardent opponents of strip-mining insist that it is incumbent upon Congress to prohibit strip-mining. Advocates of strip-mining insist that regulation and reclamation are preferable. They point out that by compelling strip miners to reclaim the land they have despoiled society can reap the benefits of strip-mining without permanently destroying the landscape.

SIGETY v. STATE BOARD OF HEALTH

Supreme Court of Montana, 1971.
482 P.2d 574.

[In 1964 the plaintiff began to make use of a sluice washing plant in his mining operations. In 1969, before he could put into use a larger plant he had purchased, a statute entitled "Dredge Mining Regulation and Land Preservation Act" was passed. It prohibited mining by sluice washing without a permit and payment of a $100 fee and filing of a $10,000 surety bond for each 10 acres or less to be so mined. Such mine operators were obliged to restore disturbed land. A violation of the law was a misdemeanor, could be enjoined, and made the violator subject to a suit for money damages. In a declaratory judgment action brought by the plaintiff the trial court held the Act unconstitutional. Defendants appealed.]

FRANK E. BLAIR, DISTRICT JUDGE. * * *

* * * Article V, Section 23 of the Montana Constitution * * * reads * * *:

"No bill, * * * shall be passed containing more than one subject, which shall be clearly expressed in its title; but if any subject shall be embraced in any act which shall not be expressed in the title, such act shall be void only as to so much thereof as shall not be so expressed."

* * *

"The reasons which prompted the enactment of * * * [this] constitutional provision are: To restrict the legislature to the enactment of laws the objects of which legislators and the public as well may be advised of, to the end that any who are interested, whether as representatives or those represented, may be intelligently watchful of the course of the pending bill. * * * to prevent legislators and the people from being misled by false or deceptive titles, and to guard against fraud in legislation by way of incorporating into a law provisions concerning which neither legislators nor the public have had any intimation through the title read or published.' " * * *

The title of said act: "The Dredge Mining Regulation and Land Preservation Act" is drafted in the simplest language. * * *

* * * [the Act regulates] in addition to * * * [dredge mining] sluice-washing * * * [which is not] included in the title of the act * * *.

* * * it is clear that a "dredge" and a "sluice-washing plant" are distinct and different objects, and because sluice-washing plants are not mentioned in the title of the bill enacting Chapter 123 of the Laws of 1969, said act violates Article V, Section 23, of the State Constitution.

* * *

Section 1 of the * * * Fourteenth Amendment * * * provides in part as follows:

" * * * No State shall make or enforce any law which shall * * * deny to any person within its jurisdiction the equal protection of the laws."

Section 3 of the Dredge Mining Act reads:

"This act shall not be construed to include any mechanical operation primarily intended for open pit mining, strip coal mining, irrigation, extraction of gravel for construction and/or road building purposes, or agricultural purposes."

This section is a clear-cut exemption of all open pit mining, strip coal mining, irrigation water exits, and extraction of gravel for construction and/or road building purposes. It is clear from * * * the evidence that none of the witnesses for either of the parties could offer any reason for differentiating between mining operations regulated under this act and those exempted therefrom concerning any damages to lands, streams or water courses, nor does the act itself contain any legislative findings offering any reasons for the classification of dredge mining operations as different from other operations which disturb the ground in or near streams or riverbeds.

* * * *to justify such discriminatory legislation, and avoid the condemnation of the Fourteenth Amendment to the federal Constitution, the classification must be reasonable—that is, must be based upon substantial distinctions which really make one class different from another.*"

* * * *the classification must rest upon some ground of difference having a fair and substantial relation to the object of the legislation, so that all persons similarly circumstanced shall be treated alike.*" * * *.

We hold that the exemptions set forth in Section 3 * * * is [sic] prohibited by the equal protection clause of the Fourteenth Amendment * * *.

* * * the judgment of the district court is * * * affirmed.

———

PROBLEMS

1. The National Materials Policy Act of 1970, Pub.L. 91–512, §§ 201–206, entrusts a seven member National Commission on Materials Policy with the task of developing "a national materials policy." The Act directs the Commission to recommend to the President and the Congress "means for the extraction, development, and use of materials which are susceptible to recycling, reuse, or self-destruction, in order to enhance environmental quality and conserve materials." What role, if any, should the Commission assign to state and local governments?

2. The federal government holds title to vast land areas containing large quantities of timber, minerals, and oil. As the demand for these resources increases the nature of the restrictions the law should place on their exploitation by the private sector warrants in-depth consideration. In arriving at an acceptable national policy, how much attention should be given to aesthetic and recreational factors?

3. Anti-strip-mining legislation must necessarily raise the cost of coal and industrial products which require the use of coal for their manufacture. Is there some point at which economic considerations outweigh aesthetic and recreational ones?

4. Plaintiff, an ardent conservationist, was in quest of evidence that the defendant, who was engaged in strip mining, was dumping refuse into a stream in violation of the Rivers and Harbors Act of 1899. To keep trespassers off his property, the defendant constructed a 10 foot high wire fence, posted large signs which read "KEEP OFF—DANGER," and set a number of traps which, when tripped, would cause a rifle to discharge. One afternoon, after having observed the defendant and all of his employees leave, the plaintiff climbed over the fence and while in search of evidence tripped a trap. The discharged shell struck him in the abdomen, causing him serious injury. He sued the defendant for compensatory and punitive damages. What judgment?

5. In the course of his strip-mining operations the defendant bulldozed and drilled mountains near the plaintiffs' homes. As a result, following a heavy rainfall, the homes, which had never before been flooded, were deluged with mud, water, and garbage. The plaintiffs sued for damages. The defendant asked the judge to instruct the jury that if it found he made use of the newest available strip-mining equipment and employed generally followed strip-mining procedures, it should return a verdict in his favor. The plaintiffs asked the court to instruct the jury that strip-mining was an extra-hazardous activity, subjecting the defendant to strict liability. The judge chose to inform the jury as to the contents of the *res ipsa loquitor* doctrine and the meaning of negligence. The jury returned a verdict in favor of the defendant. The plaintiffs appealed. What judgment?

Chapter 14

INSECTICIDES

Man and insect are constantly at war with one another. Insects threaten man's food supply, health, at times his very survival. Insects destroy crops, defoliate and decimate trees, strike down farm and ranch animals, and play a part in the transmission of such diseases as malaria, yellow fever, and encephalitis. To overcome this dangerous foe man has engaged in extensive and endless research. To date, most of man's victories have been accomplished by the use of chemical substances. But a good deal of his success has been limited, ephemeral, and not without noxious drawbacks. While directed at insects, an effective insecticide may pose a threat to wildlife, domesticated animals, and man himself. What has been said about man's struggle to vanquish insects equally applies to his efforts to destroy other types of life, such as fungi and rodents, through the use of chemical substances.

In the early part of the 1960's there was a sudden upsurge of interest in the danger insecticides, fungicides, and rodenticides pose to man, animal life, and the environment. Vigorous and persuasive demands were voiced calling upon government to take steps to control the use of substances directed at destroying pests. Congress responded by enacting the Insecticide, Fungicide and Rodenticide Act of 1964 and by amending the Food and Drug Act. State and local governments have likewise passed legislation directed at controlling pesticides.

The 1964 Act is directed at substances and devices sold to destroy a variety of pests or plant life. It uses the term "economic poison" to connote "(1) any substance or mixture of substances intended for preventing, destroying, repelling, or mitigating any insects, rodents, nematodes, fungi, weeds, and other forms of plant or animal life or viruses, except viruses on or in living man or other animals, which the * * * [Administrator of the Environmental Protection Agency] shall declare to be a pest, and (2) any substance or mixture of substances intended for use as a plant regulator, defoliant or desiccant." [1] It defines insecticides, fungicides, herbicides, and nematocides as "substances" respectively intended for "preventing, destroying, repelling, or mitigating" insects, fungi, weeds, and nematodes. [2] A "rodenticide" is said to mean "any substance or mixture of substances intended for preventing, destroying, repelling, or mitigating rodents or any other vertebrate animal which the * * * [Administrator of the Environmental Protection Agency] shall declare to be a pest." [3] The Act defines "plant regulator," "de-

1. 7 U.S.C.A. § 135(a).　　　　3. 7 U.S.C.A. § 135(e).

2. 7 U.S.C.A. §§ 135(c), (d), (f), (g).

foliant," and "desiccant" as a substance or a mixture of substances which have the described impact on plant life.[4] Insect, nematode, and fungi are defined in biological terms. Weed is defined as "any plant which grows where not wanted."[5]

The Act prohibits the misbranding of economic poisons and devices. An "economic poison" is "misbranded" if "it is an imitation of or is offered for sale under the name of another economic poison; * * * the labeling accompanying it does not contain directions for use which are necessary and if complied with adequate for the protection of the public; * * * the label does not contain a warning or caution statement which may be necessary and if complied with adequate to prevent injury to living man and other vertebrate animals, vegetation, and useful invertebrate animals; * * * the label does not bear an ingredient statement * * *; if any word, statement, or other information required * * * [by the Act] to appear on the label or labeling is not prominently placed thereon with such conspicuousness (as compared with other words, statements, designs, or graphic matter in the labeling) and in such terms as to render it likely to be read and understood by the ordinary individual under customary conditions of purchase and use; * * * in the case of an insecticide, nematocide, fungicide, or herbicide when used as directed or in accordance with commonly recognized practice it shall be injurious to living man or other vertebrate animals, or vegetation, except weeds, to which it is applied, or to the person applying such economic poison: *Provided,* That physical or physiological effects on plants or parts thereof shall not be deemed to be injury, when this is the purpose for which the plant regulator, defoliant, or desiccant was applied, in accordance with the label claims and recommendations; * * *."[6] The Act makes it unlawful to deal in misbranded economic poisons in any Territory, the District of Columbia, interstate or foreign commerce.[7] A violation of this portion of the Act is a misdemeanor and subjects one convicted under it to a fine of not more than $1,000.[8]

"Every economic poison which is distributed, sold, or offered for sale in any Territory or the District of Columbia, or which is shipped or delivered for shipment from any State, Territory, or the District of Columbia to any other State, Territory, or any foreign country * * * [must] be registered with the Administrator [of the Environmental Protection Agency]."[9] An "applicant for registration * * * [must] file with the Administrator a statement including —(1) the name and address of the applicant for registration and the name and address of the person whose name will appear on the label,

4. 7 U.S.C.A. §§ 135(h), (i), (j).

5. 7 U.S.C.A. § 135(l).

6. 7 U.S.C.A. §§ 135(z) (2) (a), (c), (d), (e), (f), (g), (h).

7. 7 U.S.C.A. § 135a(5).

8. 7 U.S.C.A. § 135f(a).

9. 7 U.S.C.A. § 135b(a).

if other than the applicant for registration; (2) the name of the economic poison; (3) a complete copy of the labeling accompanying the economic poison and a statement of all claims to be made for it, including the directions for use; and (4) if requested by the Administrator, a full description of the tests made and the results thereof upon which the claims are based." [10] If the Administrator "deems it necessary for the effective administration" of the Act, he "may require the submission of the complete formula of the economic poison."[11]

It is unlawful to deal with an economic poison in any Territory, the District of Columbia, interstate, or foreign commerce unless it is registered. It is also unlawful to deal in an economic poison "if any of the claims made for it or any of the directions for its use differ in substance from the representations made in connection with its registration, or if * * * [its] composition * * * differs from its composition as represented in connection with its registration * * *".[12] Packages of economic poisons must contain "a label bearing—(a) the name and address of the manufacturer, registrant, or person for whom manufactured; (b) the name, brand, or trademark under which * * * [it] is sold; (c) the net weight or measure of the content * * *." [13] An "economic poison which contains any substance or substances in quantities highly toxic to man" must include in its label "(a) the skull and crossbones; (b) the word 'poison' prominently (IN RED) on a background of distinctly contrasting color; and (c) a statement of an antidote for the economic poison."[14]

The failure to comply with any provision of the Act, aside from that portion of the Act which prohibits misbranding, subjects a guilty party to a fine of "not more than $500 for the first offense, and on conviction for each subsequent offense * * * not more than $1,000 or * * * [imprisonment] for not more than one year, or both * * *. *Provided*, That an offense committed more than five years after the last previous conviction * * * [is to] be considered a first offense."[15]

"If it appears to the Administrator [of the Environmental Protection Agency] that the composition of * * * [an economic poison] is such as to warrant the proposed claims for it and if * * * [it] and its labeling and other material required to be submitted comply with the requirements of * * * [the Act], he [must] register it."[16] The Act sets forth in detail the obligation of the Administrator

10.　7 U.S.C.A. § 135b(a).

11.　7 U.S.C.A. § 135b(b).

12.　7 U.S.C.A. § 135a(a) (1).

13.　7 U.S.C.A. § 135a(a) (2).

14.　7 U.S.C.A. § 135a(a) (3).

15.　7 U.S.C.A. § 135f(b).

16.　7 U.S.C.A. § 135b(b).

when he concludes that an economic poison should not be registered.[17] It prescribes the format hearings must follow [18] and provides that "any person who will be adversely affected by" an order of the Administrator "may obtain judicial review" by complying with the filing and time requirements set forth in the Act.[19]

Alert to the danger economic poisons represent to human life, Congress provided that "[n]otwithstanding any other provision * * * [of the Act having to do with the holding of a hearing], the Administrator may, when he finds that such action is necessary to prevent an imminent hazard to the public, by order, suspend the registration of an economic poison immediately. In such case, he * * * [must] give the registrant prompt notice of such action and afford the registrant the opportunity to have the matter submitted to an advisory committee and for an expedited hearing * * *. Final orders of the Administrator under * * * [this procedure are] subject to judicial review, in accordance with the provisions of * * * [the Act.]" [20]

The Administrator of the Environmental Protection Agency "is authorized to make rules and regulations for carrying out * * * [the Act]. * * * [A]fter opportunity for hearing—[he may] * * * determine economic poisons, and quantities of substances contained in economic poisons, which are highly toxic to man * * *." [21] He is "authorized to cooperate with any other department or agency of the Federal Government and with the official agricultural or other regulatory agency of any State, or any State, Territory, District, possession, or any political subdivision thereof, in carrying out * * * [the Act], and in securing uniformity of regulations."[22]

Sections 342 and 346a of Title 21 of the United States Code, entitled "Food and Drugs," reflect congressional concern with the harm pesticides can cause when found in food. Section 342 states that a "food shall be deemed to be adulterated [and hence may not be marketed] * * * (a)(1) If it bears or contains any poisons or deleterious substance which may render it injurious to health * * * or * * * (2) (A) if it bears or contains any added poisonous or added deleterious substance (other than one which is (i) a pesticide chemical in or on a raw agricultural commodity; * * * or (iv) a new animal drug which is unsafe within the meaning of section 346 of this title, or (B) if it is a raw agricultural commodity and it bears or contains a pesticide chemical which is unsafe within the meaning of section 346a(a) of this title, * * *."

17. 7 U.S.C.A. § 135b(c).

18. 7 U.S.C.A. § 135b(c).

19. 7 U.S.C.A. § 135b(d).

20. 7 U.S.C.A. § 135b(c).

21. 7 U.S.C.A. § 135d(a) (2).

22. 7 U.S.C.A. § 135k.

Section 346a(a) provides that "[a]ny poisonous or deleterious pesticide chemical, or any pesticide chemical which is not generally recognized, among experts qualified by scientific training and experience to evaluate the safety of pesticide chemicals, as safe for use," if "added to a raw agricultural commodity, shall be deemed unsafe for the purposes of * * * clause (2) of section 342(a) * * * unless—(1) a tolerance for such pesticide chemical in or on the raw agricultural commodity has been prescribed by the Administrator of the Environmental Protection Agency * * * and the quantity of such pesticide chemical in or on the raw agricultural commodity is within the limits of the tolerance * * * or (a) with respect to use in or on such raw agricultural commodity, the pesticide chemical has been exempted from the requirement of a tolerance by the Administrator * * *." Foods containing pesticide chemicals within the prescribed tolerances or exempted from the tolerance requirement are not "considered to be adulterated" under § 342(a)(1).

Section 346a. (b) empowers the Administrator to "promulgate regulations establishing tolerances. * * * In establishing * * * [them he must] give appropriate consideration, among other relevant factors, (1) to the necessity for the production of an adequate, wholesome, and economical food supply; (2) to the other ways in which the consumer may be affected by the same pesticide chemical or other related substances that are poisonous or deleterious; and (3) * * * [his opinion as to the usefulness of the pesticide which he must certify when requested by one who has registered or seeks to register an economic poison under the Federal Insecticide, Fungicide, and Rodenticide Act]." The Administrator may establish the tolerance "at zero level if the scientific data before * * * [him] does not justify the establishment of a greater tolerance." The Administrator may, when "a tolerance is not necessary to protect the public health" adopt "regulations exempting any pesticide chemical from the necessity of a tolerance with respect to use in or on any or all raw agricultural commodities."[23] Persons dissatisfied with the Administrator's action taken in regard to establishing a tolerance or the granting of an exemption are entitled to judicial review.

An agricultural commodity is not regarded as unsafe under § 342(a) if after it is processed any residue of a "pesticide chemical remaining in or on" it "has been removed to the extent possible in good manufacturing practice and the concentration of such residue in the processed food when ready to eat is not greater than the tolerance prescribed" by the Administrator.

Persons may obtain experimental permits for a pesticide chemical under the Insecticide, Fungicide, and Rodenticide Act. The Administrator may establish temporary tolerances for such substances, giving "due regard to the necessity for experimental work in develop-

---

23.   21 U.S.C.A. § 346a(c).

ing an adequate, wholesome, and economical food supply and to the limited hazard to the public involved in such work when conducted under the * * * Insecticide, Fungicide, and Rodenticide Act."[24]

State laws directed at regulating pesticide chemicals generally follow the federal approach. They may require the registration, labeling, and testing of such substances. A state body is entrusted with the task of instituting legal proceedings to seize pesticide chemicals which are not registered, insufficiently labeled, or misbranded. A license may be required before one may engage in applying pesticide chemicals by aircraft. The granting of such a license may be restricted to pesticide chemicals that are lethal to particular types of pests. Aircraft may be barred from use to apply substances which are dangerous to public health, aquatic or animal life, or public or private property. Spraying by aircraft may be restricted in terms of the aircraft which may be used, the time of day when spraying may take place, the sort of weather and wind conditions which must prevail when spraying occurs, and the minimum area size which may qualify for aerial spraying. One who operates an aircraft engaged in spraying operations may be required to carry a minimum amount of public liability and property damage insurance. Failure to comply with state law can result in the imposition of a fine or imprisonment.[25]

ENVIRONMENTAL DEFENSE FUND, INC. v. UNITED STATES DEPARTMENT OF HEALTH, EDUCATION AND WELFARE

United States Court of Appeals, District of Columbia Circuit, 1970.
428 F.2d 1083, 138 U.S.App.D.C. 391.

[Petitioners filed a petition with the Secretary of Health, Education and Welfare under 21 U.S.C.A. § 346(a) proposing that he establish a "zero tolerance" for DDT residues in or on raw agricultural commodities. Their petition was rejected on the ground that it was legally insufficient, since they had not shown any "practicable methods" of removing such residues. The Secretary refused to publish the proposal in the Federal Register, which if done, would have triggered a series of informal and formal administrative procedures, including a study of the proposal by a committee of scientists. Petitioners petitioned the Court of Appeals for review of the Secretary's order denying publication.]

J. SKELLY WRIGHT, CIRCUIT JUDGE: The pesticide DDT has been one of the most widely used chemicals to control various insect populations and to protect agricultural crops from destruction by insects. Recent scientific studies have, however, raised serious questions

24. 21 U.S.C.A. § 346a(j).

25. E. g., see Conn.Gen.Statutes Annotated, §§ 19–300m, 19–300s.

about the effect on the environment and on human health of the continued use of DDT. Some experiments have demonstrated that DDT increased the incidence of cancer in mice, and a recent Government commission on pesticides concluded that "[t]he evidence for the carcinogenicity of DDT in experimental animals is impressive."

* * *

The Commissioner of Food and Drugs, acting as the delegate of the Secretary of HEW, rejected petitioners' petition on the ground that it did not satisfy Section 408(d) (1) (E) of the FDCA, 21 U.S. C. § 346a(d) (1) (E), which requires data showing "practicable methods for removing residue which exceeds any proposed tolerance." This alleged deficiency also derives from the fact that DDT is a "persistent" pesticide, *i. e.*, it does not decay quickly, but remains in its toxic form in the environment (and increasingly in human bodies) for a period of years. * * *

In their supplement to their petition, * * * petitioners * * * suggested:

" * * * At a minimum, the Secretary should establish a zero tolerance for DDT and its residues on all raw agricultural commodities with the possible exemption from seizure of any commodities in which it can be established that any residues are the consequence of applications of DDT that were made prior to the announcement by the Secretary of the zero tolerance."

This is certainly one possible solution leading to the gradual elimination of a persistent pesticide from the environment.

* * * HEW's emphasis on the "practicability" requirement is seriously misplaced, as disclosed by the most cursory examination of the legislative history of the provision. Both House and Senate reports emphasize that the formal requirements for a petition are to be flexibly administered in the interest of safeguarding the public health: * * * In our judgment, the Commissioner of Food and Drugs failed to apply a "rule of reason" in assessing the present petition. Instead of publishing petitioners' proposal, which would begin an administrative process designed to bring forth constructive alternatives for dealing with an admittedly difficult but vitally important problem, the Commissioner chose to stop petitioners at the door. Moreover, he chose to rely on a requirement which cannot be applied literally to the present case. Everyone agrees that there is no way to remove DDT from the environment *immediately*. The questions to be answered are how great is the present danger and what steps ought to be taken immediately in response to that danger.

These are basically matters for exploration and judgment which in the last analysis will rest with HEW. * * *

* * * The administrative process, the process which Congress intended to focus on and illuminate these problems, has not been permitted to begin. In our view, the petition does comply with all statutory prerequisites, and this case must, therefore, be remanded to the Secretary of HEW with directions to file petitioners' proposal and to publish it in the Federal Register, as provided in 21 U.S.C. § 346a(d)(1).

* * *

The petition for review is granted, the order of the Secretary of HEW is reversed, and the case is remanded with instructions to publish petitioners' proposal in the Federal Register and commence the administrative process contemplated by the provisions of the Food, Drug and Cosmetic Act.

* * *

NOR–AM AGRICULTURAL PRODUCTS, INC. v. HARDIN, SECRETARY OF AGRICULTURE

United States Court of Appeals, Seventh Circuit, 1970.
435 F.2d 1151.

[Plaintiff, a distributor of fungicide products containing cyano (methylmercuri) guanadine known as Panogen, had registered them as "economic poisons" under the Federal Insecticide, Fungicide and Rodenticide Act. On February 18, 1970 the Department of Agriculture advised Nor-Am by telegram that its Panogen registration had been suspended because of a recent accident involving the ingestion of pork from a hog fed seed treated with Panogen. By letters dated February 18 and March 27 the Department stated that it had acted "[t]o prevent an imminent hazard to the public from the use of" Panogens and that Panogens caused irreversible injury to the central nervous system. On March 27, 1970 the plaintiff requested an expedited administrative hearing as provided for by the Act. Not waiting for the hearing, plaintiff filed suit on April 9, 1970 to have the suspension order set aside and immediately requested a preliminary injunction. The District Court, after holding an evidentiary hearing, found that (1) the Department's action was arbitrary, capricious, and contrary to law; (2) the plaintiff was likely to prevail on the merits; and (3) the plaintiff would suffer irreparable harm for which it had no adequate administrative or legal remedy. The injunction was granted. The defendant appealed.]

CUMMINGS, CIRCUIT JUDGE. * * * we are of the opinion that the district court lacked power to grant this relief because the plaintiffs have not exhausted their administrative remedy.

The fundamental provisions regulating judicial review of administrative actions are contained in the Administrative Procedure Act. Section 10(c) governs which agency actions shall be reviewable:

"Agency action made reviewable by statute and final agency action for which there is no other adequate remedy in a court are subject to judicial review. A preliminary, procedural, or intermediate agency action or ruling not directly reviewable is subject to review on the review of the final agency action. *   *   *"

In determining the status of the instant suspension in the light of the Administrative Procedure Act, we must turn first to the pertinent provisions of the Federal Insecticide, Fungicide and Rodenticide Act. *   *   * Congress provided for emergency action by permitting immediate suspension of registration in the face of "an imminent hazard to the public." In almost the same breath, however, Congress recognized the need for prompt determination of the accuracy of the Secretary's judgment and provided that in the wake of an emergency suspension the Secretary should

"give the registrant prompt notice of such action and afford the registrant the opportunity to have the matter submitted to an advisory committee and for an expedited hearing under this section."

*   *   * After describing the Secretary's expanded powers and their mode of exercise, Section 4(c) states that

"[f]inal orders of the Secretary under this section shall be subject to judicial review, in accordance with the provisions of subsection d. *   *   *"

Section 4(d) outlines the mechanics, forum, and character of the judicial review contemplated by Congress:

"d. In a case of actual controversy as to the validity of any order under this section, any person who will be adversely affected by such order may obtain judicial review by filing in the United States court of appeals for the circuit wherein such person resides or has his principal place of business, or in the United States Court of Appeals for the District of Columbia Circuit, within sixty days after the entry of such order, a petition praying that the order be set aside in whole or in part." *   *   *

Together, these statutory provisions do not expressly or impliedly contemplate immediate review of emergency suspensions by either district or appellate courts. *   *   *

Equally unacceptable is the contention that an emergency suspension order is a "final order" of the Secretary made reviewable by Section 4(c). That limitation on judicial review serves to avoid delay and interference with agency proceedings by confining review to orders effectively terminating administrative adjudication. *   *   * The suspension order and surrounding procedural scheme *   *   * refute the conclusion of finality under this Act. *   *   *

*   *   * the emergency suspension of registration preceding *   *   * adjudication does not constitute *   *   * a final order and is therefore not "reviewable by statute" within Section 10(c) of the Administrative Procedure Act.

Plaintiffs * * * argue that suspension of registration by the Secretary possesses sufficient "finality" as an administrative action to warrant immediate recourse to the courts * * * Suspension, they urge, immediately and drastically affects their rights and interests as greatly as formally finalized cancellation. * * *

* * * the concept of finality of administrative action encompasses a complex array of considerations which may vary in accordance with the character and activities of the administrative agency, and with the nature and role of the agency action from which judicial review is sought. * * * The flexibility of the finality concept does not, however, permit facile disregard of the purposes of congressional delegation of power and of the clear procedural scheme delineated in this particular statute. * * *

The function of the Secretary's emergency power, as well as the practical exigencies of coordinating administrative and judicial machinery, militates against avoiding the prescribed procedures. The emergency suspension of registration of an economic poison under Section 4(c) involves highly discretionary administrative action with deeply rooted antecedents in the realm of public health and safety. In subtle areas of regulation, summary emergency action frequently precedes formal administrative or judicial adjudication. * * * Where, as here, Congress follows discretionary preliminary or interlocutory agency action with specially fashioned adjudicative machinery, strict observance of the prescribed procedure prior to judicial intervention is compellingly indicated.

* * *

* * * plaintiffs urge that the equity powers of the court have been properly invoked to prevent irreparable injury caused by the suspension order.

The circumvention of clearly prescribed administrative procedures by awarding equitable relief is an exceptional practice. * * * the rule that administrative remedies may occasionally be by-passed to protect strong private interests from irreparable harm

"is not one of mere convenience or ready application. Where the intent of Congress is clear to require administrative determination, either to the exclusion of judicial action or in advance of it, a strong showing is required, both of inadequacy of the prescribed procedure and of impending harm, to permit shortcircuiting the administrative process. Congress' commands for judicial restraint in this respect are not lightly to be disregarded."

Plaintiffs have failed to establish such an irremediable threat to sufficiently strong interests to warrant equitable intercession at this juncture.

* * *

* * * Where public health and safety demand emergency removal of a commodity from the market, even unrecoverable financial

losses incurred *pendente lite* must be deemed an expense of the litigation itself. * * *

If this preliminary injunction were approved, other litigants could obtain district court threshold review by parroting plaintiffs' claim that the Secretary had acted arbitrarily and capriciously in suspending their registrations, even though Sections 4(c) and 4(d) specify that review shall only be in the courts of appeals after action by the advisory committee and then by the Secretary. We should not countenance such an evasion of the review procedure provided by Congress in this statute. In reaching this conclusion, we express no opinion on the merits of the controversy between these parties concerning the registration of Panogens.

The preliminary injunction is dissolved and the case is remanded to the district court with instructions to dismiss the complaint.

Reversed.

PROBLEMS

1. Plaintiffs, conservational groups, moved for a preliminary injunction to enjoin the Secretary of Agriculture from undertaking a cooperative federal-state program to control fire ants by aerial spraying of mirex. Fire ants adversely affect human life and impede agricultural activities. After evaluating extensive studies carried on by experts the Secretary concluded that while the presence of mirex residues in the food chain could not be avoided, the anticipated accumulation level would have no serious adverse effect on the communities involved. He considered various alternatives to the plan but rejected them, finding that each presented a more serious ecological threat than mirex. In the Secretary's opinion, the long-term agricultural productivity and human well-being offered by the spraying of mirex would outweigh any short term adverse effects on farm workers who in the course of their duties would be required to handle farm products sprayed with mirex. Plaintiffs challenged the propriety of the Secretary's conclusions. What judgment?

2. The Administrator of the Environmental Protection Agency suspended the registration of a herbicide for use in liquid form around lakes and in the home, but he refused to suspend the registration for use of its nonliquid form in the home or for its use in liquid or nonliquid form on crops. He stated that he lacked sufficient scientific data to order a suspension for the latter purposes. He concluded that the risk which might follow from consumption of food exposed to the herbicide was negligible. He made no mention of the possible adverse effect the herbicide might have on persons who would be exposed when handling the herbicide. Plaintiffs asked the court to reverse the Administrator's action on the ground that use of the herbicide created an imminent hazard to health. What judgment?

3.   The Forest Service adopted a regulation authorizing aerial spraying of a defoliant as a fire fighting weapon. Plaintiffs, living in close proximity to a large forest area, claiming that the defoliant contained materials which could be injurious to human and animal life, asked the court to enjoin its use. The Service defended its action on the ground that the regulation authorized use of the defoliant only when other fire fighting techniques were ineffective and would be used only when an uncontrolled fire posed a substantial hazard to homes and human life. What judgment?

4.   A report submitted to the United Nations concluded that on the basis of the available evidence millions of persons would be faced with famine, and malaria control programs would be seriously hampered, if there would be a worldwide ban on the use of DDT and other chlorinated hydrocarbon pesticides. Would it be proper for the Administrator of the Environmental Protection Agency to take the contents of this report into consideration when deciding whether or not the registration of a pesticide containing a chlorinated hydrocarbon should be cancelled?

5.   Plaintiff expended large sums of money to nurture a variety of trees which flourished on his property. He brought an action to enjoin enforcement of a state law which banned the use of the only pesticide classified "effective" for the destruction of pests which were destroying his trees. In the alternative, he asked for a judgment against the state awarding him compensatory damages for the cost he had incurred to nurture the trees, the decrease in the value of his property caused by the destruction of his trees, and for the mental distress caused to him by the loss of the trees. What judgment?

Chapter 15

SOLID WASTE

In the Solid Waste Disposal Act of 1965 [1] Congress attributes the nation's increased production of various forms of unwanted solid waste to (1) "progress and improvement in the methods of manufacture, packaging, and marketing of consumer products," (2) "increased industrial production," (3) "the demolition of old buildings," (4) "the construction of new buildings," (5) "the provision of highways and other avenues of transportation," and (6) "industrial, commercial, and agricultural operations." [2] Congress found that disposal of solid waste is complicated by (1) "the continuing concentration of our population in expanding metropolitan and other urban areas" [3] and (2) "inefficient and improper [disposal] methods." [4] Getting rid of solid waste presents "communities with serious financial, management, intergovernmental, and technical problems." [5] The failure to efficiently and properly dispose of solid waste results "in scenic blights, create[s] serious hazards to the public health, including pollution of air and water resources, accident hazards, and [an] increase in rodent and insect vectors of disease, * * * [has] an adverse effect on land values, create[s] public nuisances, and otherwise interfere[s] with community life and development." [6] Our "failure or inability to salvage and reuse * * * [solid waste] materials economically results in the unnecessary waste and depletion of our natural resources." [7]

In the 1965 Act Congress recognized that "the collection and disposal of solid wastes" had "become a matter national in scope and in concern and necessitate[d] Federal action," [8] but it chose to limit the federal role to "financial and technical assistance and leadership in the development, demonstration, and application of new and improved methods and processes to reduce the amount of waste and unsalvageable materials and to provide for proper and economical solid waste disposal practices." [9] Congress stated that the disposal of solid wastes "should continue to be primarily the function of State, regional, and local agencies." [10] The explicit purposes of the Act are: "(1)

1. Pub.L. 89–272, 79 Stat. 997. The Resources Recovery Act of 1970, Pub. L. 91–512, 84 Stat. 1227, introduced significant changes in the 1965 Act, as amended. Current federal policy in this area represents a composite of the 1965 and 1970 legislation.

2. 42 U.S.C.A. § 3251(a) (1), (2).

3. 42 U.S.C.A. § 3251(a) (3).

4. 42 U.S.C.A. § 3251(a) (4).

5. 42 U.S.C.A. § 3251(a) (3).

6. 42 U.S.C.A. § 3251(a) (4).

7. 42 U.S.C.A. § 3251(a) (5).

8. 42 U.S.C.A. § 3251(a) (6).

9. 42 U.S.C.A. § 3251(a) (6).

10. 42 U.S.C.A. § 3251(a) (6).

to promote the demonstration, construction, and application of solid waste management and resource recovery systems which preserve and enhance the quality of air, water, and land resources; (2) to provide technical and financial assistance to States and local governments and interstate agencies in the planning and development of resource recovery and solid waste disposal programs; (3) to promote a national research and development program for improved management techniques, more effective organizational arrangements, and new and improved methods of collection, separation, recovery, and recycling of solid wastes, and the environmentally safe disposal of nonrecoverable residues; (4) to provide for the promulgation of guidelines for solid waste collection, transport, separation, recovery, and disposal systems; and (5) to provide for training grants in occupations involving design, operation, and maintenance of solid waste disposal systems."[11]

The Administrator of the Environmental Protection Agency is directed by Congress to "conduct, and encourage, cooperate with, and render financial and other assistance to appropriate public (whether Federal, State, interstate, or local) authorities, agencies, and institutions, private agencies and institutions, and individuals in the conduct of, and [to] promote the coordination of, research, investigations, experiments, training, demonstrations, surveys, and studies relating to—(1) any adverse health and welfare effects of the release into the environment of material present in solid waste and methods to eliminate such effects; (2) the operation and financing of solid waste disposal programs; (3) the reduction of the amount of such waste and unsalvageable waste materials; (4) the development and application of new and improved methods of collecting and disposing of solid waste and processing and recovering materials and energy from solid wastes; and (5) the identification of solid waste components and potential materials and energy recoverable from such waste components."[12] The Administrator is obliged to disseminate information pertaining to research activities,[13] cooperate with those engaged in research,[14] and make grants-in-aid in accordance with the provisions set forth in the Act.[15]

The Administrator of the Environmental Protection Agency is required to "carry out investigation and study to determine—(1) means of recovering materials and energy from solid waste, recommended uses of such materials and energy for national or international welfare, including identification of potential markets for such recovered resources, and the impact of distribution of such resources on existing markets; (2) changes in current product characteristics and production and packaging practices which would reduce the

11. 42 U.S.C.A. § 3251(b).   14. 42 U.S.C.A. § 3253(b) (2).

12. 42 U.S.C.A. § 3253(a).   15. 42 U.S.C.A. § 3253(b) (3).

13. 42 U.S.C.A. § 3253(b) (1).

amount of solid waste; (3) methods of collection, separation, and containerization which will encourage efficient utilization of facilities and contribute to more effective programs of reduction, reuse, or disposal of wastes; (4) the use of Federal procurement to develop market demand for recovered resources; (5) recommended incentives (including Federal grants, loans, and other assistance) and disincentives to accelerate the reclamation of recycling of materials from solid wastes, with special emphasis on motor vehicle hulks; (6) the effect of existing public policies, including subsidies and economic incentives and disincentives, percentage depletion allowances, capital gains treatment and other tax incentives and disincentives, upon the recycling and reuse of materials, and the likely effect of the modification or elimination of such incentives and disincentives upon the reuse, recycling, and conservation of such materials; and (7) the necessity and method of imposing disposal or other charges on packaging, containers, vehicles, and other manufactured goods, which charges would reflect the cost of final disposal, the value of recoverable components of the item, and any social costs associated with nonrecycling or uncontrolled disposal of such items. The Administrator * * * [is required] from time to time, but not less frequently than annually, [to] report the results of such investigation[s] and stud[ies] to the President and the Congress. * * * [He] is also authorized to carry out demonstration projects to test and demonstrate methods and techniques developed * * * [with regard to each of the seven enumerated areas.]"[16]

"The Administrator * * * [is required], in cooperation with appropriate State, Federal, interstate, regional, and local agencies, allowing for public comment by other interested parties, * * * [to recommend] to appropriate agencies and publish in the Federal Register guidelines for solid waste recovery, collection, separation, and disposal systems (including systems for private use), which * * * [are] consistent with public health and welfare, and air and water quality standards and adaptable to appropriate land-use plans."[17] The Administrator is required to "recommend model codes, ordinances, and statutes which are designed to implement * * * [his guidelines and the Act[18] and to] issue to appropriate Federal, interstate, regional, and local agencies information on technically feasible solid waste collection, separation, disposal, recycling, and recovery methods, including data on the cost of construction, operation, and maintenance of such methods."[19] Federal executive agencies are directed to comply with the Administrator's guidelines and the purposes of the Act.[20] So that Congress might draw upon the expertise and the knowledge accumulated by the Environmental Protection Agency the

16. 42 U.S.C.A. §§ 3253a(a), (b).

17. 42 U.S.C.A. § 3254c(a).

18. 42 U.S.C.A. § 3254c(b) (1).

19. 42 U.S.C.A. § 3254c(b) (2).

20. 42 U.S.C.A. § 3254(e).

Administrator is directed to "submit to Congress * * *, a comprehensive report and plan for the creation of a system of national disposal sites for the storage and disposal of hazardous waste, including radioactive toxic chemical, biological, and other wastes which may endanger public health or welfare. Such report * * * is to include: (1) a list of materials which should be subject to disposal in any such site; (2) current methods of disposal of such materials; (3) recommended methods of reduction, neutralization, recovery, or disposal of such materials; (4) an inventory of possible sites including existing land or water disposal sites operated or licensed by Federal agencies; (5) an estimate of the cost of developing and maintaining sites including consideration of means for distributing the short- and long-term costs of operating such sites among the users thereof; and (6) such other information as may be appropriate."[21]

Consistent with its conclusion that the Federal government has a role to play in solid waste disposal, but that this area is to be regarded as "primarily the function of State, regional, and local agencies," the Administrator of the Environmental Protection Agency is directed "to encourage cooperative activities by the States and local governments in connection with solid-waste disposal programs; encourage, where practicable, interstate, interlocal, and regional planning for, and the conduct of interstate, interlocal, and regional solid-waste disposal programs; and encourage the enactment of improved and, so far as practicable, uniform State and local laws governing solid-waste disposal."[22]

State and local governments are considering or are already making use of one or more of the following means to reduce the accumulation of solid waste or to help cope with disposal problems: (1) requiring that those who market goods in glass containers charge a deposit fee, the fee being returnable to the consumer when the glass container is returned; (2) prohibiting the use of non-returnable glass or metal containers; (3) placing a tax on containers made of materials that are not biodegradable or are especially difficult to dispose of; (4) prohibiting the use of metal containers with throw-away rings; (5) granting tax benefits to those who construct facilities designed to facilitate the disposal of solid waste; (6) making use of shredders; (7) recycling of waste paper, metals, and glass; (8) construction of giant incinerators designed to protect air quality, located at some distance from densely populated areas, which generate steam and in turn electric power as a by-product of the garbage disposal process; (9) treating solid wastes in such a fashion that they can be used as sanitary landfill; (10) sustaining a demand for recycled goods by purchasing such items for use in governmental activities; (11) establishment of composting plants so that organic garbage can be converted into useful agricultural compost; and (12) requiring those

21. 42 U.S.C.A. § 3254(f).   22. 42 U.S.C.A. § 3254.

who are disposing of solid wastes to separate their refuse into distinct categories to facilitate recycling and disposal.

Industry is searching for new means which individuals, enterprise, and government could use to curb the flow of solid waste and to facilitate its elimination. Among the techniques now being considered or in production are: (1) use of plastic containers that disintegrate after serving their intended purpose; (2) treating solid waste so that it can be used in the construction of buildings, roads, or pavement; (3) use of pneumatic tubes to gather garbage; (4) use of compacters; and (5) converting garbage into liquid fertilizer.

SOCIETY OF THE PLASTICS INDUSTRY, INC.
v. CITY OF NEW YORK

Supreme Court, New York County, New York, 1971.
326 N.Y.S.2d 788.

[The New York State Enabling Act, Tax Law § 1201, characterized by its proponents as a "Recycling Incentive Tax" Law, authorized municipalities to tax "the sale of containers made in whole or in part of rigid or semi-rigid paper board, fibre, glass, metal, plastic or any combination of such materials * * * intended for use in packing or packaging any product intended for sale." Section 1201 requires municipalities enacting such legislation to allow specified credits against taxes for containers composed in part of recycled materials. The defendant, with the stated purpose of raising revenue and promoting recycling, enacted Law No. 43 which placed a 2¢ tax on the sale of every rigid or semi-rigid plastic container by a seller or supplier to a retailer, allowing a 1¢ credit for each taxable container manufactured with a minimum of 30% recycled material. The Law exempted from taxation all containers made of metal, glass, fibre, and paper board. Plaintiffs, an association of plastic container manufacturers and individual plastic container manufacturers, contending that Law No. 43 violated § 1201 and denied them equal protection of the laws and due process, brought an action asking the Court to declare it invalid and unconstitutional and to enjoin its enforcement.]

SAUL S. STREIT, JUSTICE. * * * The * * * authorization of Tax Law § 1201 does permit New York City to impose * * * a tax on rigid and semi-rigid containers made of five specified types of materials. The contention that each type of container material may thus be the subject of a separate tax strains the plain meaning of the law and contravenes the tenet of strict construction of tax statutes. * * *

* * * the legislative history * * * supports the conclusion that the State Legislature intended to impose a tax on all the enumerated container materials. Indeed, the entire scheme of the tax

authorized by the State Legislature   *   *   *   is premised upon the taxation of all such containers.   *   *   *

Unless the tax were imposed upon all the enumerated types of container materials there could be no "incentive" to recycle containers nor to reduce significantly the amount of solid waste or the cost of its disposal. The only "incentive" created by a tax on one, rather than all types of containers, would be the incentive to switch from the taxed type to the exempted types, with no reduction in the volume of containers used and no recycling.

*   *   *   *Nothing in the   *   *   *   Act or its legislative history supports the contention that the Legislature contemplated or authorized the resulting destruction of the plastic container industry, for the ultimate benefit of the paper, glass and metal industries in New York City.*

*   *   *   Local Law No. 43 exceeds the authorization granted by the State Legislature,   *   *   *   and is, therefore, invalid.

*   *   *

*   *   *   Defendants assert that the differences between plastic containers and all the other types is so obvious as to justify their separate classification for tax purposes.

This court perceives no *obvious* distinction between plastic containers and all other types and, in line with impressive precedents, has put the parties to their proof on this question.

*   *   *

Plaintiffs' assertion that the discrimination against plastic containers was an arbitrary one appears valid. Plaintiffs' further assertion that this discrimination was not grounded on any difference having a fair and substantial relation to the object of the legislation was established by an overwhelming preponderance of the credible evidence presented.

I find the expert testimony established that it costs no more, and probably less, to collect plastic containers than to collect paper, metal or glass containers. The significant cost factor in the municipal collection of solid waste is the weight of the refuse load. Plaintiffs' expert witness conclusively demonstrated that plastics, being lighter than the other materials, was easier to lift and carry, thus increasing the productivity of sanitationmen. It follows that if the enforcement of this law resulted in the substitution of paper, glass or metal containers for plastic containers, the costs of solid waste collection would increase rather than decrease.

Once collected, the City's solid wastes are disposed of by two methods—incineration and sanitary landfill. Expert testimony established that plastic containers are cheaper to dispose of by incineration than glass or metal containers. These latter types do not burn and some thirty percent of the cost of incineration is removal of the residue left after incineration. * * * defendants failed to establish that plastic containers cause any damage or increase in repair costs to the City's incinerators.

Expert testimony also established that plastic containers occupy no more space in the City's collection trucks or in the City's sanitary landfills than an equal number of glass, metal or paper containers and may well occupy less space therein. It is conceded by plaintiffs that plastics are not biodegradable. * * * it was established that neither glass nor metal are biodegradable.

* * * plaintiffs have demonstrated by convincing proof that the discrimination against plastic containers does not rest upon any ground of difference having any relation to the objective of the legislation to reduce the City's cost of solid waste disposal.

With respect to the objective of recycling containers, it has already been noted that the Local Law not only fails to induce or require recycling of present containers made of glass, metal, paperboard and fibre, but logically will lead to an increase of such containers in use, defeating both objectives of the * * * Act.

It thus appears that the discrimination against plastic containers does not rest on any reasonable basis in relation to the objective of promoting the recycling of containers, plastic or otherwise.
　　　* * *

I find * * * that Local Law No. 43 will operate arbitrarily to damage or destroy plaintiffs' businesses without serving any permissible public objective and thus deprives plaintiffs of property without due process of law in violation of the Federal and State Constitutions and is, therefore, invalid * * *.

Plaintiffs assert a further basis for their claim of denial of due process, namely that the statute is unduly vague. * * * the Local Law gives no standards by which the terms "rigid or semi-rigid plastic" can be defined. The Enabling Act is of no assistance here, since it also fails to define these terms. * * * The only reference cited to the Court by defense counsel was "any dictionary". Indeed, one of defendants' experts confessed that he did not know what was intended by these terms and sought a definition from the Court.

* * * "[A] statute which either forbids or requires the doing of an act in terms so vague that men of common intelligence must necessarily guess at its meaning and differ as to its application violates the first essential of due process of law."

For the additional reason of vagueness, then, I find that Local Law No. 43 is violative of the Due Process Clauses of the Federal and State Constitutions.
　　　* * *

I * * * declare that Local Law No. 43 * * * is unconstitutional * * *. Defendants * * * are permanently enjoined from enforcing * * * said Local Law.

PROBLEMS

1.   An ordinance imposed a 2¢ sales tax on nonbiodegradable containers used in connection with or as part of a sale to a consumer. The tax was payable by the wholesaler or supplier, the retailer having to pay the tax only if neither a wholesaler nor a supplier did so. Out-of-state wholesalers were exempt from the tax, retailers purchasing from such wholesalers themselves being required to keep records of their purchases and to pay the tax.   In an action brought to enjoin enforcement of the law, the plaintiff, an out-of-state wholesaler, argued that the ordinance denied him due process and contravened the interstate commerce clause of the Constitution since retailers would favor local suppliers in order to avoid the ordinance's extensive record keeping provisions.   What judgment?

2.   The Solid Waste Disposal Act directs the Secretary of Health, Education and Welfare to conduct an investigation to determine the relationship between packaging methods, cost of final disposal, and any social costs associated with non-recycling or uncontrolled disposal of containers.   Does the Act bar state legislation directed at controlling the disposal and recycling of packaging materials?

3.   State law provided that state agencies, whenever possible, should purchase only items which contained a "substantial" quantity of recycled material.   Plaintiff, a manufacturer and non-user of recycled material, who for more than half a century had been supplying state agencies with a variety of items, claimed the statute denied him due process and equal protection of the laws.   What judgment?

4.   The preamble to a state recycling incentive statute recited that there was an economic cost disadvantage when one transported scrap steel and iron rather than iron ore.   The statute provided that a "transportation equalization subsidy" would be paid by the state environmental agency to businesses which made use of scrap steel and iron in the manufacture of consumer goods so that their transportation cost would not exceed that paid by businesses which used iron ore.   Plaintiff, a taxpayer, challenged the constitutionality of the statute.   What judgment?

5.   Local law prohibited the sale and distribution of malt beverages, including beer and ale, and soft drinks, in metal cans or non-returnable glass bottles.   The law exempted dairy products and fruit drink beverages.   Plaintiff sold glass bottles and metal cans to manufacturers of beer, ale, and soft drinks.   He asked the court to declare the statute unconstitutional.   What judgment?

Chapter 16

RADIATION

Prior to the advent of the atomic bomb concern with the hazards posed by radiation was confined to those who worked with radioactive substances in laboratories, administered or made use of radiation for medicinal purposes, or as patients were exposed to radiation. The discovery of means to harness and use atomic energy opened the door to military as well as non-military use of nuclear power. The hydrogen bombs which exploded over Japan in 1945 made it clear that for whatever purpose nuclear energy might be used, be it bellicose or peaceful, it would have to be carefully regulated. The failure to wisely oversee the use of nuclear energy can result in the death of all forms of life on earth.

The Atomic Energy Act, proclaiming that "[a]tomic energy is capable of application for peaceful as well as military purposes" states that "[i]t is declared to be the policy of the United States—that (a) the development, use, and control of atomic energy shall be directed so as to make the maximum contribution to the general welfare, subject at all times to the paramount objective of making the maximum contribution to the common defense and security; and (b) the development, use, and control of atomic energy shall be directed so as to promote world peace, improve the general welfare, increase the standard of living, and strengthen free competition in private enterprise."[1] The Act enumerates findings made by Congress which necessitate federal involvement in "the development, use, and control of atomic energy."[2] Mention is made of "military" and "all other purposes * * * vital to the common defense and security"[3] as well as the need to protect "the health and safety of the public."[4] Congress asserted that "[t]he processing and utilization of source, by-product, and special nuclear material affect interstate and foreign commerce and must be regulated in the national interest."[5] It found it to be the responsibility of the United States to regulate "the production and utilization of atomic energy and of the facilities used in connection" with such activities.[6] Congress stated that it would be necessary for the federal government to make funds available "for the development and use of atomic energy under conditions which will provide for the common defense and security and promote the

---

1. This portion of the Act was passed in 1946 and amended in 1954 when Congress directed that it should be known as the "Atomic Energy Act of 1954." 42 U.S.C.A. § 2011.

2. 42 U.S.C.A. § 2012.

3. 42 U.S.C.A. § 2012(a).

4. 42 U.S.C.A. § 2012(d).

5. 42 U.S.C.A. § 2012(c).

6. 42 U.S.C.A. § 2012(e).

general welfare"[7] and to "make funds available for a portion of the damages suffered by the public from nuclear incidents, and * * * [to] limit the liability of those persons liable for such losses."[8]

The Act creates the Atomic Energy Commission. Included among the Commission's powers is authority "(i) to issue licenses to transfer, deliver, acquire, possess, own, receive possession of or title to, import or export * * * special nuclear material, (ii) to make special nuclear material available for the period of the license, and, (iii) to distribute special nuclear material within the United States to qualified applicants requesting such material—(1) for the conduct of research and development activities * * * ["relating to—(1) nuclear processes; (2) the theory and production of atomic energy, * * *; (3) utilization of special nuclear material and radioactive material for medical, biological, agricultural, health, or military purposes; (4) utilization of special nuclear material, atomic energy, and radioactive material and processes entailed in the utilization or production of atomic energy or such material for all other purposes, including industrial or commercial uses, the generation of usable energy, and the demonstration of advances in the commercial or industrial application of atomic energy; and (5) the protection of health and the promotion of safety during research and production activities * * * to make grants and contributions to the cost of construction and operation of reactors and other facilities and other equipment to colleges, universities, hospitals, and eleemosynary or charitable institutions for the conduct of educational and training activities relating to the * * * [above five enumerated] fields * * *.[9]]; (2) for use in the conduct of research and development activities or in medical therapy under a license issued * * * [by the Commission]; (3) for use under a license issued * * * [under the Act for] utilization or production facilities for industrial or commercial purposes; (4) for such other uses as the Commission determines to be appropriate to carry out the purposes of the" Act.[10]

The Act defines "special nuclear material" as "(1) plutonium, uranium enriched in the isotope 233 or in the isotope 235, and any other material which the Commission, pursuant to the provisions of * * * [the Act], determines to be special nuclear material, but does not include source material; or (2) any material artificially enriched by any of the foregoing, but does not include source material."[11] "Source material" is defined as "(1) uranium, thorium, or any other material which is determined by the Commission pursuant to the * * * [terms of the Act] to be source materials; or (2) ores containing one or more of the foregoing materials, in such concentra-

7. 42 U.S.C.A. § 2012(g).

8. 42 U.S.C.A. § 2012(j).

9. 42 U.S.C.A. § 2051.

10. 42 U.S.C.A. § 2073(a).

11. 42 U.S.C.A. § 2014(aa).

tion as the Commission may by regulation determine from time to time."[12] Section 2091 of Title 42 provides that "[t]he Commission may determine from time to time that other material is source material in addition to those specified in the definition of source material." [13]

The Commission is empowered to "cooperate with any nation by distributing special nuclear material and to distribute such special nuclear material" under the conditions set forth in the Act.[14] "[T]o the extent it deems necessary to effectuate the provisions of" the Act the Commission may "acquire any special nuclear material." [15]

The Act prohibits persons from transferring, delivering, acquiring, owning, possessing, receiving possession of or title to, or importing into or exporting from "the United States any special nuclear material" unless they are authorized by the Commission to carry on such an activity.[16] It also bans persons from directly or indirectly engaging "in the production of any special nuclear material outside of the United States" unless authorized by law or "upon authorization by the Commission after a determination that such activity will not be inimical to the interest of the United States."[17]

The Commission is empowered to issue licenses to persons for the manufacture, production, transfer, acquisition, ownership, possession, importing, or exporting of "byproduct materials." [18] The Act defines such materials as "any radioactive material (except special nuclear material) yielded in or made radioactive by exposure to the radiation incident to the process of producing or utilizing special nuclear material."[19]

The Act requires persons who wish to operate a facility which makes use of special nuclear materials to first obtain a license from the Commission.[20]

One who violates any of the Act's licensing provisions is "subject to a civil penalty, to be imposed by the Commission, of not to exceed $5,000 for such violation." The total penalty however may not "exceed $25,000 for all violations by such person occurring within any period of thirty consecutive days. If any violation is a continuing one, each day of such violation * * * [constitutes] a separate violation for the purpose of computing the applicable civil penalty.

12. 42 U.S.C.A. § 2014(2).

13. By authorizing the Commission to make use of its expertise in this area Congress patently intended to have the definition of the term reflect the current state of knowledge.

14. 42 U.S.C.A. § 2074.

15. 42 U.S.C.A. § 2075.

16. 42 U.S.C.A. § 2077(a).

17. 42 U.S.C.A. § 2077(b).

18. 42 U.S.C.A. § 2111.

19. 42 U.S.C.A. § 2014(e).

20. 42 U.S.C.A. §§ 2133, 2134.

The Commission   *   *   *   [may] compromise, mitigate, or remit such penalties."[21]

If in the Commission's judgment one has or is about to violate the Act or any of the Commission's regulations, the Attorney General may seek temporary as well as permanent injunctive relief.[22]

Subchapter VIII of Title 42 of the United States Code is entitled "Military Application of Atomic Energy." Here Congress details the role of the Commission and the President in regard to atomic weapons. "The Commission is authorized to—(1) conduct experiments and do research and development work in the military application of atomic energy; and (2) engage in the production of atomic weapons, or atomic weapons parts, except that such activities shall be carried on only to the extent that the express consent and direction of the President of the United States has been obtained, which consent and direction   *   *   *   [must] be obtained at least once each year."[23] The President may override a Commission decision to detonate an atomic warhead. The President may direct the Commission to make atomic weapons or special nuclear material available to the Department of Defense[24] and authorize the Commission or the Department of Defense to make available to other nations in accordance with the terms of the Act, "source, byproduct, or special nuclear material for research on, development of, production of, or use in utilization facilities for military applications; and   *   *   *   for research on, development of, or use in atomic weapons."[25]

Both military and peaceful uses of atomic energy, if not discreetly and stringently regulated, patently represent a grave threat to man and the environment. There is even some question as to whether regardless of the care taken it can ever be said with certainty that an atomic explosion is "safe." In every instance in which other than a very minor atomic blast occurs damage is done at or beneath the earth's surface. Usually a quantum of wildlife and vegetation are destroyed. Inadequate safeguards can result in an atomic explosion filling the air with radioactive particles which can cause great injury to human life. Utilization of atomic energy for the production of other forms of energy, such as electricity, likewise requires great care be taken to prevent the discharge of radioactive rays into the atmosphere. The Act imposes on the Atomic Energy Commission the task of establishing "by rule, regulation, or order, such standards and instructions to govern the possession and use of special nuclear material, source material, and byproduct material as the Commission may deem necessary or desirable to promote the common defense and security or to protect health or to minimize danger to life or property."[26]

21. 42 U.S.C.A. § 2282(a).

22. 42 U.S.C.A. § 2280.

23. 42 U.S.C.A. §§ 2121(a), 2121(b).

24. 42 U.S.C.A. § 2121(b).

25. 42 U.S.C.A. §§ 2121(c) (3), 2121(c) (4).

26. 42 U.S.C.A. § 2201(b).

Because of the threat atomic weaponry poses to national security, Congress, under the heading of "Control of Information", entrusts the Atomic Energy Commission, in cooperation with other named branches of the Federal Government, to limit access to Restricted Data. The Act defines Restricted Data as "all data concerning (1) design, manufacture, or utilization of atomic weapons; (2) the production of special nuclear material; or (3) the use of special nuclear material in the production of energy, but * * * [does] not include data declassified or removed from the Restricted Data category pursuant to * * * [the terms of the Act]."[27]

Congress directs that "[i]t shall be the policy of the Commission to control the dissemination and declassification of Restricted Data in such a manner as to assure the common defense and security."[28] The Commission is authorized to "exchange * * * Restricted Data with other nations"[29] only as authorized by the President in accordance with the Act.[30] So far as data not classified as Restricted is concerned, consistent with the demands of "common defense and security," the Act calls upon the Commission to permit and encourage "[t]he dissemination of scientific and technical information relating to atomic energy * * * so as to provide that free interchange of ideas and criticism which is essential to scientific and industrial progress and public understanding and to enlarge the fund of technical information."[31]

The Atomic Energy Act makes explicit provision for safeguarding the confidentiality of information, but it shuns a totally secretive approach. It sets forth procedures which must be followed to insure that information which warrants revelation is not kept from the public.[32] This congressional stance is understandable in a society which values the free flow of information. Not all governmental officials, however, place the same value on the dissemination of information. A clash between confidentiality and disclosure marks military matters, but is not confined to this area. There are instances in which it is apparent to most, if not all persons, that it is proper for government to impose a cloak of secrecy on particular types of information. But cases in which non-disclosure is necessary are comparatively few in number when measured in terms of the lengths to which some governmental officials go to keep information from the public. In cases in which an official possesses the power to decide whether or not to withhold information the delicate decision-making process in which he must engage is seldom free from what might be viewed as irrelevant considerations. Yet such factors may weigh most heavily on his deliberations. Personal predilection, fear of making known a

27. 42 U.S.C.A. § 2014(y).

28. 42 U.S.C.A. § 2161.

29. 42 U.S.C.A. § 2161(a).

30. 42 U.S.C.A. § 2164(a).

31. 42 U.S.C.A. § 2161(b).

32. 42 U.S.C.A. § 2162(a), (b).

personal mistake or one of a subordinate, revealing a flaw in the administrative process, making known a program's shortcomings, and political ambitions have historically played a critical behind the scene role in agency decisions not to release information. An official who is hostile to environmental protection or has little or no interest in the environment may find it expedient to resort to a supposed need for secrecy when his decision is challenged on environmental grounds. The Freedom of Information Act, signed on July 4, 1966, is designed to facilitate the flow of information from government to individual.[33]

In Soucie v. David,[34] the Court of Appeals for the District of Columbia wrote that "Congress passed the Freedom of Information Act to strengthen the disclosure requirements of the Administrative Procedure Act (APA). Each federal agency subject to the APA [the Atomic Energy Act makes the Atomic Energy Commission subject to the Administrative Procedure Act except for Restricted Data or defense information[35]] must now make its records, with certain specific exceptions, available to 'any person' who requests them; district courts have jurisdiction to order the production of any 'identifiable record' which is 'improperly withheld' and 'the burden is on the agency to sustain its action.' * * *."

"The Act enumerates nine specific exemptions to its general requirement of disclosure * * * [They are set forth below]."

"It has been argued that courts may recognize other grounds for non-disclosure, apart from the statutory exemptions. At least one court has held that the Act's grant of 'jurisdiction to enjoin' improper withholding of agency records leaves district courts with discretion to deny relief on general equitable grounds, even when no exemption is applicable. But Congress clearly has the power to eliminate ordinary discretionary barriers to injunctive relief, and we believe that Congress intended to do so here."

"Prior to the Freedom of Information Act, the disclosure provisions of the APA allowed the agencies to withhold information 'in the public interest,' or 'for good cause shown,' or on the ground that the person seeking the record was not 'properly and directly concerned.' The chief purpose of the new Act was to increase public access to governmental records by substituting limited categories of privileged material for these discretionary standards, and providing an effective judicial remedy. The Act rejects the usual principle of deference to administrative determinations by requiring a trial 'de novo' in the district court. By directing disclosure to any person, the Act precludes consideration of the interests of the party seeking relief. Most significantly, the Act expressly limits the grounds for non-disclosure to those specified in the exemptions. Through the general disclosure

33. Pub.L. 89–487, 80 Stat. 250, 5 U.S.
    C.A. § 552.

34. 448 F.2d 1067, (D.C.D.C.1971).

35. 42 U.S.C.A. § 2231.

requirement and specific exemptions, the Act thus strikes a balance among factors which would ordinarily be deemed relevant to the exercise of equitable discretion, *i. e.*, the public interest in freedom of information and countervailing public and private interests in secrecy. Since judicial use of traditional equitable principles to prevent disclosure would upset this legislative resolution of conflicting interests, we are persuaded that Congress did not intend to confer on district courts a general power to deny relief on equitable grounds apart from the exemptions in the Act itself. There may be exceptional circumstances in which a court could fairly conclude that Congress intended to leave room for the operation of limited judicial discretion, but no such circumstance appears in the present record of this case. [The plaintiffs in this case were "[t]wo citizens" who sought "to compel the Director of the Office of Science and Technology * * * to release to them a document, * * * which evaluates the Federal Government's program for development of a supersonic transport aircraft (SST)."]"

The 1966 Act exempts from compulsory disclosure information which falls into one of the following categories:

"(1) specifically required by Executive order to be kept secret in the interest of the national defense or foreign policy;

"(2) related solely to the internal personnel rules and practices of an agency;

"(3) specifically exempted from disclosure by statute;

"(4) trade secrets and commercial or financial information obtained from a person and privileged or confidential;

"(5) inter-agency or intra-agency memorandums or letters which would not be available by law to a party other than an agency in litigation with the agency;

"(6) personnel and medical files and similar files the disclosure of which would constitute a clearly unwarranted invasion of personal privacy;

"(7) investigatory files compiled for law enforcement purposes except to the extent available by law to a party other than an agency;

"(8) contained in or related to examination, operating, or condition reports prepared by, on behalf of, or for the use of an agency responsible for the regulation or supervision of financial institutions; or

"(9) geological and geophysical information and data, including maps, concerning wells." [36]

The Act specifically provides that it "does not authorize withholding of information or limit the availability of records to the public, except as specifically stated" therein.[37] The Act expressly bars of-

---

36. 5 U.S.C.A. § 552(b).   **37.** 5 U.S.C.A. § 552(c).

ficials from treating it as "authority to withhold information from Congress."[38]

In Soucie v. David the court acknowledged that the district court, on rehearing the case, might still bar disclosure if the agency established that the constitutional privilege of "executive privilege" was applicable. The doctrine of executive privilege, the court asserted, is in "some degree inherent in the constitutional requirement of separation of powers." The Constitution establishes three branches of government, executive, legislative, and judicial. While the Constitution does call for a system of checks and balances it has not been interpreted to authorize one branch of government to take such action as may undermine the effectiveness or impair the integrity of another branch of government.

When applicable, the privilege bars a court from compelling the executive branch of the federal government to produce military or diplomatic secrets or "intra-governmental documents reflecting advisory opinions, recommendations and deliberations comprising part of a process by which governmental decisions and policies are formulated."[39] In instances in which a litigant requests a court to direct an executive or administrative official to produce one or more documents and the official invokes the privilege, the court must evaluate the competing interests served by disclosure on the one hand and "public needs for confidentiality" on the other. Attention must also be paid to the fact that judges are not free " 'to probe the mental processes' of an executive or administrative officer." The court must weigh "the detrimental effects of disclosure against the necessity for production."[40] To determine whether the circumstances are appropriate to direct disclosure, a court may not force "a disclosure of the very thing the privilege is designed to protect."[41] It "may not properly require an *in camera* inspection as a matter of course before accepting a claim of executive privilege. * * * [A]n *in camera* examination should be afforded only where a suitable occasion therefor sufficiently appears. * * * Such an inspection should not be directed without a definite showing of 'facts indicating reasonable cause for requiring such a submission.' "[42]

38. 5 U.S.C.A. § 552(c).

39. Stiftung v. V.E.B. Carl Zeiss, Jena (D.C.D.C.1966) 40 F.R.D. 318.

40. Stiftung v. V.E.B. Carl Zeiss, Jena (D.C.D.C.1966) 40 F.R.D. 318.

41. United States v. Reynolds, 73 S.Ct. 528, 345 U.S. 1, 97 L.Ed. 727 (1953).

42. Stiftung v. V.E.B. Carl Zeiss, Jena (D.C.D.C.1966) 40 F.R.D. 318.

CALVERT CLIFFS' COORDINATING COMMITTEE, INC.
v. UNITED STATES ATOMIC ENERGY COMMISSION

United States Court of Appeals, District of Columbia Circuit, 1971.
449 F.2d 1109.

[The defendant's procedural rules (1) require applicants for a construction or operation permit to submit an environmental report and in such cases require Commission regulatory staff members to prepare a statement of environmental costs, benefits, and alternatives, but the rules prohibit a hearing board from considering nonradiological environmental issues unless affirmatively raised by an outside party or staff member, (2) provide that unless the notice of hearing appeared in the Federal Register after March 4, 1971 a hearing board may not take into account nonradiological environmental issues, (3) provide that in cases in which other responsible agencies have certified that their own environmental standards have been satisfied a hearing board is to treat all environmental standards as having been satisfied, and (4) provide that if a construction permit was issued prior to the passage of the National Environmental Policy Act (NEPA) the Commission would not formally consider environmental factors or require changes in proposed facilities until it considers an application for an operating license. Petitioners challenged these rules, asserting that they failed to satisfy NEPA.]

J. SKELLY WRIGHT, CIRCUIT JUDGE: * * *

NEPA * * * takes the major step of requiring all federal agencies to consider values of environmental preservation in their spheres of activity, and it prescribes certain procedural measures to ensure that those values are in fact fully respected. * * *

* * * Section 101 sets forth the Act's basic substantive policy: that the federal government "use all practicable means and measures" to protect environmental values. Congress did not establish environmental protection as an exclusive goal; rather, it desired a reordering of priorities, so that environmental costs and benefits will assume their proper place along with other considerations. * * *

* * * the general substantive policy of the Act is a flexible one. It leaves room for a responsible exercise of discretion and may not require particular substantive results in particular problematic instances. * * *, the Act also contains very important "procedural" provisions—provisions which are designed to see that all federal agencies do in fact exercise the substantive discretion given them. These provisions are not highly flexible. Indeed, they establish a strict standard of compliance.

NEPA, first of all, makes environmental protection a part of the mandate of every federal agency and department. * * * Perhaps the greatest importance of NEPA is to require the Atomic Energy

Commission and other agencies to *consider* environmental issues just as they consider other matters within their mandates. *   *   *

*   *   * In general, all agencies must use a "systematic, interdisciplinary approach" to environmental planning and evaluation "in decisionmaking which may have an impact on man's environment." *   *   * NEPA mandates a rather finely tuned and "systematic" balancing analysis in each instance.

To ensure that the balancing analysis is carried out and given full effect, *   *   * [NEPA] requires that responsible officials of all agencies prepare a "detailed statement" covering the impact of particular actions on the environment, the environmental costs which might be avoided, and alternative measures which might alter the cost-benefit equation. The apparent purpose of the "detailed statement" is to aid in the agencies' own decision making process and to advise other interested agencies and the public of the environmental consequences of planned federal action. *   *   *

Of course, all of these *   *   * [agency] duties are qualified by the phrase "to the fullest extent possible." *   *   * the requirement of environmental consideration "to the fullest extent possible" sets a high standard for the agencies, a standard which must be rigorously enforced by the reviewing courts.

*   *   *

We conclude, *   *   * that *   *   * NEPA mandates a particular sort of careful and informed decisionmaking process and creates judicially enforceable duties. The reviewing courts probably cannot reverse a substantive decision on its merits, *   *   *, unless it be shown that the actual balance of costs and benefits that was struck was arbitrary or clearly gave insufficient weight to environmental values. But if the decision was reached procedurally without individualized consideration and balancing of environmental factors —conducted fully and in good faith—it is the responsibility of the courts to reverse. *   *   *

*   *   * The question here is *   *   * whether it is enough that environmental data and evaluations merely "accompany" an application through the review process, but receive no consideration whatever from the hearing board.

We believe that the Commission's crabbed interpretation of NEPA makes a mockery of the Act. *   *   * NEPA was meant to do more than regulate the flow of papers in the federal bureaucracy. *   *   * It must, *   *   * be read to indicate a congressional intent that environmental factors, as compiled in the "detailed statement," be *considered* through agency review processes.

*   *   *

*   *   * NEPA establishes environmental protection as an integral part of the Atomic Energy Commission's basic mandate. The primary responsibility for fulfilling that mandate lies with the Com-

mission. Its responsibility is not simply to sit back, like an umpire, and resolve adversary contentions at the hearing stage. Rather, it must itself take the initiative of considering environmental values at every distinctive and comprehensive stage of the process beyond the staff's evaluation and recommendation.

Congress passed the final version of NEPA in late 1969, and the Act went into full effect on January 1, 1970. Yet the Atomic Energy Commission's rules prohibit any consideration of environmental issues by its hearing boards at proceedings officially noticed before March 4, 1971. * * * The result is that major federal actions having a significant environmental impact may be taken by the Commission, without full NEPA compliance, more than two years after the Act's effective date. In view of the importance of environmental consideration during the agency review process, * * * such a time lag is shocking.

* * *

* * * the Commission's long delay seems based upon what it believes to be a pressing national power crisis. Inclusion of environmental issues in pre-March 4, 1971 hearings might have held up the licensing of some power plants for a time. But the very purpose of NEPA was to tell federal agencies that environmental protection is as much a part of their responsibility as is protection and promotion of the industries they regulate. Whether or not the spectre of a national power crisis is as real as the Commission apparently believes, it must not be used to create a blackout of environmental consideration in the agency review process. NEPA compels a case-by-case examination and balancing of discrete factors. Perhaps there may be cases in which the need for rapid licensing of a particular facility would justify a strict time limit on a hearing board's review of environmental issues; but a blanket banning of such issues until March 4, 1971 is impermissible under NEPA.

* * *

* * * NEPA mandates a case-by-case balancing judgment on the part of federal agencies. In each individual case, the particular economic and technical benefits of planned action must be assessed and then weighed against the environmental costs; alternatives must be considered which would affect the balance of values. * * *

Certification by another agency that its own environmental standards are satisfied involves an entirely different kind of judgment. Such agencies, without overall responsibility for the particular federal action in question, attend only to one aspect of the problem: the magnitude of certain environmental costs. * * *

The Atomic Energy Commission, abdicating entirely to other agencies' certifications, neglects the mandated balancing analysis. Concerned members of the public are thereby precluded from raising a wide range of environmental issues in order to affect particular

Commission decisions. And the special purpose of NEPA is subverted.

* * *

* * * NEPA does not permit the sort of total abdication of responsibility practiced by the Atomic Energy Commission.

* * *

By refusing to consider requirement of alterations until construction is completed, the Commission may effectively foreclose the environmental protection desired by Congress. It may also foreclose rigorous consideration of environmental factors at the eventual operating license proceedings. If "irreversible and irretrievable commitment[s] of resources" have already been made, the license hearing (and any public intervention therein) may become a hollow exercise. This hardly amounts to consideration of environmental values "to the fullest extent possible."

* * *

* * * the Commission must go farther than it has in its present rules. It must consider action, as well as file reports and papers, at the pre-operating license stage. As the Commission candidly admits, such consideration does not amount to a retroactive application of NEPA. Although the projects in question may have been commenced and initially approved before January 1, 1970, the Act clearly applies to them since they must still pass muster before going into full operation. All we demand is that the environmental review be as full and fruitful as possible.

We hold that, * * * the Commission must revise its rules governing consideration of environmental issues. We do not impose a harsh burden on the Commission. For we require only an exercise of substantive discretion which will protect the environment "to the fullest extent possible." No less is required if the grand congressional purposes underlying NEPA are to become a reality.

Remanded for proceedings consistent with this opinion.

* * *

PROBLEMS

1. Plaintiff, a public utility producing and selling electrical energy to consumers located in several states obtained a permit from the Atomic Energy Commission to construct an atomic energy generating plant. Pending action on its application to the Commission for a license to begin to operate the plant, the state in which the plant was located granted the plaintiff a permit to discharge cooling water and liquid waste into the Mississippi River but only if specified state disposal standards were satisfied. Plaintiff, in a declaratory judgment action challenging the imposition of state-established standards,

claimed that the federal government had preempted the field. In part plaintiff relied on the federal law which created the Commission. It provides that the Commission has the "authority and responsibility * * * [with respect to] * * * construction and operation of any production or utilization facility." The state defended its right to act on the ground that its standards were more demanding than those prescribed by the Commission. What judgment?

2. The Atomic Energy Commission purchased a parcel of land one-half mile square. It contained an abandoned salt mine which the Commission planned to use to entomb "high level" radioactive wastes generated by commercial atomic power plants. Plaintiff, who operated a motel two miles from the mine, brought an action asking for an injunction banning the planned use of the mine and alternatively for a judgment awarding him money damages equivalent to the reasonable value of his motel and the land on which it was situated. He claimed that fear of contamination would keep persons away from his motel. The Commission's experts testified that storage procedures would guarantee that the wastes would cause no harm to human beings or animals. What judgment?

3. A contractor who had built a portion of a nuclear power plant wrote a letter to the Atomic Energy Commission stating that the plant was unsafe and an operating permit should not be granted. Attached to his letter was an elaborate detailed statement of his position and how he arrived at his conclusion. Two experts in the employ of the Commission, after having examined the statement, reported that "the facts contained in the statement fail to support the author's conclusions. We reaffirm our original conclusion that the plant will be a safe producer of much needed electrical power." When notified of the report, the contractor demanded a hearing so he could personally present his position to the Commission. His request was refused. He appealed. What judgment?

4. How much weight should the Atomic Energy Commission assign to the respective priorities involved when balancing the anticipated harm thermal pollution would cause to wildlife and a recognized need for electrical power which, if not satisfied, would probably produce "brown outs?"

5. Plaintiffs, objecting to the carrying out of a planned underground nuclear explosion on the ground that the Atomic Energy Commission had failed to take into account adverse reports submitted to it by some members of its staff, asked the court to direct the Commission to make the reports public. The Commission refused, pleading executive privilege. What judgment?

Chapter 17

LAND USE

Europeans who first settled on the North American continent as well as immigrants who subsequently followed them to the New World regarded land as an endless natural resource. As late as the close of the Civil War a vast expanse of the United States was yet to be settled. Even the so-called "closing of the West" which had occurred by the end of the nineteenth century did not substantially modify the comforting attitude of most persons toward the quantity of land at the nation's disposal. The notion that the land supply was inexhaustible lingered on well into the twentieth century. And with good reason. Arizona retained territorial status until 1913. Except for the exigencies which confronted a relatively small number of large metropolitan areas, pre-World War I United States could afford the luxury of paying little attention to the question of land use.

During the past several decades a variety of factors have appeared, converged, and congealed which have made necessary adoption of a new attitude toward land. An exponential-like increase in population; shifts in the national demographic pattern; unprecedented visibility of and concern with minorities and the indigent; espousal of a demanding, ever more embracing egalitarian philosophy; formulation of an assortment of legal principles directed at protecting and expanding civil rights; the impact of technology on life styles and the physical, mental, and emotional well-being of persons; and individual and group reactions to what is and what is not taking place across the nation in cities, towns, and rural areas, have helped to shape a point of view toward land which is almost the very antithesis of the approach generally accepted but half a century ago. Land is now commonly recognized as a finite resource. It is in the national interest that individuals be obliged to use land in ways consistent with contemporary and presumed future societal needs and aspirations.

In Village of Euclid v. Ambler Realty Co.[1] decided in 1926 the Supreme Court of the United States commented on building zone laws, labeling them as "of modern origin." Speaking of the appearance of such laws and their constitutionality, the Court said: "They began in this country about twenty-five years ago. Until recent years, urban life was comparatively simple; but with the great increase and concentration of population, problems have developed, and constantly are developing, which require, and will continue to require, additional restrictions in respect of the use and occupation of private lands in urban communities. Regulations, the wisdom, necessity and

1. 47 S.Ct. 114, 272 U.S. 365, 71 L.Ed. 303.

validity of which, as applied to existing conditions, are so apparent that they are now uniformly sustained, a century ago, or even half a century ago, probably would have been rejected as arbitrary and oppressive. Such regulations are sustained, under the complex conditions of our day, for reasons analogous to those which justify traffic regulations, which, before the advent of automobiles and rapid transit street railways, would have been condemned as fatally arbitrary and unreasonable. And in this there is no inconsistency, for while the meaning of constitutional guaranties never varies, the scope of their application must expand or contract to meet the new and different conditions which are constantly coming within the field of their operation. In a changing world, it is impossible that it should be otherwise. But although a degree of elasticity is thus imparted, not to the *meaning*, but to the *application* of constitutional principles, statutes and ordinances, which, after giving due weight to the new conditions, are found clearly not to conform to the Constitution, of course, must fall."

"The ordinance now under review, and all similar laws and regulations, must find their justification in some aspect of the police power, asserted for the public welfare. The line which in this field separate the legitimate from the illegitimate assumption of power is not capable of precise determination. It varies with circumstances and conditions. A regulatory zoning ordinance, which would be clearly valid as applied to the great cities, might be clearly invalid as applied to rural communities. In solving doubts, the maxim *sic utere tuo ut alienum non laedas* [use your property in such a manner as not to injure that of another], which lies at the foundation of so much of the common law of nuisance, ordinarily will furnish a fairly helpful clew. And the law of nuisances, likewise, may be consulted, not for the purpose of controlling, but for the helpful aid of its analogies in the process of ascertaining the scope of, the power. Thus the question whether the power exists to forbid the erection of a building of a particular kind or for a particular use, like the question whether a particular thing is a nuisance, is to be determined, not by an abstract consideration of the building or of the thing considered apart, but by considering it in connection with the circumstances and the locality. * * * A nuisance may be merely a right thing in the wrong place, —like a pig in the parlor instead of the barnyard. If the validity of the legislative classification for zoning purposes be fairly debatable, the legislative judgment must be allowed to control. * * * [Sustaining the constitutionality of the ordinance the Court found that it] can not be said that the ordinance * * * 'passes the bounds of reason and assumes the character of a merely arbitrary fiat.' "

The Court asserted that it was proper for an ordinance to exclude "from residential districts, [such things as] apartment houses, business houses, retail stores and shops, [hotels] and other like establishments." It concluded that such legislation "bears a rational relation to the health and safety of the community" since it promotes "the health and security from injury of children and others by separating dwelling houses from territory devoted to trade and industry;" suppresses and prevents "disorder;" facilitates "the extinguishment of fires, and the enforcement of street traffic regulations and other general welfare ordinances;" aids "the health and safety of the community by excluding from residential areas the confusion and danger of fire, contagion and disorder which in greater or less degree attach to the location of stores, shops and factories. Another ground is that the construction and repair of streets may be rendered easier and less expensive by confining the greater part of the heavy traffic to the streets where business is carried on."

Addressing itself directly to the propriety of treating apartment houses as a distinct category of housing, the Court said: "With particular reference to apartment houses, it is pointed out that the development of detached house sections is greatly retarded by the coming of apartment houses, which has sometimes resulted in destroying the entire section for private house purposes; that in such sections very often the apartment house is a mere parasite, constructed in order to take advantage of the open spaces and attractive surroundings created by the residential character of the district. Moreover, the coming of one apartment house is followed by others, interfering by their height and bulk with the free circulation of air and monopolizing the rays of the sun which otherwise would fall upon the smaller homes, and bringing, as their necessary accompaniments, the disturbing noises incident to increased traffic and business, and the occupation, by means of moving and parked automobiles, of larger portions of the streets, thus detracting from their safety and depriving children of the privilege of quiet and open spaces for play, enjoyed by those in more favored localities,—until, finally, the residential character of the neighborhood and its desirability as a place of detached residences are utterly destroyed. Under these circumstances, apartment houses, which in a different environment would be not only entirely unobjectionable but highly desirable, come very near to being nuisances."

The Court recognized that the legislative branch of government enjoyed a broad latitude of discretion in the formulation of zoning legislation. It is not within the province of the judiciary to insist that it be demonstrated that such legislation is predicated on "wisdom or sound policy in all respects." A zoning ordinance must be sustained so long as "the reasons [in favor of the law] are sufficiently cogent to preclude * * * [the court] from saying, as it must be said before the ordinance * * * [could] be declared unconstitutional, that such provisions are clearly arbitrary and unreasonable, having no substantial relation to the public health, safety, morals, or general welfare."

To be constitutional a zoning ordinance must be rationally related to a constitutionally permissible objective. Almost a decade before *Euclid*, in Buchanan v. Warley,[2] the Supreme Court struck down a City of Louisville ordinance that prohibited the new occupancy by blacks in those parts of the City in which whites already occupied a greater number of residences than blacks and barred whites from entering into occupancy in those parts of the City where more blacks were residing than whites. The Court found no merit in the argument that this legislation was a proper exercise of the City's police power because it "tends to promote the public peace by preventing racial conflicts; * * * it tends to maintain racial purity; * * * it prevents the deterioration of property owned and occupied by white people, * * *. But * * * [declared the Court] the police power, broad as it is, cannot justify the passage of a law or ordinance which runs counter to the limitations of the Federal Constitution." Addressing itself to racism, the Court wrote "[t]hat there exists a serious and difficult problem arising from a feeling of race hostility which the law is powerless to control, and to which it must give a measure of consideration, * * *. But its solution cannot be promoted by depriving citizens of their constitutional rights and privileges." The Court concluded: "We think this attempt to prevent alienation of the property in question to a person of color was not a legitimate exercise of the police power of the State, and is in direct violation of the fundamental law enacted in the Fourteenth Amendment of the Constitution preventing state interference with property rights except by due process of law." Elsewhere in the opinion the Court, speaking of the Fourteenth Amendment, stated that "[w]hile a principal purpose of the * * * Amendment was to protect persons of color, the broad language used was deemed sufficient to protect all persons, white or black, against discriminatory legislation by the States." The Court concluded that the ordinance could not stand.

Euclid viewed zoning as a function of contemporary values, concerns, demands, and aspirations. To be valid zoning legislation must be rationally related to a legitimate societal interest. *Buchanan* placed the breadth of the zoning power in constitutional perspective. Societal values, concerns, demands, and aspirations and constitutional directives which initially made their appearance in the late 1950's and 1960's have precipitated the formulation of an assortment of new criteria which jurists are now obliged to use to test the lawfulness of zoning legislation. Additional standards of propriety are certain to appear in the years which lie ahead. Some courts have already tested the lawfulness of zoning legislation by post-1950 standards. Others are now doing so. The new yardsticks are varied, not always easy to apply, and oftentimes controversial. For the most part they are intertwined with undoing zoning which is racist, snobbish, or class oriented.

2. 38 S.Ct. 16, 245 U.S. 60, 62 L.Ed. 149.

Large lot zoning bans the construction of single family dwellings on less than a specified minimum land area. This prohibition might be based on *bona fide* health, safety, or aesthetic reasons. It may also be done in order to keep out middle class white and nonwhite persons. A person of limited financial means might be capable of paying for a home built on a quarter or a half acre site. He would be unable to purchase a single family dwelling built on a five acre site. An ordinance which prohibits the construction of multiple dwellings effectively keeps out middle or lower class persons with large families who cannot afford a private home. It likewise prevents working and non-working poor who, with welfare assistance, might be able to otherwise find apartment house accommodations. Banning mobile homes and trailer parks denies those who cannot afford a conventional type home from enjoying a semblance of a one family dwelling. A town which sets aside all or most of the remaining open land within its boundaries for park or recreational purposes may satisfy the wishes of the local citizenry. But it precludes those who wish to move into the town from doing so unless they can find a vacancy in an existing structure. Some courts have struck down one or more of the above types of zoning.

Various levels and agencies of government pursuing policies intended to promote racial and class integration and in quest of housing for the shelter deprived have undertaken to put an end to a rigid compartmentalized approach to single family and multiple residences. The concept of spot zoning permits construction of a multiple dwelling in an area otherwise set aside for other purposes. Scatter site zoning calls for the building of premises intended to provide homes for the poor and near poor in an area predominantly populated by middle class persons. Fiscal zoning, like scatter site zoning, is concerned with the poor. It connotes governmental action which denies funds for urban renewal projects unless the proposed plans make suitable provision for meeting the needs of indigent persons.

There is almost universal agreement that care must be taken to insure that in heavily populated cities and sprawling suburbs available land is used in a planned and orderly fashion so that existing and future needs and aspirations can be satisfied. What disagreement does exist usually centers on the nature of the objectives to be selected and the means to be employed to attain them. A variety of considerations having to do with health, safety, aesthetics, and social policies have to be weighed and accommodated. A great deal of the decision-making takes place in the political arena. It is from this sphere of activity that constitutional amendments and legislation emanate. Within the discretion granted to them executive and agency officials are obliged to carry out selected legislative policies. The courts interpret and apply the constitution, statutes, ordinances, and agency regulations. Illustrative of this multifaceted approach to land use is application of that portion the National Environmental Policy

Act's provision which calls for an impact statement whenever governmental action affects the environment. Under this mandate of the Act it is now necessary for a federal agency involved in making changes in land use to prepare a statement which sets forth the affect the planned action will have on the environment. This requirement has already forced agency officials to pay heed to the fact that land is a limited resource and whatever is done to alter or destroy existing structures or to construct new ones calls for a decision as to what use should or should not be made of the available land supply.

Not directly related to zoning, yet in a sense a form of zoning, is the manner in which a municipality treats persons who reside in different parts of the city. It has been commonplace for local governments to give preferential treatment to some parts of a community and to neglect other parts. The United States Court of Appeals for the Fifth Circuit, in Hawkins v. Town of Shaw,[3] described such disparity of treatment as follows: "Referring to a portion of town or a segment of society as being 'on the other side of the tracks' has for too long been a familiar expression to most Americans. Such a phrase immediately conjures up an area characterized by poor housing, overcrowded conditions and, in short, overall deterioration." The Court was not confronted with a frontal attack on all forms of disparity, only one—racial. The Court asserted: "While there may be many reasons why such areas exist in nearly all of our cities, one reason that cannot be accepted is the discriminatory provision of municipal services based on race." On examining the facts at hand, the Court found that "97% of all those who live[d] in homes fronting on unpaved streets * * * [were] black * * * all of the *better* lighting that exist[ed] in Shaw * * * [could] be found *only* in the white parts of town * * * [w]hile 99% of white residents * * * [were] served by sanitary sewer system, nearly 20% of the black population * * * [were] not so served * * * [the problem of water drainage, while affecting] both the black and white sections of town * * * [were] far more serious * * * [in the black community] * * * [and] the two areas where the water pressure * * * [was] most inadequate * * * [were] black and constitute[d] 63% of the town's black population." The Court found that the Fourteenth Amendment had been violated in spite of the fact that there was "no direct evidence aimed at establishing bad faith, ill will or an evil motive on the part of the Town of Shaw and its public officials." It stated that "[i]n a civil rights suit alleging racial discrimination in contravention of the Fourteenth Amendment, actual intent or motive need not be directly proved, for: 'equal protection of the laws' means more than merely the absence of governmental action designed to discriminate; * * * we now firmly recognize that the arbitrary quality of thoughtlessness can be as disastrous and unfair to private rights and the public interest as

3.   437 F.2d 1286 (5th Cir. 1971).

the perversity of a willful scheme.' " Finding that "no compelling state interests can possibly justify the discriminatory *results* of Shaw's administration of municipal services" the Court concluded "that a violation of equal protection * * * [had] occurred." The Town of Shaw was ordered to "submit a plan for the court's approval detailing how it propose[d] to cure the results of the long history of discrimination which the record reveal[ed]."

CONLON v. TOWN OF FARMINGTON

Superior Court of Connecticut, Hartford County, 1971.
280 A.2d 896, 29 Conn.Sup. 230.

[Plaintiffs, four children, brought suit against the Town to recover damages for illness and other consequences they suffered as a result of storm water and sewage backing up and entering their parents' home. In their complaint they alleged that the backing up of the water and sewage was due to the Town's faulty and inadequate sewer system which they charged constituted a private or public nuisance. The defendant demurred.]

FITZ GERALD, JUDGE.

* * *

There are two classifications of nuisance: public and private. * * * The minor plaintiffs are not suing as members of the general public. " 'Nuisances are public where they violate public rights, and produce a common injury,' and where they constitute an obstruction to public rights, 'that is, the rights enjoyed by citizens as part of the public.' * * * "To be considered public, the nuisance must affect an interest common to the general public, rather than peculiar to one individual, or several." * * * The minor children have not alleged sufficient facts to spell out, as to them, a public nuisance.

Nor have the minor children alleged facts sufficient to sustain a cause of action in private nuisance. At the most, they were living on premises owned by their parents, * * * with the consent of both parents. "A private nuisance exists only where one is injured in relation to a right which he enjoys by reasons of his ownership of an interest in land." * * * "[I]t is the prevailing rule that any one who has no interest in the property affected, such as a licensee, an employee or a lodger on the premises, cannot maintain an action based on a private nuisance. In perhaps the greater number of cases, this has been held to include members of the possessor's family, who have no property rights. A few courts have permitted them to recover for personal injuries, in an action which was said to be one for the nuisance. Such decisions apparently overlook the fact that the existence of a nuisance to the land does not preclude an independent tort action for the interference with the bodily security of the individual, and seem to have allowed an entirely proper recovery for ordinary negligence, under the wrong theory." * * *

To go no further, the defendant's interposed demurrer * * * is, sustained in toto.

APPEAL OF KIT–MAR BUILDERS, INC.

Supreme Court of Pennsylvania, 1970.
268 A.2d 765, 439 Pa. 466.

[Kit-Mar Builders, Inc. agreed to purchase a 140 acre tract of land contingent on Concord Township rezoning it to permit construction of single-family homes on one acre lots. As zoned, lots of no less than two acres were required along existing roads and no less than three acres in the interior. The Township denied a request for rezoning and a building permit. Appealing to the Zoning Board of Adjustment Kit-Mar attacked the constitutionality of the zoning ordinance. The Board upheld the minimum lot requirements. Kit-Mar appealed to the Court of Common Pleas which took no additional testimony but made new findings of fact and reversed the Board. The Township appealed.]

ROBERTS, JUSTICE. * * * Initially we must note that the trial court erred in making new findings of fact without taking additional testimony. Without an independent taking of evidence the trial court could not properly make its own findings of fact, but could only review the decision of the board to determine if an abuse of discretion or an error of law had been committed. * * * However, it remains within the province of this Court to affirm the action of the trial court, even if that action was based on an erroneous procedure, if there are independent grounds for affirmance. * * * We conclude that, even accepting the findings of the zoning board, the ordinance here in question is unconstitutional under the test set forth in our decision in *National Land* * * *.

We decided in *National Land* that a scheme of zoning that has an exclusionary purpose or result is not acceptable in Pennsylvania. We do not intend to say, of course, that minimum lot size requirements are inherently unreasonable. Planning considerations and other interests can justify reasonably varying minimum lot sizes in given areas of a community. "At some point along the spectrum, however, the size of lots ceases to be a concern requiring public regulation and becomes simply a matter of private preference." The two and three acre minimums imposed in this case are no more reasonable than the four acre requirements struck down in *National Land*. As we pointed out in *National Land*, there are obvious advantages to the residents of a community in having houses built on four—or three—acre lots. However, minimum lot sizes of the magnitude required by this ordinance are a great deal larger than what should be considered as a *necessary* size for the building of a house, and are therefore not the proper subjects of public regulation. * * * Absent some extraordinary justification, a zoning ordinance with minimum lot sizes such as those in this case is completely unreasonable.

As the primary justification for the zoning ordinance now before us the township contends that lots of a smaller size will create a potential sewerage problem. It was on this question that the zoning board and the trial court made conflicting findings of fact. Whether a potential sewerage problem exists or not is irrelevant, however, since we *explicitly rejected* the argument that sewerage problems could excuse exclusionary zoning in *National Land*.

* * *

* * * We in effect held in *National Land* that because there were alternative methods for dealing with nearly all the problems that attend a growth in population, including sewage problems, zoning which had an exclusive purpose or effect could not be allowed. * * * "This is not to say that the village may not, pursuant to its other and general police powers [i. e. not zoning power], impose other restrictions or conditions on the granting of a building permit to plaintiff, such as a general assessment for reconstruction of the sewage system, granting of building permits * * * in stages, or perhaps even a moratorium on the issuance of any building permits, reasonably limited as to time. But, whatever the right of a municipality to impose ' "a * * * temporary restraint of beneficial enjoyment * * * where the interference is necessary to promote the ultimate good either of the municipality as a whole or of the immediate neighborhood" ', such restraint must be kept ' "within the limits of necessity" ' and may not prevent permanently the reasonable use of private property for the only purposes to which it is practically adapted [citations omitted]."

* * * We * * * refuse to allow the township to do precisely what we have never permitted—keep out people, rather than make community improvements.

The implication of our decision in *National Land* is that communities must deal with the problems of population growth. They may not refuse to confront the future by adopting zoning regulations that effectively restrict population to near present levels. It is not for any given township to say who may or may not live within its confines, while disregarding the interests of the entire area. If Concord Township is successful in unnaturally limiting its population growth through the use of exclusive zoning regulations, the people who would normally live there will inevitably have to live in another community, and the requirement that they do so is not a decision that Concord Township should alone be able to make.

While our decision in *National Land* requires municipalities to meet the challenge of population growth without closing their doors to it, we have indicated our willingness to give communities the ability to respond with great flexibility to the problems caused by suburban expansion. Most notable in this regard is our decision in Village 2 at New Hope, Inc. Appeals, in which we approved planned unit development. * * * Effective interrelations between the various component needs of the community can now be more easily realized. For instance, various types of housing, schools, and recreational facilities can be planned not only for the immediate needs of the community, but also to effectuate broad social purposes. The adverse economic impact of large-scale development can be mitigated if not entirely eliminated by the judicious juxtapositioning of revenue-producing development with residential and public uses. In this manner, achievement of good traffic separation, public transportation, visual enjoyment, and a host of other desiderata can be realized as [sic] much reduced economic cost."

* * * New and exciting techniques are available to the local governing bodies of this Commonwealth for dealing with the problems of population growth. Neither Concord Township * * * nor any other local governing unit may retreat behind a cover of exclusive zoning. We fully realize that the overall solution to these problems lies with greater regional planning; but until the time comes that we have such a system we must confront the situation as it is. The power currently resides in the hands of each local governing unit, and we will not tolerate their abusing that power in attempting to zone out growth at the expense of neighboring communities.

       * * *

Thinly veiled justifications for exclusionary zoning will not be countenanced by this Court. We rejected them in *National Land* * * * and we reject them here.

       Decree affirmed.

       * * *

PROBLEMS

1. To promote the construction of theaters and museums an ordinance included an "incentive" zoning provision which granted one who built such a structure broader latitude in the utilization of his land site than otherwise allowed. Plaintiff, desirous of erecting an apartment-office building complex challenged the constitutionality of the statute. What judgment?

2. A state income tax law authorized one who had donated land to an organization or governmental body for a use "consistent with the demands of a healthy environment" to treat the transfer as a charitable contribution and to state the value of his contribution at twice the land's market value on the day of the transfer. Plaintiff, a

taxpayer, who had contributed a large parcel of land to a religious organization, under the law was limited to stating the value of his contribution at its assessed value on the day of the transfer. He challenged the constitutionality of the statute. What judgment?

3. A state statute empowered municipalities to condemn and raze blighted "land" areas within their boundaries. Plaintiff owned a commercial structure located in the heart of the city's business district. It was built in the air space above railroad tracks. Finding the tracks a blight, the municipality ordered the condemnation of plaintiff's property. He challenged the action, claiming that the statute authorized the condemnation of "land" but not air space. What judgment?

4. An executive order directed that prior to a federal agency erecting a facility it make certain that there was adequate integrated low-income housing in the area for future federal employees and other persons. Plaintiff, an association of blacks and Puerto Ricans, asked the court to enjoin a federal agency from carrying out a contract calling for the construction of a new agency office building on the ground that integrated low-income housing was not available in the immediate area. The agency established that such housing was available within a commuting zone of one and a half hours (round trip) and that public transportation was generally available. What judgment?

5. A local ordinance barred mobile homes and communal residences from all areas zoned "residential." Plaintiffs, members of a commune which owned a mobile home, challenged the constitutionality of the statute. What judgment?

6. Would an ordinance be constitutional if it made it a misdemeanor for a landlord to refuse to rent an apartment to an applicant because of the applicant's age or because the applicant was the parent of one or more children under the age of 12 years?

7. After the state legislature repealed its anti-abortion law, the defendant, a physician, established an abortion center on his property which was located in an area zoned "residential and commercial, but not industrial." Plaintiff, claiming that the center constituted a nuisance, brought an action to enjoin the defendant from making such use of his property. What judgment? Would occupation of residential property exclusively by transsexuals or homosexuals constitute a nuisance?

Chapter 18

HIGHWAYS

Urbanization, suburbanization, interdependence of persons to satisfy their needs for goods and services, and the relatively small cost of owning and operating a motor vehicle have generated widespread support for the construction and maintenance of elaborate highway systems. In legislation which established the Department of Transportation, Congress declared "that the general welfare, the economic growth and stability of the Nation and its security require the development of national transportation policies and programs conducive to the provision of fast, safe, efficient, and convenient transportation at the lowest cost consistent therewith and with other national objectives, including the efficient utilization and conservation of the Nation's resources."[1] Congress simultaneously recognized the mischief highways do to the environment, declaring it "to be the national policy that special effort should be made [when highways are constructed] to preserve the natural beauty of the countryside and public park and recreation lands, wildlife and waterfowl refuges, and historic sites."[2]

Like all federal agencies, the Department of Transportation is obliged to satisfy the requirements of the National Environmental Policy Act. In addition, Congress has directed the Secretary of Transportation to "cooperate and consult with the Secretaries of the Interior, Housing and Urban Development, and Agriculture, and with the States in developing transportation plans and programs that include measures to maintain or enhance the natural beauty of the lands traversed. * * * [He is directed not to] approve any program or project which requires the use of any publicly owned land from a public park, recreation area, or wildlife and waterfowl refuge of national, State, or local significance as so determined by such officials unless (1) there is no feasible and prudent alternative to the use of such land, and (2) such program includes all possible planning to minimize harm to such park, recreational area, wildlife and waterfowl refuge, or historic site resulting from such use."[3]

Aware of the need to recognize and coordinate the availability of suitable transportation facilities, housing, urban growth, and planning, Congress has directed the Secretary of Transportation "and the Secretary of Housing and Urban Development * * * [to] consult and exchange information regarding their respective transportation policies and activities; carry on joint planning, research and other activities; and [to] coordinate assistance for local transportation

1. 49 U.S.C.A. § 1651(a). 3. 49 U.S.C.A. § 1653(f).

2. 49 U.S.C.A. § 1651(b) (1).

183

projects * * * [to] jointly study how Federal policies and programs can assure that urban transportation systems most effectively
serve both national transportation needs and the comprehensively
planned development of urban areas * * * [to] annually
* * * report to the President, for submission to the Congress, on
their studies and other activities [in the stated areas] including any
legislative recommendations which they determine to be desirable."[4]

Demand for the expansion of existing highways and the construction of additional ones is to a large extent a function of the
number of persons who due to predilection or the absence of a viable
alternative use individually owned and operated automobiles to satisfy their transportation needs. One way to curtail the incessant clam-
or for improving and building highways is to make available attractive, inexpensive, and reliable forms of mass transportation in those
portions of the country in which it can effectively be utilized. In the
Urban Mass Transportation Act adopted in 1964 Congress acknowledged that there existed a critical need for the development of such
forms of transportation. This need continues unabated.

In the declaration of findings included in the Urban Mass Transportation Act, Congress declared that "the predominant part of the
Nation's population is located in its rapidly expanding metropolitan
and other urban areas, which generally cross the boundary lines of local jurisdictions and often extend into two or more States;[5]
* * * that the welfare and vitality of urban areas, the satisfactory movement of people and goods within such areas, and the effectiveness of housing, urban renewal, highway, and other federally aided programs are being jeoparized by the deterioration or inadequate
provision of urban transportation facilities and services, the intensi-
fication of traffic congestion, and the lack of coordinated transportation and other development planning on a comprehensive and continuing basis; * * *."[6] Congress found "that the rapid urbanization
and the continued dispersal of population and activities within urban
areas * * * [had] made the ability of all citizens to move quickly and at a reasonable cost an urgent national problem."[7] It saw the
federal role as primarily fiscal, asserting that success required "a
Federal commitment for the expenditure of at least $10,000,000,000
over a twelve-year period to permit confident and continuing local
planning, and greater flexibility in program administration."[8] The
expressed purposes of the Act were stated to be "to assist in the development of improved mass transportation facilities, equipment,
techniques, and methods,[9] with the cooperation of mass transporta-

4. 49 U.S.C.A. § 1653(g).

5. 49 U.S.C.A. § 1601(a) (1).

6. 49 U.S.C.A. § 1601(a) (2).

7. 49 U.S.C.A. § 1601a.

8. 49 U.S.C.A. § 1601a.

9. 49 U.S.C.A. § 1601(b) (1).

tion companies both public and private; [10] * * * to encourage the planning and establishment of areawide urban mass transportation systems needed for economical and desirable urban development, with the cooperation of mass transportation companies both public and private; * * * to provide assistance to State and local governments and their instrumentalities in financing such systems, to be operated by public or private mass transportation companies as determined by local needs * * * [11] [and] to create a partnership which permits the local community, through Federal financial assistance, to exercise the initiative necessary to satisfy its urban mass transportation requirements."[12]

To further the stated objectives of the Act the Secretary of Transportation, when the standards of eligibility set forth in the Act are satisfied, may "make grants or loans * * * to assist States and local and public bodies and agencies * * * in financing the acquisition, construction, reconstruction, and improvement of facilities and equipment for use, by operation or lease or otherwise, in mass transportation service in urban areas and in coordinating such service with highway and other transportation in such areas."[13] Under specified circumstances the Secretary is authorized to extend financial assistance to private mass transportation companies.[14] He "is authorized to undertake research, development, and demonstration projects in all phases of urban mass transportation (including the development, testing, and demonstration of new facilities, equipment, techniques, and methods) which he determines will assist in the reduction of urban transportation needs, the improvement of mass transportation service, or the contribution of such service toward meeting total urban transportation needs at minimum cost. He may undertake such projects independently or by grant or contract (including working agreements with other Federal departments and agencies)."[15] The Act provides the conditions under which the Secretary may make grants "to States and local public bodies and agencies * * * for the planning, engineering, and designing of urban mass transportation projects, and for other technical studies, to be included, or proposed to be included, in a program (completed or under active preparation) for a unified or officially coordinated urban transportation system as a part of the comprehensively planned development of the urban area."[16]

The search for viable forms of mass transportation has engendered the following recommendations: (1) end the practice of earmarking federal and state gasoline taxes exclusively for highway im-

10.   49 U.S.C.A. § 1601(b) (2).

11.   49 U.S.C.A. § 1601(b) (3).

12.   49 U.S.C.A. § 1601a.

13.   49 U.S.C.A. § 1602(a).

14.   49 U.S.C.A. § 1602(e).

15.   49 U.S.C.A. § 1605(a).

16.   49 U.S.C.A. § 1607(a).

provement and construction and use such funds to promote and underwrite mass transportation; (2) improve existing highways rather than construct new ones; (3) use federal, state, and local funds to subsidize the improvement and operation of private and publicly owned forms of mass transit; (4) construct new subway systems and establish new bus routes; (5) offer mass transit services at little or no cost; (6) encourage commuters who do not use mass transit to organize car pools; (7) reduce or excuse the payment of tolls by those who commute as members of a car pool; (8) establish "speed lanes" for buses and cars used by those who are part of a car pool; (9) in urban areas impose a parking tax or parking fee at a rate which would deter the use of automobiles in particular parts of the city; (10) ban the use of automobiles in congested urban areas.

CITIZENS TO PRESERVE OVERTON PARK, INC. v. VOLPE

Supreme Court of the United States, 1971.
91 S.Ct. 814, 401 U.S. 402, 28 L.Ed.2d 136.

[The Secretary of Transportation announced that he concurred with the judgment of local officials that a portion of a six-lane high-speed interstate expressway, I–40, should pass through Overton Park, a public park located in Memphis, Tennessee. He authorized the expenditure of federal funds for its construction. At the time the park contained, in addition to other features, a zoo, nature trails, picnic areas, and 170 acres of forest. As planned, the highway would sever the zoo from the rest of the park and would destroy 26 acres of parkland. It would provide some residents of Memphis with more ready access to the downtown area.

Petitioners, private citizens and local and national conservational groups, challenged the Secretary's action. They claimed that he violated the Department of Transportation Act of 1966 and the Federal-Aid Highway Act of 1968 which prohibit him from authorizing the use of federal funds to finance construction of a highway through a public park if a "feasible and prudent alternative route exists." These statutes allow him to approve construction through a park only if there has been "all possible planning to minimize harm to the park." The Secretary never stated why he believed there were no feasible and prudent alternative routes or why design changes could not be made to reduce harm to the park.

The District Court granted the Secretary's motion for summary judgment. The Court of Appeals affirmed. Certiorari and a stay halting construction were granted.]

Opinion of the Court by MR. JUSTICE MARSHALL, announced by MR. JUSTICE STEWART.

The growing public concern about the quality of our natural environment has prompted Congress in recent years to enact legislation designed to curb the accelerating destruction of our country's natural beauty. We are concerned in this case with § 4(f) of the Department of Transportation Act of 1966, as amended, and § 18(a) of the Federal-Aid Highway Act of 1968 (hereinafter § 138) * * *

     *   *   *

Petitioners contend that the Secretary's action is invalid without * * * formal findings and that the Secretary did not make an independent determination but merely relied on the judgment of the Memphis City Council. They also contend that it would be "feasible and prudent" to route I–40 around Overton Park either to the north or to the south. And they argue that if these alternative routes are not "feasible and prudent," the present plan does not include "all possible" methods for reducing harm to the park. * * *

The District Court and the Court of Appeals found that formal findings by the Secretary were not necessary and refused to order the deposition of the former Federal Highway Administrator because those courts believed that probing of the mental processes of an administrative decisionmaker was prohibited. And, believing that the Secretary's authority was wide and reviewing courts' authority narrow in the approval of highway routes, the lower courts held that the affidavits contained no basis for a determination that the Secretary had exceeded his authority.

We agree that formal findings were not required. But we do not believe that in this case judicial review based solely on litigation affidavits was adequate.

     *   *   *

Section 4(f) of the Department of Transportation Act and § 138 of the Federal-Aid Highway Act are clear and specific directives. Both the Department of Transportation Act and the Federal-Aid to Highway Act provide that the Secretary "shall not approve any program or project" that requires the use of any public parkland "unless (1) there is no feasible and prudent alternative to the use of such land, and (2) such program includes all possible planning to minimize harm to such park * * *." * * * This language is a plain and explicit bar to the use of federal funds for construction of highways through parks—only the most unusual situations are exempted.

Despite the clarity of the statutory language, respondents argue that the Secretary has wide discretion. They recognize that the requirement that there be no "feasible" alternative route admits of little administrative discretion. For this exemption to apply the Secretary must find that as a matter of sound engineering it would not be feasible to build the highway along any other route. Respondents argue, however, that the requirement that there be no other "prudent" route requires the Secretary to engage in a wide-ranging balancing of competing interests. They contend that the Secretary should weigh the detriment resulting from the destruction of parkland against the cost of other routes, safety considerations, and other factors, and determine on the basis of the importance that he attaches to these other factors whether, on balance, alternative feasible routes would be "prudent."

But no such wide-ranging endeavor was intended. It is obvious that in most cases considerations of cost, directness of route, and community disruption will indicate that parkland should be used for highway construction whenever possible. Although it may be necessary to transfer funds from one jurisdiction to another, there will always be a smaller outlay required from the public purse when parkland is used since the public already owns the land and there will be no need to pay for right-of-way. And since people do not live or work in parks, if a highway is built on parkland no one will have to leave his home or give up his business. Such factors are common to substantially all highway construction. Thus, if Congress intended these factors to be on an equal footing with preservation of parkland there would have been no need for the statutes.

Congress clearly did not intend that cost and disruption of the community were to be ignored by the Secretary. But the very existence of the statutes indicates that protection of parkland was to be given paramount importance. The few green havens that are public parks were not to be lost unless there were truly unusual factors present in a particular case or the cost or community disruption resulting from alternative routes reached extraordinary magnitudes. If the statutes are to have any meaning, the Secretary cannot approve the destruction of parkland unless he finds that alternative routes present unique problems.

* * *

Undoubtedly, review of the Secretary's action is hampered by his failure to make such findings, but the absence of formal findings does not necessarily require that the case be remanded to the Secretary. Neither the Department of Transportation Act nor the Federal-Aid Highway Act requires such formal findings. Moreover, the Administrative Procedure Act requirements that there be formal findings in certain rule-making and adjudicatory proceedings do not apply to the Secretary's action here. * * * And, although formal findings may be required in some cases in the absence of statutory directives when the nature of the agency action is ambiguous, those situations are rare. * * * Plainly, there is no ambiguity here; the Secretary has approved the construction of I–40 through Overton Park and has approved a specific design for the project.

* * *

* * * The lower courts based their review on the litigation affidavits that were presented. These affidavits were merely "*post hoc*" rationalizations, which have traditionally been found to be an inadequate basis for review. And they clearly do not constitute the "whole record" compiled by the agency: the basis for review required by § 706 of the Administrative Procedure Act. * * *

Thus it is necessary to remand this case to the District Court for plenary review of the Secretary's decision. That review is to be based on the full administrative record that was before the Secretary at the time he made his decision. But since the bare record may not disclose the factors that were considered or the Secretary's construction of the evidence it may be necessary for the District Court to require some explanation in order to determine if the Secretary acted within the scope of his authority and if the Secretary's action was justifiable under the applicable standard.

The court may require the administrative officials who participated in the decision to give testimony explaining their action. Of course, such inquiry into the mental processes of administrative decisionmakers is usually to be avoided. And where there are administrative findings that were made at the same time as the decision, * * * there must be a strong showing of bad faith or improper behavior before such inquiry may be made. But here there are no such formal findings and it may be that the only way there can be effective judicial review is by examining the decisionmakers themselves.

The District Court is not, however, required to make such an inquiry. It may be that the Secretary can prepare formal findings * * * that will provide an adequate explanation for his action. Such an explanation will, to some extent, be a "*post hoc* rationalization" and thus must be viewed critically. If the District Court decides that additional explanation is necessary, that court should consider which method will prove the most expeditious so that full review may be had as soon as possible.

Reversed and remanded.

PROBLEMS

1. Defendant, a large city plagued with difficult transportation problems, enacted an ordinance requiring employers to establish work schedules in accordance with a plan devised to maximize use of mass transportation, minimize commuter discomfort, and promote the use of car pools. Failure to comply with the ordinance constituted a misdemeanor. Plaintiff corporation, employing 400 persons in the city, incorporated and having its home office in a nearby state, challenged the law's constitutionality. What judgment?

2. Several Congressmen, favoring construction of the Three Sisters Bridge, blocked the appropriation of funds for a rapid transit system in the District of Columbia over the opposition of the Secretary of Transportation. They informed the Secretary that they

would not relent unless he approved construction of the Bridge. Shortly thereafter he announced his approval. Opponents of the Bridge challenged his action. The district court, granting an injunction pending the Secretary's reconsideration of the matter, found (1) "extraneous pressure intruded into the calculus of considerations on which the Secretary's decision was based;" (2) the Congressmen hold strong views "on the desirability of building the bridge, * * * [and assumedly were] acting with the interests of the public at heart," (3) assumedly they had not acted illegally, with impropriety, or without authority to exert pressure, and (4) the Secretary had not "acted in bad faith or in deliberate disregard of his statutory duties." What judgment on appeal?

3. The Uniform Relocation Assistance Act of 1970 requires federal officials to prepare relocation plans for persons displaced due to agency action. Action was brought to enjoin construction of an interstate highway on the ground that it would displace almost 5,000 Mexican-Americans without any plans having been made for their acquiring new residences. What judgment?

4. During legislative hearings bus operators insisted that Congress should authorize use of wider buses on the nation's highways so more comfortable buses could be built. In turn more persons would use mass transportation facilities. Opponents said the wider bus would present automobile drivers with a new highway hazard and would in time lead to wider trucks. How should this dispute be resolved?

5. Plaintiffs sued to enjoin the construction of a new exit from a 7 year old six lane expressway. The planned exit would be located one-half mile from their homes. They charged that the exit would precipitate an endless stream of noise-making pollution-causing automobiles which would endanger the lives of their children. The highway commission insisted that the exit was necessary to satisfy the "unquestionable" needs of many thousands of drivers. What judgment?

Chapter 19

RECREATION

Ours is a technological society. It allows individuals time to engage in recreational activities which can provide them with needed exercise and relief from stress. But some of the very same factors which make time available for recreational purposes decrease the availability of places where pleasurable and fruitful forms of recreation can take place. Today many officials recognize that if recreational areas are to be generally available to the citizenry, broad-based governmental involvement is necessary. Should government fail to affirmatively respond, the door may forever be closed to the types of recreational pursuits which require the use of land or the utilization of some of the unique offerings of nature.

To make it possible for persons to engage in the sort of recreational pursuits that can only be carried on outdoors, national, state, and local governments have enacted laws which foster and shield from disruption such forms of activity. In the Wilderness Act of 1964 Congress established a National Wilderness Preservation System with the stated purpose of preserving and protecting wilderness areas "in their natural condition * * * [so as to secure] for the American people of present and future generations the benefits of an enduring resource of wilderness."[1] Congress directed that such areas, to be owned by the federal government, and to be known as "wilderness areas," are to "be administered for the use and enjoyment of the American people in such manner as will leave them unimpaired for future use and enjoyment as wilderness, and so as to provide for the protection of these areas, the preservation of their wilderness character * * *."[2] For the purposes of the Act, Congress defined a wilderness as an area which "in contrast with those areas where man and his own works dominate the landscape, is * * * an area where the earth and its community of life are untrammeled by man, where man himself is a visitor who does not remain * * * an area of undeveloped Federal land retaining its primeval character and influence, without permanent improvements or human habitation, which is protected and managed so as to preserve its natural conditions * * *."[3] The Act directs the Secretary of Agriculture, "within ten years after September 3, 1964, [to] review, as to its suitability, each area in the national forests classified on September 3, 1964 by the Secretary * * * or the Chief of the Forest Service as 'primitive' and report his findings to the President."[4] The Secretary of the Interior is directed to act in a sim-

1. 16 U.S.C.A. § 1131(a).   3. 16 U.S.C.A. § 1131(c).

2. 16 U.S.C.A. § 1131(a).   4. 16 U.S.C.A. § 1132(b).

ilar fashion in regard to "every roadless area of five thousand contiguous acres or more in the national parks, monuments and other units of the national park system * * * [and] the national wildlife refuges and game ranges.[5] The Act details the obligations of the Secretaries of Agriculture and Interior, as well as of the President and the Congress, in carrying out the purposes of the Act.[6] "[C]ommercial enterprise" except "to the extent necessary for activities which are proper for realizing the recreational or other wilderness purposes of the areas" [7] and "permanent" roads are barred from wilderness areas "except as necessary to meet minimum requirements for the administration of the area * * * [and] required in emergencies involving the health and safety of persons within the area."[8] Likewise prohibited are temporary roads, motor vehicles, motorized equipment, motorboats, the "landing of aircraft, * * * other form[s] of mechanical transport," and structures and installations.[9] Aircraft or motorboats, if their use had been established prior to the passage of the Act, may be continued if consented to by the Secretary of Agriculture if he "deems" their continued use "desirable."[10] Measures necessary to "control fire, insects, and diseases" may be carried on if deemed "desirable" by the Secretary.[11] The Act exempts, "until midnight December 31, 1983, existing mining laws pertaining to mineral leasing which were in effect prior to September 3, 1964" but it makes subject to "reasonable regulations" of the Secretary of Agriculture such things as means of "ingress and egress," employment of mining equipment, and the use of land for "transmission lines, waterlines, telephone lines, or [mining] facilities."[12]

In 1968 Congress enacted the National Trails System Act [13] "to provide for the ever-increasing outdoor recreation needs of an expanding population and * * * to promote public access to, travel within, and enjoyment and appreciation of the open-air, outdoor areas of the Nation [by establishing] trails * * * (i) primarily, near the urban areas of the Nation, and (ii) secondarily, within established scenic areas more remotely located."[14] The Act calls for attaining the stated "objectives by instituting a national system of recreation and scenic trails."[15] It designated "the Appalachian Trail and the Pacific Crest Trail as the initial components of * * * [the national] system."[16] The Act sets forth "the methods by which, and standards according to which, additional components may be added to

---

5. 16 U.S.C.A. § 1132(c).

6. 16 U.S.C.A. § 1132(b), (c).

7. 16 U.S.C.A. § 1133(d) (6).

8. 16 U.S.C.A. § 1133(c).

9. 16 U.S.C.A. § 1133(c).

10. 16 U.S.C.A. § 1133(d) (1).

11. 16 U.S.C.A. § 1133(d) (1).

12. 16 U.S.C.A. § 1133(d) (3).

13. Pub.L. 90–543, 82 Stat. 99.

14. 16 U.S.C.A. § 1241(a).

15. 16 U.S.C.A. § 1241(b).

16. 16 U.S.C.A. § 1241(b).

the system."[17] The Secretaries of Agriculture and Interior are authorized to "establish and designate national recreation trails"[18] in lands under their administration under conditions set forth in the Act. "The Secretary of the Interior is directed to encourage States to consider, in their comprehensive statewide outdoor recreation plans and proposals for financial assistance for State and local projects submitted pursuant to the Land and Water Conservation Fund Act, needs and opportunities for establishing park, forest, and other recreation trails on lands owned or administered by States, and recreation trails on lands in or near urban areas * * * [and] to encourage States, political subdivisions, and private interests, including nonprofit organizations, to establish such trails."[19] The Secretary of Agriculture is directed to act in a similar fashion.[20] "The Secretary of Housing and Urban Development is directed, in administering the program of comprehensive urban planning and assistance under * * * [federal law], to encourage the planning of recreation trails in connection with the recreation and transportation planning for metropolitan and other urban areas."[21]

In the Wild and Scenic Rivers Act[22] passed in 1968 Congress "declared [it] to be the policy of the United States that certain selected rivers of the Nation which, with their immediate environments, possess outstandingly remarkable scenic, recreational, geologic, fish and wildlife, historic, cultural, or other similar values, * * * be preserved in free-flowing condition, and that they and their immediate environments * * * be protected for the benefit and enjoyment of present and future generations."[23] To implement the stated policy Congress instituted "a national wild and scenic rivers system, by designating the initial components of that system, and by prescribing the methods by which and standards according to which additional components may be added to the system from time to time."[24] Congress directed that "[t]he Secretary of the Interior or, where national forest lands are involved, the Secretary of Agriculture or, in appropriate cases, the two Secretaries jointly * * * study and from time to time submit to the President and the Congress proposals for the addition to the national wild and scenic rivers system of rivers."[25] The Act details the criteria and procedures the Secretaries must follow when preparing and submitting such proposals.[26] They are also authorized to acquire land by condemnation to further the stated purposes of the Act under the circumstances prescribed in the Act.[27]

17. 16 U.S.C.A. §§ 1241(b), 1244(b), (c).

18. 16 U.S.C.A. § 1243(a).

19. 16 U.S.C.A. § 1247(a).

20. 16 U.S.C.A. § 1247(c).

21. 16 U.S.C.A. § 1247(b).

22. Pub.L. 90–542, 82 Stat. 906 (1968).

23. 16 U.S.C.A. § 1271.

24. 16 U.S.C.A. § 1272.

25. 16 U.S.C.A. § 1275(a).

26. 16 U.S.C.A. § 1275(a).

27. 16 U.S.C.A. § 1277(a), (b), (c).

"Each component of the national wild and scenic rivers system * * * [is to] be administered in such manner as to protect and enhance the values which caused it to be included in * * * [the] system without, insofar as is consistent therewith, limiting other uses that do not substantially interfere with public use and enjoyment of these values * * * primary emphasis * * * [is to] be given to protecting its esthetic, scenic, historic, archeologic, and scientific features. Management plans for any such component may establish varying degrees of intensity for its protection and development, based on the special attributes of the area."[28] Federal agencies "charged with the administration of any component of the national wild and scenic rivers system * * * [are authorized to] enter into written cooperative agreements" with appropriate state and local officials so that they can participate "in the administration of the component * * * [state and local governments are to] be encouraged to cooperate in the planning and administration of components of the system which include or adjoin State- or county-owned lands."[29]

In the Housing Act of 1961[30] Congress asserted that it had found "that the rapid expansion of the Nation's urban areas and the rapid growth of the population within such areas * * * [had] resulted in severe problems of urban and suburban living for the preponderant majority of the Nation's present and future population, including the lack of valuable open-space for recreational and other purposes[31] * * *. [It found] that there is a need for the additional provision of parks and other open space in the built-up portions of urban areas especially in low income neighborhoods and communities and a need for greater and better coordinated State and local efforts to make available and improve open-space land throughout entire urban areas."[32] It stated that it chose to act to assist "State and local public bodies in taking prompt action to (1) provide, preserve, and develop open-space land in a manner consistent with the planned long-range development of the Nation's urban areas, (2) acquire, improve, and restore areas, * * * and (3) develop and improve open space and other public urban land, in accordance with programs to encourage and coordinate local public and private efforts toward this end."[33] The Act authorizes the Secretary of Housing and Urban Development "to make grants to State and local public bodies to help finance (1) the acquisition of title to, or other interest in, open-space land in urban areas and (2) the development of open-space or other land in urban areas for open-space uses."[34] The federal contribution may in no instance exceed more than fifty percent of the acquisition cost.[35]

28.   16 U.S.C.A. § 1281(a).

29.   16 U.S.C.A. § 1281(e).

30.   Pub.L. 87–70, 75 Stat. 183.

31.   42 U.S.C.A. § 1500(a).

32.   42 U.S.C.A. § 1500(b).

33.   42 U.S.C.A. § 1500(d).

34.   42 U.S.C.A. § 1500a(a).

35.   42 U.S.C.A. § 1500a(a).

The Act specifies the criteria and procedures the Secretary must follow when carrying out its stated objectives.[36]

States have passed legislation authorizing the acquisition of open-space lands. This authority may be vested in municipal governments. States have empowered local zoning boards to withhold building permits from a home developer unless the developer sets aside a portion of the land on which he plans to erect dwellings for recreational or park purposes.

ASSOCIATED HOME BUILDERS OF THE GREATER EAST BAY, INCORPORATED v. CITY OF WALNUT CREEK

Supreme Court of California, 1971.
94 Cal.Rptr. 630, 484 P.2d 606, 4 Cal.3d 633.

[Section 11546 of the California Business and Professions Code authorizes a city to require a subdivider, as a condition for the approval of a subdivision plan, to dedicate land for park or recreational purposes or pay fees in lieu thereof. The plaintiff, in a class action, asking for declaratory and injunctive relief, challenged the constitutionality of § 11546 and § 10–1.516 of the defendant's ordinance implementing § 11546. Section 10–1.516 provided that if a park or recreational facility indicated on the defendant's general plan falls within a proposed subdivision the builder must dedicate two and one-half acres of land for park or recreational purposes for each 1,000 new residents in the subdivision. If a park is not designated on the plan and the subdivision is within three-fourths of a mile radius of a park or a proposed park, or the dedication of land is not feasible, the subdivider must pay a fee equal to the value of the land which he would have been required to dedicate. The trial court dismissed the complaint. The plaintiff appealed.]

MOSK, JUSTICE. * * * Associated's primary contention is that section 11546 violates the equal protection and due process clauses of the federal and state Constitutions in that it deprives a subdivider of his property without just compensation. It is asserted that the state is avoiding the obligation of compensation by the device of requiring the subdivider to dedicate land or pay a fee for park or recreational purposes, that such contributions are used to pay for public facilities enjoyed by all citizens of the city and only incidentally by subdivision residents, and that all taxpayers should share in the cost of these public facilities. * * *

In order to avoid these constitutional pitfalls, claims Associated, a dedication requirement is justified only if it can be shown that the need for additional park and recreational facilities is attributable to the increase in population stimulated by the new subdivision alone

36. 42 U.S.C.A. § 1500a(b), (c), (d), (e).

and the validity of the section may not be upheld upon the theory that all subdivisions to be built in the future will create the need for such facilities.

In Ayres v. City Council of City of Los Angeles, we rejected similar arguments. * * *

We held that the city was not acting in eminent domain but, rather, that a subdivider who was seeking to acquire the advantages of subdivision had the duty to comply with reasonable conditions for dedication so as to conform to the welfare of the lot owners and the general public. We held, further, that the conditions were not improper because their fulfillment would incidentally benefit the city as a whole or because future as well as immediate needs were taken into consideration and that potential as well as present population factors affecting the neighborhood could be considered in formulating the conditions imposed upon the subdivider. * * *

Even if it were not for the authority of *Ayres* we would have no doubt that section 11546 can be justified on the basis of a general public need for recreational facilities caused by present and future subdivisions. The elimination of open space in California is a melancholy aspect of the unprecedented population increase which has characterized our state in the last few decades. Manifestly governmental entities have the responsibility to provide park and recreation land to accommodate this human expansion despite the inexorable decrease of open space available to fulfill such need. * * *

The legislative committee which recommended the enactment of section 11546 emphasized that land pressure due to increasing population has intensified the need for open space, that parks are essential for a full community life, and that local officials have been besieged by demands for more park space. * * *

These problems are not confined to contemporary California. It has been estimated that by the year 2000 the metropolitan population of the United States will increase by 110 to 145 million, that 57 to 75 million of the increase will occur in areas which are now unincorporated open land encircling metropolitan centers, and that the demand for outdoor recreation will increase tenfold over the 1956 requirement. Walnut Creek is a typical growth community. Located minutes' distance by motor vehicle from the metropolitan environs of Oakland and East Bay communities, the city population rose from 9,903 in 1960 to 36,606 in 1970, an increase of more than 365 percent in a decade.

We see no persuasive reason in the face of these urgent needs caused by present and anticipated future population growth on the one hand and the disappearance of open land on the other to hold that a statute requiring the dedication of land by a subdivider may be justified only upon the ground that the particular subdivider upon whom an exaction has been imposed will, solely by the development of his subdivision, increase the need for recreational facilities to such an extent that additional land for such facilities will be required.

        *   *   *

Another assertion by Associated is that the only exactions imposed upon subdividers which may be valid are those directly related to the health and safety of the subdivision residents and necessary to the use and habitation of the subdivision, such as sewers, streets and drainage facilities. While it is true that such improvements are categories directly required by the health and safety of subdivision residents, it cannot be said that recreational facilities are not also related to these salutary purposes. So far as we are aware, no case has held a dedication condition invalid on the ground that, unlike sewers or streets, recreational facilities are not sufficiently related to the health and welfare of subdivision residents to justify the requirement of dedication.   *   *   *

Associated next poses as an eventuality that, if the requirements of section 11546 are upheld as a valid exercise of the police power on the theory that new residents of the subdivision must pay the cost of park land needs engendered by their entry into the community, a city or county could also require contributions from a subdivider for such services as added costs of fire and police protection, the construction of a new city hall, or even a general contribution to defray the additional cost of all types of governmental services necessitated by the entry of the new residents.

This proposition overlooks the unique problem involved in utilization of raw land. Undeveloped land in a community is a limited resource which is difficult to conserve in a period of increased population pressure. The development of a new subdivision in and of itself has the counterproductive effect of consuming a substantial supply of this precious commodity, while at the same time increasing the need for park and recreational land. In terms of economics, subdivisions diminish supply and increase demand.   *   *   *

The rationale of   *   *   *   cases affirming constitutionality indicate the dedication statutes are valid under the state's police power. They reason that the subdivider realizes a profit from governmental approval of a subdivision since his land is rendered more valuable by the fact of subdivision, and in return for this benefit the city may require him to dedicate a portion of his land for park purposes whenever the influx of new residents will increase the need for park and recreational facilities.   *   *   *   Such exactions have been compared to admittedly valid zoning regulations such as minimum lot size and setback requirements.   *   *   *

Turning from the state statute to the Municipal Code, Associated argues that the fees the subdivider must pay in lieu of dedicating land are, under the city's ordinance, determined arbitrarily and without a reasonable relationship to principles of equality. It is claimed, for example, that a subdivider who develops high-density land may be required to pay a higher fee in lieu of dedication than one who develops low-density land even though both builders may be responsible for bringing the same number of new residents into the community. This may be true because the higher-density land is frequently more valuable and the fee is measured by the amount of land required by the number of persons in the subdivision.

While the owner of more valuable land which will support a greater number of living units may be required to pay a higher fee for each new resident than the owner of less valuable land with a lower density, it does not follow that there is no reasonable relationship between the use of the facilities by future residents and the fee charged the subdivider. It is a proper assumption that persons occupying housing in a high-density area will use the public recreational facilities more consistently than those residents in single family homes who have private yards and more open space readily at their individual disposal.

*   *   *

It may come to pass, as Associated states, that subdividers will transfer the cost of the land dedicated or the in-lieu fee to the consumers who ultimately purchase homes in the subdivision, thereby to some extent increasing the price of houses to newcomers. While we recognize the ominous possibility that the contributions required by a city can be deliberately set unreasonably high in order to prevent the influx of economically depressed persons into the community, a circumstance which would present serious social and legal problems, there is nothing to indicate that the enactments of Walnut Creek in the present case raise such a spectre. The desirability of encouraging subdividers to build low-cost housing cannot be denied and unreasonable exactions could defeat this object, but these considerations must be balanced against the phenomenon of the appallingly rapid disappearance of open areas in and around our cities. We believe section 11546 constitutes a valiant attempt to solve this urgent problem, and we cannot say that its provisions or the city's enactments pursuant to the section are constitutionally deficient.

The judgment is affirmed.

*   *   *

ALLEN v. HICKEL

United States Court of Appeals, District of Columbia, 1970.
424 F.2d 944, 138 U.S.App.D.C. 31.

[On December 15, 1969 the President threw a switch thereby lighting the National Christmas Tree located across the street from the White House in a park operated by the National Park Service. Adjacent to the Tree were 57 other trees, a reindeer, a burning Yule log, and an illuminated life-size crèche or Nativity scene, all part of an annual Christmas Pageant of Peace. Plaintiffs, an Episcopal minister, a Catholic priest, a rabbi, the president of the American Ethical Union, and an officer of the National Humanist Association, brought a suit against the Secretary of the Interior, in whose Department the National Park Service is housed, and the Christmas Pageant of Peace, Inc., a non-profit corporation which co-sponsored the Pageant. They asked the District Court to enjoin the construction and maintenance of the crèche, claiming that its presence violated the First Amendment. On September 30, 1969 the Court dismissed the suit on the ground that the plaintiffs lacked standing, and alternatively, granted the defendants' motion for summary judgment, denying a preliminary injunction. On December 12, 1969 plaintiffs' motion for an injunction *pendente lite* was denied. They appealed.]

LEVENTHAL, CIRCUIT JUDGE: * * * In the present case we conclude that the issues under the Free Exercise and Establishment Clauses are presented by plaintiffs who have standing, who present an injury, in the impairment of non-economic values, giving them a "personal stake in the outcome of the controversy," as contrasted with mere airing of "generalized grievances about the conduct of the government." An aspect of the case that underscores the standing of the plaintiffs is their allegation that the defendants are proposing to devote Government park property to uses inconsisent with the Free Exercise and Establishment Clauses. Park lands are dedicated to public use and enjoyment.

Plaintiffs are all residents of the metropolitan area of the District of Columbia served by park lands in the District. And in a broader sense the * * * park serves all citizens of the nation who come to the Nation's Capital not merely to present grievances but also, and indeed more typically, to visit its sites and monuments as one means of maintaining and strengthening their ties with the nation's values and heritage. Citizens may sue to enjoin a government holding land in trust as a park from impermissibly diverting the use so as to destroy their beneficial interests as park uses. They likewise have standing to complain when the park lands are impermissibly devoted to uses that contravene the Establishment Clause.

Since a claim under the Establishment Clause does not require a showing that plaintiffs' religious freedom is infringed, a claim that park land which plaintiff has a beneficial right be maintained for public purposes is being devoted to the use of an established religion is sufficient personal involvement to provide standing.

The standing issue was perhaps clarified, in terms of perspective, when Government counsel put it at argument that if the plaintiffs didn't like to look at the crèche, they could avoid walking near the * * * [park] while it was occupied by the crèche. Plaintiffs were entitled, as members of the public, to enjoy the park land and its devotion to permissible public use; a government action cannot infringe that right or require them to give it up without access to the court to complain that the action is unconstitutional.

The Government contends that the use of the crèche objected to by the plaintiffs is wholly secular, and therefore avoids any entanglement with the First Amendment. That surely overstates the matter. The crèche is not wholly secular. On the contrary, as set forth in the official pamphlet of the Christmas Pageant of Peace: "The *spiritual* meaning of Christmas is offered in the form of a life-sized Nativity Scene * * *" (emphasis added). But the first Amendment does not require the Government to ignore the existence of certain beliefs and customs on the part of large numbers of its citizens. In Zorach v. Clauson, the Court, per Justice Douglas, noted: "We are a religious people * * *" As Justice Brennan stated in his concurring opinion in School District of Abington Township, Pa. v. Schempp, "Nothing in the Constitution compels the organs of government to be blind to what everyone else perceives—that religious differences among Americans have important and pervasive implications for our society."

The applicable rule may fairly be stated thus: The Government may depict objects with spiritual content, but it may not promote or give its stamp of approval to such spiritual content. * * *

The crèche * * * was related to the celebration of a holiday season that has a clearly secular half; the visual demonstration as a whole included definitely secular symbols of the secular holiday—reindeer, the Yule log, the Christmas trees; * * * As such its purpose is no more objectionable than that of a postage stamp bearing a reproduction of a religious painting or a Government-sponsored museum display illustrating various religious or holiday customs.

It is not only the purpose but also the effect of the crèche that must be considered. "The test may be stated as follows: What are the purpose and the primary effect of the enactments? If either is the advancement or inhibition of religion then the enactment exceeds the scope of legislative power as circumscribed by the Constitution."

However, our inquiry into the effect of the crèche is hampered by the fact that there has been no trial to provide an opportunity for airing this question. * * *

Plaintiffs submit that the placement and size of the crèche (described as "life-sized") give it a significant religious impact even assuming the kind of secular purpose claimed by the defendants. This is underscored, they say, by the national television coverage of the scene portrayed throughout the land at the time of the tree-lighting ceremonies. The danger to be apprehended is that it will appear to the public, those on the scene and those seeing it second-hand, that the government has given a stamp of approval to the religious content of the Nativity scene, * * *.

The duty of the courts is to strike the proper balance. The area is a sensitive one, involving questions of degree. The question is not whether there is any religious effect at all, but rather whether that effect, if present, is substantial. Obviously, brief references to the Deity in courtroom ceremony, in oaths of office taken by public officials, and on coins of the realm are modest in impact—it may be more accurate to say that they usually go unnoticed altogether.

Whatever our own personal impressions as residents of the area we cannot say as a court, on the record before us and in the absence of evidence, that it is conclusive beyond dispute that the visual impact of the crèche does not entail substantial religious impact. * * *

We imply no present judgment * * * but we think that the issues are substantial enough to require attentive examination by the Park Service and by the District Court in the context of a presentation of pertinent evidence.

The problem which we consider here is a recurrent one. The program has been in effect for many years, and there is every indication that it will continue unless court action forbids. The case is thus not moot. * * *

We vacate the judgment entered for defendants and remand to the District Court for an evidentiary hearing and a determination of the effect of the crèche * * * .

So ordered.

PROBLEMS

1. Objection was made to a builder's proposed open space subdivision plan on the ground that the acreage set aside for recreational or park purposes was "the least attractive and least valuable" part of the subdivision. Does the objection merit consideration by the board of zoning?

2. Do individuals who make use of a public recreational area have standing to challenge a determination of the Secretary of Transportation which would deny them future use of the area if in his decision the Secretary provided for the establishment of "a roughly comparable recreational site" 10 miles distant?

3. Defendants were landowners whose property completely enclosed a 100 acre lake which was not suitable for boat or vessel navigation but was nonetheless a "fine spot for swimming." They refused to permit members of the general public to cross their land to swim in the lake. Plaintiffs established that the lake was the only "decent water recreational site for at least 100 miles." They insisted that it was "a public recreational area." They asked the court for an order directing the defendants not to interfere with their making use of the lake for swimming purposes during reasonable hours of the

day during the months of June, July, August, and September. What judgment?

4. When a municipality dedicates land for recreational purposes, is it required to supply free transportation for indigent persons who wish to make use of the facility?

5. At what point would a state sponsored recreational facility which would cause destruction of trees and diversion of streams constitute an improper invasion of a citizen's right to enjoy nature's offerings undisturbed by man?

6. Plaintiff challenged the constitutionality of an ordinance which taxed privately owned property used for recreational purposes at a rate 80% lower than that imposed on private property used for other purposes. What judgment?

7. An ordinance barred the use of municipal beaches, parks, lakes, and golf courses by non-residents. Is the law constitutional?

Chapter 20

WILDLIFE

Legislation designed to manage the population of some types of wildlife or to shield particular species of wildlife from extinction is predicated on such dissonant considerations as the desirability of keeping a broad variety of animal life alive, and, if necessary, even nurtured; mankind's respect for and interest in the survival of certain, if not of all forms of wildlife; and insuring that a continuous supply of wildlife is available for those persons who wish to take part in the stalking, capturing, or destruction of some sorts of wildlife in their pursuit of economic gain or recreation. While many persons might treat each of the cited considerations as a valid reason for the enactment of wildlife statutes, ardent conservationists would view economic and recreational purposes as unworthy if not inhumane. Because of the disparity of objectives which engender the passage of wildlife protection laws, officials charged with administering such legislation oftentimes find themselves under attack from members of opposing camps who favor such legislation but differ as to what should be achieved. Legislation invariably favors one objective of wildlife preservation over others. A person who is devoted to the preservation of all forms of wildlife could not help but object to a legislative mandate directed at managing rather than totally protecting wildlife population. He would be opposed to a legislative policy which directed responsible agency officials to establish an optimum level of killing for particular animals. On the other hand, a sportsman would find unpalatable a policy which calls for the nurturing and preservation of all members of a particular species of wildlife and outlaws the killing of any member of the species.

In the Fish and Wildlife Coordination Act [1] Congress states that "[f]or the purpose of recognizing the vital contribution of our wildlife resources to the Nation, the increasing public interest and significance thereof due to expansion of our national economy and other factors, and to provide that wildlife conservation shall receive equal consideration and be coordinated with other features of water-resource development programs through the effectual and harmonious planning, development, maintenance and coordination of wildlife conservation and rehabilitation for the purposes of * * * [the Act], the Secretary of the Interior is authorized (1) to provide assistance to, and cooperate with, Federal, State, and public or private agencies and organizations in the development, protection, rearing, and stocking of all species of wildlife, resources thereof, and their habitat, in controlling losses of the same from disease or other causes,

---

1. Pub.L. 85–624, 72 Stat. 563 (1958).

in minimizing damages from overabundant species, in providing public shooting and fishing areas, including easements across public
lands for the access thereto, and in carrying out other measures necessary to effectuate the purposes of * * * [the Act]; (2) to
make surveys and investigations of the wildlife of the public domain,
including lands and waters or interests therein acquired or controlled
by any agency of the United States; and (3) to accept donations of
land and contributions of funds in furtherance of the purposes of
* * * [the Act]."[2]

To promote the Act's stated objectives, Congress directed that
except for "those projects for the impoundment of water where the
maximum surface area of such impoundments is less than ten acres,
* * * or [for] activities * * * in connection with programs
primarily for land management and use carried out by Federal agencies with respect to Federal lands under their jurisdiction"[3] in cases
in which "the waters of any stream or other body of water are proposed or authorized to be impounded, diverted, the channel deepened,
or the stream of other body of water otherwise controlled or modified
for any purpose whatever, including navigation and drainage, by any
department or agency of the United States, or by any public or private agency under Federal permit or license, such department or
agency [must] first * * * consult with the United States Fish
and Wildlife Service, Department of the Interior, and with the head
of the agency exercising administration over the wildlife resources of
the particular State wherein the impoundment, diversion, or other
control facility is to be constructed, with a view to the conservation
of wildlife resources by preventing loss of and damage to such resources as well as providing for the development and improvement
thereof in connection with such water-resource * * *."[4] Should
it be decided that the proposed action be carried out, then the involved "department or agency of the United States" must make "adequate provision, consistent with the primary purposes of such impoundment, diversion, or other control, for the use thereof, together
with any areas of land, water, or interests therein, acquired or administered by a Federal agency in connection therewith, for the conservation, maintenance, and management of [the] wildlife resources
thereof, and its habitat thereon, including the development and improvement of such wildlife resources pursuant to the * * *
[Act]."[5] The Secretary of Interior is obliged to study the impact of
projects on wildlife and submit reports and recommendations pertaining to a project's effect on wildlife.[6] When recommending to Congress that it authorize new projects involving the control of water the
Secretary must at the same time submit "an estimation of the wild-

2. 16 U.S.C.A. § 661.   5. 16 U.S.C.A. § 663(a).

3. 16 U.S.C.A. § 662(h).   6. 16 U.S.C.A. § 662(b).

4. 16 U.S.C.A. § 662(a).

life benefits or losses to be derived therefrom including benefits to be derived from measures recommended specifically for the development and improvement of wildlife resources, the cost of providing wildlife benefits (including the cost of additional facilities to be installed or lands to be acquired specifically for that particular phase of wildlife conservation relating to the development and improvement of wildlife), the part of the cost of joint-use facilities allocated to wildlife, and the part of such costs, if any, to be reimbursed by non-Federal interests."[7]

The Act authorizes "[t]he Secretary of the Interior, through the Fish and Wildlife Service and the Bureau of Mines, * * * to make such investigations as he deems necessary to determine the effects of domestic sewage, mine, petroleum, and industrial wastes, erosion silt, and other polluting substances on wildlife, and to make reports to the Congress concerning such investigations and of recommendations for alleviating dangerous and undesirable effects of such pollution. These investigations * * * [are to] include (1) the determination of standards of water quality for the maintenance of wildlife; (2) the study of methods of abating and preventing pollution, including methods for the recovery of useful or marketable products and byproducts of wastes; and (3) the collation and distribution of data on the progress and results of such investigations for the use of Federal, State, municipal, and private agencies, individuals, organizations, or enterprises."[8]

For the purpose of carrying out the Act the Secretary of the Interior "in accordance with general plans approved jointly by the Secretary * * * and the head of the department or agency exercising primary administration of * * * [affected] areas" may promulgate "rules and regulations for the conservation, maintenance, and management of wildlife, resources * * * [found in such areas] and * * * habitat[s located in such areas.]"[9] One found guilty of violating any such rule or regulation may be "fined not more than $500 or [be imprisoned] * * * for not more than one year, or both."[10]

Under the Act specified states are authorized "to enter into compacts or agreements, not in conflict with any law of the United States, for cooperative effort and mutual assistance for the uniform, common, or mutual regulation of fishing or of any species of fish, mollusks, or crustacea in the territorial waters and bays and inlets of the Atlantic Ocean on which such States border or to which their jurisdiction otherwise extends and of anadromous fish spawning in the inland waters of those States."[11] Other states "which have juris-

7.   16 U.S.C.A. § 662(f).

8.   16 U.S.C.A. § 665.

9.   16 U.S.C.A. § 664.

10. 16 U.S.C.A. § 666a.

11. 16 U.S.C.A. § 667a.

diction over inland waters frequented by anadromous fish of the sea" may do likewise.[12]

"For the purposes of conserving and protecting the fish and shellfish resources in the coastal waters of the United States and * * * Puerto Rico, and promoting and safeguarding water-based recreation for present and future generations in these waters, the Secretary of the Interior is authorized to cooperate with, and provide assistance to, the States in controlling and eliminating jellyfish, commonly referred to as 'sea nettles,' and other such pests and in conducting research for the purposes of controlling floating seaweed in such waters."[13]

In the Endangered Species Conservation Act of 1969[14] Congress declared "that one of the unfortunate consequences of growth and development in the United States has been the extermination of some native species of fish and wildlife; that serious losses in other species of native wild animals with educational, historical, recreational, and scientific value have occurred and are occurring; and that the United States has pledged itself, pursuant to migratory bird treaties * * *, to conserve and protect, where practicable, the various species of native fish and wildlife, including game and nongame migratory birds, that are threatened with extinction." The Act establishes a "program for the conservation, protection, restoration, and propagation of selected species of native fish and wildlife, including migratory birds, that are threatened with extinction."[15] It states that it is "the policy of Congress that the" Secretaries of Interior, Agriculture and Defense "together with the heads of bureaus, agencies, and services within their departments, * * * seek to protect species of native fish and wildlife, including migratory birds, that are threatened with extinction, and, insofar as is practicable and consistent with the primary purposes of such bureaus, agencies, and services, * * * [must] preserve the habitats of such threatened species on lands under their jurisdiction."[16]

"A species of native fish and wildlife * * * [is to be] regarded as threatened with extinction whenever the Secretary of the Interior finds, after consultation with the affected States, that its existence is endangered because its habitat is threatened with destruction, drastic modification, or severe curtailment, or because of overexploitation, disease, predation, or because of other factors, and that its survival requires assistance. In addition to consulting with the States, the secretary * * * [is required], from time to time, [to] seek the advice and recommendations of interested persons and organizations including, but not limited to, ornithologists, ichthyolo-

12. 16 U.S.C.A. § 667a.

13. 16 U.S.C.A. § 1201.

14. Pub.L. 91–135, 83 Stat. 283.

15. 16 U.S.C.A. § 668aa(a).

16. 16 U.S.C.A. § 668aa(b).

gists, ecologists, herpetologists, and mamalogists. He * * * [is directed to] publish in the Federal Register the names of the species of native fish and wildlife found to be threatened with extinction * * *."[17] The Act defines "fish and wildlife" as "any wild mammal, fish, wild bird, amphibian, reptile, mollusk, or crustacean."[18]

The Act authorizes the Secretary of the Interior to adjudge that a species or subspecies of fish or wildlife is "threatened with worldwide extinction."[19] His determination must be "based on the best scientific and commercial data available to him" and may be made only "after consultation, in cooperation with the Secretary of State, with the foreign country or countries, in which such fish or wildlife are normally found and, to the extent practicable, with interested persons and organizations and other interested Federal agencies, that the continued existence of such species or subspecies of fish or wildlife is, in the judgment of the Secretary, endangered due to any of the following factors: (1) the destruction, drastic modification, or severe curtailment, or the threatened destruction, drastic modification, or severe curtailment, of its habitat, or (2) its overutilization for commercial or sporting purposes, or (3) the effect on it of disease or predation, or (4) other natural or man-made factors affecting its continued existence."[20] The Secretary is obliged to keep "a list in the Federal Register of such fish or wildlife" and to "at least once every five years * * * review [it]."[21] One who "imports from any foreign country into the United States any species or subspecies of fish or wildlife" contained in the list, unless expressly permitted by a permit issued by the Secretary, may "be assessed a civil penalty by the Secretary of not more than $5,000 for each * * * violation."[22] So as "to minimize undue economic hardship to" persons engaged in the business of importing listed fish or wildlife "under any contract entered into prior to the date of publication of" the Secretary's "determination in the Federal Register" the Secretary, if requested, should, if convinced that not to do so would cause a "hardship * * * permit such person to import such" fish or wildlife "in such quantities and for such periods, not to exceed one year, as he determines to be appropriate."[23] With the consent of the Secretary listed fish and wildlife may be imported for "zoological, educational, and scientific purposes, and for the propagation of such fish or wildlife in captivity for preservation purposes, unless such importation is prohibited by any other Federal law or regulation."[24]

The Secretary of the Interior, "through the Secretary of State," is directed to "encourage foreign countries to provide protection to

17.　16 U.S.C.A. § 668aa(c).

18.　16 U.S.C.A. § 668aa(d).

19.　16 U.S.C.A. § 668cc–3.

20.　16 U.S.C.A. § 668cc–3.

21.　16 U.S.C.A. § 668cc–3.

22.　16 U.S.C.A. § 668cc–4.

23.　16 U.S.C.A. § 668cc–3(b).

24.　16 U.S.C.A. § 668cc–3(c).

species and subspecies of fish or wildlife threatened with worldwide extinction * * * and [to cooperate] with such countries in providing technical assistance in developing and carrying out programs to provide such protection."[25]

"The Secretary of the Interior is authorized to cooperate with * * * States, * * * in wildlife-restoration projects."[26] Federal funds, not to exceed 75% of the cost of a state's wildlife-restoration project may be authorized by the Secretary of the Interior,[27] if the project complies with federal law and the Secretary's rules and regulations and if the State has "passed laws for the conservation of wildlife which * * * include a prohibition against the diversion of license fees paid by hunters for any other purpose than the administration of * * * [the State's] fish and game department * * *. The Secretary of the Interior and the State fish and game department of each State accepting * * * [federal funds must] agree upon the wildlife-restoration projects to be aided in such State under the terms of * * * [federal law] and all projects * * * [must] conform to the standards fixed by the Secretary of the Interior."[28]

The Fur Seal Act of 1966 [29] makes it "unlawful" unless authorized by federal law "or by regulation of the Secretary of the Interior, for any person or vessel subject to the jurisdiction of the United States to engage in the taking of fur seals in the North Pacific Ocean or on lands or waters under the jurisdiction of the United States, * * * or for any person to transport, import, offer for sale, or possess at any port or place or on any vessel, subject to the jurisdiction of the United States, fur seals or the parts thereof, * * * taken contrary to * * * [law], or for any person subject to the jurisdiction of the United States to refuse to permit, except within the territorial waters of the United States, a duly authorized official of Canada, Japan, or the Union of Soviet Socialist Republics to board and search any vessel which is outfitted for the harvesting of living marine resources and which is subject to the jurisdiction of the United States to determine whether such vessel is engaged in sealing contrary to the provision of * * * [the] Convention [to which the stated nations are parties]."[30]

The Act specifies the circumstances under which "Indians, Aleuts, and Eskimos who dwell on the coasts of the North Pacific Ocean are permitted to take fur seals and dispose of their skins."[31] The Secretary of the Interior is directed to conduct "scientific re-

25. 16 U.S.C.A. § 668cc–5(a).

26. 16 U.S.C.A. § 669.

27. 16 U.S.C.A. § 669e.

28. 16 U.S.C.A. § 669.

29. Pub.L. 89–702, 80 Stat. 1091.

30. 16 U.S.C.A. § 1151.

31. 16 U.S.C.A. § 1152.

search and investigations on the fur seal resources" and to "permit, subject to such terms and conditions as he deems desirable, the taking, transportation, importation, exportation, or possession of fur seals or their parts for educational, scientific, or exhibition purposes." [32]

Federal law prohibits persons from taking, possessing, selling, purchasing, bartering, offering "to sell, purchase, or barter, transport, export, or import, at any time or in any manner, any bald eagle commonly known as the American eagle, or any golden eagle, alive or dead, or any part, nest or egg thereof, of * * * [such] eagles" unless permission is granted by the Secretary of the Interior.[33] The Secretary may grant such permission if "after investigation * * * [he] determines that" such behavior "is compatible with the preservation of the bald eagle or the golden eagle" and is "for the scientific or exhibition purposes of public museums, scientific societies, and zoological parks, or for the religious purposes of Indian tribes, or that it is necessary * * * for the protection of wildlife or of agricultural or other interests in any particular locality * * * [and so far as the golden eagle is concerned] on the request of the Governor of any State, the Secretary * * * [may] authorize the taking of golden eagles for the purpose of seasonally protecting domesticated flocks and herds in such State * * * [for such periods and under such terms] as the Secretary determines to be necessary to protect such interests * * *."[34]

State legislatures have passed statutes comparable to the laws enacted by Congress to protect the sorts of wildlife which they have decided warrant the protection of the law.

A. E. NETTLETON COMPANY v. DIAMOND

Court of Appeals of New York, 1970.
315 N.Y.S.2d 625, 264 N.E.2d 118, 27 N.Y.2d 182.

[The plaintiff, for more than 90 years engaged in the manufacture, sale, and distribution of men's footwear made from alligator, crocodile, and caiman skins, brought an action against Diamond, the Commissioner of the State's Environmental Conservation Department, and several other State officials, asking for a judgment declaring the Mason Law, § 358–a of the New York Agriculture and Markets Law, unconstitutional. Parties representing the spotted fur industry, retailers selling products covered by § 358–a, and persons engaged in selling reptile products intervened on the side of the plaintiff. The trial court ruled in favor of the plaintiff and the interve-

32. 16 U.S.C.A. § 1153. 34. 16 U.S.C.A. § 668a.

33. 16 U.S.C.A. § 668.

nors collectively referred to below as "the Industry." The defendants appealed.]

SCILEPPI, JUDGE.

* * *

This appeal presents a problem of critical importance. Throughout history, man has relied upon the lower forms of life for food, clothing and shelter. Indeed, long before the advent of what historians have come to term the Commercial Revolution, the skins and pelts of animals had played an essential role in the development of man and his trade. In recent years, however, the scientific community has warned that since the year 1600, 130 animal species and 228 subspecies have become extinct and numerous other species will soon be lost to the world forever unless something is done to curtail man's commercial exploitation of the wildlife of the world. While it is not our function here to engage in any form of biblical exegesis, it is obvious that man has only too readily acceded to the blessing enunciated in Genesis encouraging him to " 'be masters of the fish of the sea, the birds of heaven, the cattle, all the wild beasts and all the reptiles that crawl upon the earth' " (Genesis, ch. 1, verse 26, Jerusalem Bible, p. 16).

It was in response to the great need to preserve wildlife that the Legislature, sharing the concern expressed by the people of our State, Nation and planet, * * * enacted * * *

* * * section 358–a to the Agriculture and Markets Law (hereinafter referred to as the Mason Law) which provides that after September 1, 1970: "1. *No part of the skin or body, whether raw or manufactured, of the following species of wild animals or the animal itself may be sold or offered for sale by any individual, firm, corporation, association or partnership within the state of New York* after the effective date of this section: * * * Alligators, Caiman or Crocodile of the Order Crocodylia, * * *.

* * *

The Industry has made a two-fold attack on the power of the State to promulgate legislation in the area of wildlife preservation arguing that the Mason Law violates both the Supremacy Clause (art. VI, § 2) and the Commerce Clause (art. I, § 8, cl. 3) of the Federal Constitution. * * *

Taking the Supremacy issue first, it is argued by the Industry that the recent Federal Endangered Species Conservation Act of 1969 (Public Law 91–135, 83 U.S. Stat. 275) is an elaborate, comprehensive and pervasive scheme of Federal regulations which necessitates the conclusion that State power has been curtailed and that the field of wildlife preservation has been pre-empted by Congress * * * This argument was rejected by the court below and we are in agreement with that court's resolution of this issue.

It is true that the Federal Act is a piece of comprehensive legislation which provides for the systematic prohibition of the importation into our country of certain species designated as endangered by the Secretary of the Interior (§ 3 of the Act), and requires the Secretary of State to promote the protection of threatened species in their countries of origin and regulates the importation of other species of animals by restricting points of entry and requiring documentation of origin (§ 4).

* * * Turning to the first test (State power to legislate), there is no real conflict between the Federal statute and the Mason Law. While it is true that our State statute includes species which are not on the Federal list * * * there has been no showing that compliance with both the Federal and State law is an impossibility. Nor has it been demonstrated that the Mason Law could not be enforced without impairing the effectiveness of the Federal Act. The Industry has not shown that wildlife conservation is a matter exclusively within the sphere of Federal competence. On the contrary, it is almost axiomatic that wildlife conservation has been a matter traditionally left to the States. Thus, it would seem that the pre-emption question narrows down to whether Congress by the 1969 Act has evidenced its design to exclude State action. We think it has not. Federal displacement of the "historic police powers of the States" should not be decreed "unless that was the clear and manifest purpose of Congress" * * *. We find no such mandate. On the contrary, the Federal statute specifically provides for the enforcement of State laws such as the Mason Law. Section 7 of the Federal Act makes any person who: "(a) * * * (2) delivers, carries, transports, or ships, by any means whatever, or causes to be delivered, carried, transported, or shipped for commercial or noncommercial purposes or sells or causes to be sold in interstate or foreign commerce *any wildlife taken, transported, or sold in any manner in violation of any law or regulation of any State or foreign country*; or (b) * * * (2) sells or causes to be sold in interstate or foreign commerce any products manufactured, made, or processed from *any wildlife taken, transported, or sold in any manner in violation of any law or regulation of a State or a foreign country*" (emphasis added) subject to the enforcement provisions of the Act. Moreover, the regulations promulgated by the Secretary of Interior which preceded the Federal list of Endangered Species also indicate that: "§ 17.16 Other laws applicable. Nothing in this part, nor any permit, exception, or permission issued hereunder, shall be construed to relieve any person from any provision of any other laws, rules, or regulations of the States or the United States." (35 Federal Register 8495.)

* * *

* * * the Mason Act merely prohibits the sale, or offer for sale, within New York State, of skins or products made from the for-

bidden species and it is our view that the Industry's Commerce Clause argument is untenable.

     *   *   *

     *   *   * "[t]he police power of the State is the least limitable of all the powers of government" and we have sustained its application to the conservation of fish and wildlife and other areas of beauty and esthetics   *   *   * "The police power is not to be limited to guarding merely the physical or material interests of the citizen. His moral, intellectual and spiritual needs may also be considered. The eagle is preserved, not for its use but for its beauty."

Since wildlife conservation is within the police power, our inquiry is limited to the question whether the means employed are reasonable. A strong presumption of validity attaches to legislative enactments and a party who is attacking the constitutionality of a statute bears the heavy burden of establishing unconstitutionality beyond a reasonable doubt.

We find that in the instant case, the Industry has not met its burden.   *   *   * "The police power is 'very broad and comprehensive' and in its exercise 'the conduct of an individual and the use of property may be regulated so as to interfere, to some extent, with the freedom of the one and the enjoyment of the other.' But, in order for an exercise of the police power to be valid, there must be 'some fair, just and reasonable connection' between it and the promotion of the health, comfort, safety and welfare of society." Viewed in this light, the Mason Law would be an unreasonable exercise of the police power only if we are able to say that it is *unreasonable* for the State of New York to declare that the interdiction of all sales, or offers for sale, of skins of certain animals or products made therefrom is necessary for the continued existence of those animals. Such a conclusion is not warranted in the instant case. The wildlife of the world is a vital assert to the people of this State.   *   *   * The protection of the animals listed in the Mason Act is necessary not only for their natural beauty and for the purpose of biological study, but for the key role that they play in the maintenance of the life cycle. Thus, the protection of these animals is essential for the welfare of our society, and we do not agree with the Industry that the Mason Law goes too far.

     *   *   * The wisdom of a particular statute is beyond the scope of judicial review   *   *   * and we should not substitute our judgment for that employed by the Legislature in enacting the statute in question.   *   *   *

While it is true that the banning of "alligators, Caiman or Crocodile of the Order Crocodylia" may include some reptiles which are in adequate supply, it is clear that the Legislature did so because it is practically impossible to determine, without expert detection at great expense, whether a given skin is from a threatened species or one that is not threatened. Thus, by preventing the sale, or offer for sale, within the State of skins or products made from the skins of animals listed in the Mason Law, one market for these goods is removed and the killing of these animals is rendered less lucrative. * * * If the Industry wishes to take issue with this view, it is our opinion that the proper procedure is for them to seek amendment of the statute. Furthermore, the Mason Law should provide an impetus to the Industry to develop methods of sustained yield breeding which would guarantee the existence of their business in the years to come.

* * * the evil in the instant case which the Legislature sought to prevent is as broad as the statute itself. All the listed animals need protection either because they are endangered or, in the case of the crocodiles, because processed skins of endangered animals for all practical purposes are indistinguishable from those in abundant supply. * * *

As to the Industry's contention that the Mason Law is confiscatory in that it bars all sales, or offers for sale, after September 1, 1970 thus rendering valueless the inventory on hand and imported into the State while it was legal to do so, we do not think that such a result was the intent of the Legislature. Such a prohibition could in no way effectuate the purpose of the Mason Law since it could not afford protection to the animals already destroyed. It is, therefore, our view that the Mason Law does not apply to skins, hides, or products therefrom which arrived in the United States of America on or before August 31, 1970, providing that the time of arrival shall be documented either by official U.S. Customs records or authentic inventory or shipment records of the holder or any predecessor in title which is a United States corporation, firm, or person regularly engaged in the business of handling the products on August 31, 1970.

Accordingly, the judgment appealed from should be reversed, without costs, and the matter remitted * * * for the entry of a judgment declaring section 358–a * * * constitutional.

* * *

ALFORD v. FINCH

Supreme Court of Florida, 1963.
155 So.2d 790.

[Without the consent of or compensation to the appellees, owners of a 700 acre tract of land, the appellants, members of the State Game and Fresh Water Fish Commission, issued an order closing the tract to all hunting for an indefinite period. Appellants did not issue a similar order for other tracts of private property located in the same vicinity. In an action appellees brought for a declaratory decree the trial court found the order unconstitutional. Appellants appealed.]

CALDWELL, JUSTICE. * * * Recognizing the power of the Commission to * * * regulate the taking of game, the trial judge found that regulations which impose burdens on some but not upon other citizens like situated, with no just basis for the classification, constitute a denial of equal protection of the law; that the orders complained of here denied the * * * (appellees) privileges which neighbors in the area enjoy, and held:

"[T]he effect is the destruction of plaintiffs' rights to hunt on their land in order that others having rights or privileges in nearby lands of substantially the same habitat qualities may better enjoy their hunting privileges. This is not a reasonable basis for discrimination and serves to deny plaintiffs equal protection of the law."

The court further held that the indefinite prohibition of hunting on the lands of the * * * (appellees), under the facts of the case, constituted "a taking of private property for public use and since no compensation has been paid is itself a violation of Sec. 12, Declaration of Rights, and Sec. 29, Art. XVI, Fla.Const., which prohibits deprivation of property without due process of law and taking of private property without just compensation."

This cause necessitates the determination of whether, under * * * the Florida Constitution, the Commission has the power to close to hunting for a period of years, without consent or compensation, the private property of one owner, leaving unaffected in the same vicinity the private property of others. The Court can take judicial notice of the fact that vast acreages are maintained in Florida by owners for the principal, if not the sole, purpose of preserving, protecting and shooting game thereon.

The exclusive common law right of a landowner to take game on his land, known as property ratione soli, was defined * * * in an early English case as "the common law right which every owner of land has to kill and take such animals * * * as may from time to time be found on his land." This right has been recognized throughout the history of common law, with one exception: Following the Norman Conquest the King contended that he was lord paramount of the field, possessed of the right to the universal soil and of the exclusive right to take the game, but the irate landowners, vehemently objecting, quickly and decisively recaptured their rights and reestablished the common law.

American cases are in harmony with the common law rule. * * *

The appellant has confused the ownership of the game in its wild state with the ownership of the right to pursue the game. The landowner is not the owner of the game, * * * but he does own, as private property, the right to pursue game upon his own lands. That right is property, just as are the trees on the land and the ore in the ground, and is subject to lease, purchase and sale in like manner. * * *

* * * It is our view that the Commission is empowered to regulate the taking of game and to acquire property, by purchase and gift, for its use but * * * it is not, under the guise of regulation or otherwise, empowered to take private property for public purpose without just compensation. There is no Florida precedent for a contrary view and such federal precedent as there may be is less than persuasive. We are not yet ready in this State to embrace the "managed economy" theory of government.

* * * all doubt should be resolved in favor of the Constitutional interdiction against the taking of private property without compensation. Recognizing the laudable purpose of the Game Commission and its regulatory powers in an increasingly complex society we must conclude that the adjective advantage of game preservation cannot overshadow the mischief to be achieved by the circumvention of the Bill of Rights.

* * *

We find: * * * That appellant has no constitutional authority, express or otherwise, to exercise the police power to classify private property as a refuge without compensation to the owner.

It is not compatible with sound jurisprudence that the Commission be permitted to invade the owners' right and to cloud the title of his land by the imposition of the order in controversy. If, as is claimed, the chief value of the land of the appellees is the right of the owners to pursue the game thereon then, obviously, when they are deprived of that right they are deprived of property and about all that is left to them is the privilege of paying taxes thereon. * * * The salutary purpose of the Commission will not be well served by the exercise of authority achieved by this Court's strained construction of the Constitution.

Affirmed.

* * *

PROBLEMS

1. One purpose of The Wilderness Act of 1964, 16 U.S.C.A. § 1132(b), is to preserve aspects of our "natural environment from the progressive, destructive and hasty inroads of man, usually commercial in nature." The Act designates the Gore Range "a preserved wilderness" and bars the sale of timber in the Range without the prior approval of the President and Congress. It authorizes the President to recommend to Congress that it enlarge the Range. Without presidential and legislative approval the United States Forest Service entered into a contract to sell trees on land adjoining the Range. In a suit to enjoin enforcement of the contract the Service maintained that the sale was not covered by the Act. Plaintiff contended that since the sale would preclude future presidential and leg-

islative action to enlarge Gore Range the act's provisions had to be satisfied. What judgment?

2. A state statute delegated to timber owners and operators the exclusive power to formulate forest practice rules which, when adopted, would have the force and effect of law. The statute contained no guidelines or standards to prevent abuse, vesting absolute discretion in forest practice committees composed of timber owners and operators. The constitutionality of the law was challenged on the ground that it permitted persons with a pecuniary interest to act as final arbiters. What judgment?

3. The Multiple Use-Sustained Yield Act, 16 U.S.C.A. §§ 528–531 declares: "[i]t is the policy of Congress that the national forests are established and shall be administered for outdoor recreation, range timber, watershed, and wildlife and fish purposes." The Act calls for the management and utilization of resources to "best meet the needs of the American people" and for achieving and maintaining "in perpetuity * * * a high level of regular periodic output of the various renewable resources of the national forests without impairment of the productivity of the land." Plaintiffs brought suit to enjoin the sale of trees located in one of the national forests, charging that the forest was being administered "predominantly for timber production." The Forest Service insisted that since Congress had not indicated the weight to be assigned to each of the Act's values it must be assumed that the decision was left to the sound discretion and expertise of the Service. Plaintiffs insisted that it was for the court to interpret the statute and to assign relative weights to each value. Are they correct?

4. Plaintiff had been engaged in whaling for almost half a century. After the whale was added to the federal government's list of endangered species his request that his whaling license be renewed was denied. He sued for damages for the deprivation of his business and for the loss of his livelihood, "present and future." The government defended its action as a proper exercise of its police power and contended that once whale herds reached optimum population levels whaling permits would again be issued. Expert witnesses agreed that the whale population would probably reach such a size in about 50 to 100 years. What judgment?

5. A state wildlife protection statute listed several wild animals as members of an endangered species, shielding them from destruction. The plaintiffs, sheep raisers, regarded such animals as predators since they attacked and devoured sheep. They challenged the constitutionality of the statute, insisting that it deprived them of their property without due process of law. What judgment?

Chapter 21

WETLANDS

An estuary is that area located at the mouth of a river or a bay where fresh and salt water meet and mix. The wetlands adjoining estuaries, commonly referred to as estuarian wetlands, as well as inland wetlands, serve a variety of purposes. They are a locale in which diverse sorts of plants and animals live. Nutrients, manufactured in wetlands, are used in the food chain which ultimately produces food for human consumption. Wetlands play a part in the natural removal of waste products. They absorb many times their volume in water and thereby help to control floods. Wetlands offer man an august vista of natural beauty and a striking opportunity for recreational activity.

Congress has expressly found that "estuaries   *   *   *   are rich in a variety of natural, commercial, and other resources   *   *   * [and has declared that they] are of immediate and potential value to the present and future generations of Americans."[1] In 1968 it enacted legislation which provides for a "general study and inventory of estuaries and their natural resources."[2] It directs that the study "focus attention on whether any land or water area within an estuary and the Great Lakes should be acquired or administered by the Secretary [of Interior] or by a State or local subdivision thereof, or whether such land or water area may be protected adequately through local, State, or Federal laws or other methods without Federal land acquisition or administration."[3] Congress calls upon the Secretary of Interior to "encourage States and local subdivisions thereof to consider, in their comprehensive planning and proposals   *   *   * [prepared with a view toward receiving federal financial assistance under other federal laws], the needs and opportunities for protecting and restoring estuaries   *   *   *."[4] Congress asserted that it was the policy of the United States to consider "the need to protect, conserve, and restore   *   *   *   estuaries in a manner that adequately and reasonably maintains a balance between the national need for such protection in the interest of conserving natural resources and natural beauty of the Nation and the need to develop   *   *   *   estuaries to further the growth and development of the Nation."[5] Congress also stated that it was the policy of that body "to recognize, preserve, and protect the responsibilities of the States in protecting, conserving, and restoring the estuaries in the United States."[6]

1. 16 U.S.C.A. § 1221.

2. 16 U.S.C.A. § 1222(a).

3. 16 U.S.C.A. § 1222(b).

4. 16 U.S.C.A. § 1225.

5. 16 U.S.C.A. § 1221.

6. 16 U.S.C.A. § 1221.

In 1970 Congress proclaimed that it found "that it is in the public interest to preserve, restore, and improve the wetlands of the Nation, and thereby to conserve surface waters, to preserve and improve habitat for migratory waterfowl and other wildlife resources, to reduce runoff, soil and wind erosion, and contribute to flood control, to contribute to improved water quality and reduce stream sedimentation, to contribute to improved subsurface moisture, to reduce acres of new land coming into production and to retire lands now in agricultural production, to enhance the natural beauty of the landscape, and to promote comprehensive and total water management planning."[7] Congress authorized and directed the Secretary of Agriculture "to formulate and carry out a continuous program to prevent the serious loss of wetlands, and to preserve, restore, and improve such lands, * * *."[8] Congress set forth the circumstances under which the Secretary could enter into agreements with land owners to conserve water and wetlands under established conservation plans.[9] Those who lost the enjoyment of their property under such agreements would be entitled to compensation for such loss.[10] To * * * [insure that] the Secretary's efforts and those of others concerned with wetlands [are] coordinated, Congress directed that he "consult with the Secretary of the Interior" and also "consult with and utilize the technical and related services of appropriate local, State, Federal, and private conservation agencies."[11]

The State of Connecticut's approach is illustrative of state wetland legislation. The Connecticut Legislature has declared "that much of the wetlands of * * * [the] state has been lost or despoiled by unregulated dredging, dumping, filling and like activities and that the remaining wetlands of * * * [the] state are all in jeopardy of being lost or despoiled by these and other activities; that such loss or despoilation will adversely affect, if not entirely eliminate, the value of such wetlands as sources of nutrients to finfish, crustacea and shellfish of significant economic value; that such loss or despoilation will destroy such wetlands as habitats for plants and animals of significant economic value and will eliminate or substantially reduce marine commerce, recreation and aesthetic enjoyment; and that such loss or despoilation will, in most cases, disturb the natural ability of tidal wetlands to reduce flood damage and adversely affect the public health and welfare; that such loss or despoilation will substantially reduce the capacity of such wetlands to absorb silt and thus will result in the increased silting of channels and harbor areas to the detriment of free navigation. Therefore, it is * * *

7. 16 U.S.C.A. § 1301.   10. 16 U.S.C.A. § 1302.

8. 16 U.S.C.A. § 1301.   11. 16 U.S.C.A. § 1309.

9. 16 U.S.C.A. §§ 1302–1306.

[the announced] public policy of this state to preserve the wetlands and to prevent the despoilation and destruction thereof."[12]

The Connecticut Legislature, for the purpose of regulating activity in wetland areas, has defined wetland as follows: "'wetland' means those areas which border on or lie beneath tidal waters, such as, but not limited to banks, bogs, salt marsh, swamps, meadows, flats, or other low lands subject to tidal action, including those areas now or formerly connected to tidal waters, and whose surface is at or below an elevation of one foot above local extreme high water; and upon which may grow or be capable of growing some, but not necessarily all, of the following: Salt meadow grass * * *, spike grass * * *, black grass * * *, saltmarsh grass * * *, saltworts * * *, Sea Lavendar * * *, saltmarsh bulrushes * * *, sand spurrey * * *, switch grass * * *, tail cordgrass * * *, hightide bush * * *, cuttails * * *, spike rush * * *, chairmaker's rush * * *, bent grass * * *, and sweet grass * * *." The sorts of activities which Connecticut outlaws from taking place in wetlands without prior approval are: "Draining, dredging, excavation, or removal of soil, mud, sand, gravel, aggregate of any kind or rubbish from any wetland or the dumping, filling or depositing thereon of any soil, stones, sand, gravel, mud, aggregate of any kind, rubbish or similar material, either directly or otherwise, and the erection of structures, driving of pilings, or placing of obstructions, whether or not changing the tidal ebb and flow." [13]

Persons wishing to make use of wetlands in Connecticut must apply to the Commissioner of Agriculture and Natural Resources for a permit. The Commissioner "[i]n granting, denying or limiting any permit * * * [must] consider the effect of the proposed * * * [activity in a wetland area] with reference to the public health and welfare, marine fisheries, shell-fisheries, wildlife, the protection of life and property from flood, hurricane and other natural disasters, and * * * [the State's stated public policy], inclusive. Notice to the commissioner that the state board of fisheries and game is in the process of acquisition of any tidal wetlands by negotiation or condemnation * * * [is a] sufficient basis for denial of any permit. In granting a permit the commission may limit or impose conditions or limitations designed to carry out the [State's] public policy. The commissioner may require a bond in an amount and with surety and conditions satisfactory to him securing to the state compliance with the conditions and limitations set forth in the permit. The commissioner may suspend or revoke a permit if * * * [he] finds that the applicant has not complied with any of the conditions or lim-

12. Conn.Gen.Statutes Annotated § 22–7h.

13. Conn.Gen.Statutes Annotated § 22–7i.

itations * * * or [has done something other than the authorized form of activity]."[14]

The cited statute is designed to protect tidal wetlands. States have enacted comparable legislation to shield inland wetlands from destruction.

———

BARTLETT v. ZONING COMMISSION OF THE TOWN OF OLD LYME

Supreme Court of Connecticut, 1971.
282 A.2d 907, 161 Conn. 24.

[In 1961, when the plaintiff acquired four acres of tidal marshland for investment purposes for a nominal sum of cash, local zoning regulations prohibited construction or the placing of fill on the land or its being paved without a permit from the defendant. In 1964 the defendant denied the plaintiff's request for a permit to fill the land. In 1968 the defendant held a public hearing to consider amending the ordinance. The plaintiff appeared and objected to the proposed change on the ground that it would amount to a confiscation of his land without just compensation. Subsequently the defendant altered the zoning regulations so as to restrict the use of plaintiff's land to wooden walkways, wharves, duck blinds, public boat landings and public ditches unless special permission were granted to permit the digging of a channel and erection of a boat house on piles sufficient to accommodate a boat, if the plaintiff owned one, and for the erection of piers, docks, piles for life lines, rafts, or jetties. The plaintiff appealed from the Board's action. The trial court ruled in favor of the plaintiff. The defendant appealed.]

ALCORN, CHIEF JUSTICE. * * *

Undeniably, the defendant's objective to preserve marshlands from encroachment or destruction is a laudable one. The preservation of our natural environment is of critical concern. Indeed, the General Assembly, has recognized this fact but has provided for the determination of reasonable compensation for land taken. The purpose to be served is not the issue on this appeal, however. The issue is whether that purpose can be accomplished in the manner attempted here.

Zoning regulations are a legitimate subject for the exercise of the police power provided they are not such an unreasonable exercise of that power as to become arbitrary, destructive or confiscatory and so unconstitutional. Whether the amendments adopted in this case meet the test of a constitutional exercise of the police power must be determined in the light of the circumstances shown to exist. The ul-

14. Conn.Gen.Statutes Annotated § 22–7m.

timate question is whether the amendments which the defendant adopted are so unreasonable and confiscatory as to amount, for all practical purposes, to a taking of the plaintiff's property for a public use without just compensation. If they are, then they violate both the fifth and fourteenth amendments to the constitution of the United States and § 11 of article first of the constitution of Connecticut. The trial court concluded that, as to the plaintiff's property, the action complained of was unreasonable, confiscatory and unconstitutional and we agree with that conclusion.

It is unnecessary to repeat the extreme restrictions which the defendant has placed on the plaintiff's use of his property. Other than public boat landings and ditches, neither of which would appear to be a private activity, the plaintiff's use of his property is practically nonexistent unless he happens to own a boat and even that use purports to be conditioned on the exercise of the very broad powers vested in the zoning board of appeals.

There is no error.

* * *

STATE v. JOHNSON

Supreme Judicial Court of Maine, 1970.
265 A.2d 711.

[Maine's Wetlands Act prohibits the alteration or use of coastal wetlands, defined so as to include salt water marshes, without a permit issued by a municipality and the State Wetlands Control Board. Appellants, owners of a tract of land extending across a salt water marsh, with notice to the Board, applied to municipal officials for a permit to fill a portion of the marsh. The Board denied their request. They appealed to this Court, challenging the constitutionality of the Act. The case (Case No.1) was remanded so that the Board could gather evidence as to the nature of the land and the benefits or harm to be expected from the Board's action. The appellants proceeded to deposit fill on the marsh. The State requested, and the trial court granted, an injunction restricting the alteration and use of the marsh by the appellants (Case No. 2). They appealed.]

MARDEN, JUSTICE. * * * It is stipulated that the evidence in this case should be accepted as the evidence lacking in (Case No. 1) and that the two cases be consolidated for final determination of both.

The record establishes that the land which the appellants propose to build up by fill and build upon for sale, or to be offered for sale to be built upon, are coastal wetlands within the definition of the Act and that the refusal by the Board to permit the deposit of such fill prevents the development as proposed. The * * * [trial] Justice found that the property is a portion of a salt marsh area, a valuable natural resource of the State, that the highest and best use for the land, so filled, is for housing, and that unfilled it has no commercial value.

The issue is the same in both, namely, whether the denial of permit (Case No. 1) and the injunction (Case No. 2) so limit the use to plaintiffs of their land that such deprivation of use amounts to a taking of their property without constitutional due process and just compensation.

* * *

It is "the constitutional guaranty that no person shall be deprived of * * * property for arbitrary reasons, such a deprivation being constitutionally supportable only if the conduct from which the deprivation flows is proscribed by reasonable legislation (that is, legislation the enactment of which is within the scope of legislative authority) reasonably applied (that is, for a purpose consonant with the purpose of the legislation itself)."

* * *

The constitutional aspect of the current problem is to be determined by consideration of the extent to which appellants are deprived of their usual incidents of ownership,—for the conduct of the public authorities with relation to appellants' land is not a "taking" in the traditional sense. * * *

* * * Broadly speaking, deprivation of property contrary to constitutional guaranty occurs "if it deprives an owner of one of its essential attributes, destroys its value, restricts or interrupts its common necessary, or profitable use, hampers the owner in the application of it to the purposes of trade, or imposes conditions upon the right to hold or use it and thereby seriously impairs its value."

Conditions so burdensome may be imposed that they are equivalent to an outright taking, although the title to the property and some vestiges of its uses remain in the owner.

A guiding principle appears in the frequently cited case of Pennsylvania Coal Company v. Mahon et al., where Mr. Justice Holmes declared:

"Government hardly could go on if to some extent values incident to property could not be diminished without paying for every such change in the general law. As long recognized some values are enjoyed under an implied limitation and must yield to the police power. * * * One fact for consideration in determining such limits is the extent of the diminution. When it reaches a certain magnitude, in most if not in all cases there must be an exercise of eminent domain and compensation to sustain the act. So the question depends upon the particular facts."

*   *   *   *   *   *   *   *   *   *

"We are in danger of forgetting that a strong public desire to improve the public condition is not enough to warrant achieving the desire by a shorter cut than the constitutional way of paying for the change. As we already have said this is a question of degree—and therefore cannot be disposed of by general propositions."

Confrontation between public interests and private interests is common in the application of zoning laws, with which the Wetlands Act may be analogized, and the great majority of which, upon their facts, are held to be reasonable exercise of the police power. There are, however, zoning restrictions which have been recognized as equivalent to a taking of the property restricted.

* * *

Between the public interest in braking and eventually stopping the insidious despoliation of our natural resources which have for so long been taken for granted, on the one hand, and the protection of appellants' property rights on the other, the issue is cast.

Here the single Justice has found that the area of which appellants' land is a part "is a valuable natural resource of the State of Maine and plays an important role in the conservation and development of aquatic and marine life, game birds and waterfowl," which bespeaks the public interest involved and the protection of which is sought by * * * the Act. With relation to appellants' interest the single Justice found that appellants' land absent the addition of fill "has no commercial value whatever." * * *

* * * To leave appellants with commercially valueless land in upholding the restriction presently imposed, is to charge them with more than their just share of the cost of this state-wide conservation program, granting fully its commendable purpose. * * *

The application of the Wetlands restriction in the terms of the denial of appellants' proposal to fill, and enjoining them from so doing deprives them of the reasonable use of their property and is both an unreasonable exercise of police power and equivalent to taking within constitutional considerations.

* * *

Holding, as we do, that the prohibition against the filling of appellants' land, upon the facts peculiar to the case, is an unreasonable exercise of police power, it does not follow that the restriction as to draining sanitary sewage into coastal wetlands is subject to the same infirmity. Additional considerations of health and pollution which are "separable from and independent of" the "fill" restriction may well support validity of the Act in those areas of concern. * * *

* * * the denial of the permit to fill (Case No. 1) and the injunction (Case No. 2) are "set aside."

* * *

PROBLEMS

1.   State law prohibited the use of wetlands without a permit issued by the state environmental commission. A privately owned and
operated airport, having been the site of several aircraft mishaps,
was directed by the Federal Aviation Administration to lengthen its
runways and to install signal towers. The plan approved by the Administration required the towers to be located in a wetland area.
Without securing a permit from the state commission the airport operator proceeded to build the towers. The commission brought an action in a state court to enjoin the installation. What judgment?

2.   State law empowered towns to prohibit the use of marshlands for purposes which would be detrimental to public health or
safety. The defendant town's zoning commission denied plaintiff's
request for a permit to excavate and fill a waterfront marsh located
on his property on the ground that the town desired to preserve the
marsh in an "unspoiled state for public enjoyment." He appealed.
What judgment?

3.   A vast wetlands area owned by private persons constituted
50% of the open land remaining in a town located 25 miles from a
heavily populated city. The town council enacted an ordinance which
set aside town funds for the purchase of all of the wetlands located in
the town "in order to preserve this necessary natural resource."
Plaintiffs, owners of many acres of wetlands, challenged the constitutionality of the law, charging that intentionally or inadvertently it
"foreclosed to those in need of housing a decent place to live." What
judgment?

4.   A town, holding title to an area rich in wetlands, agreed to
sell the area to housing developers. Its action was intended to obtain needed funds and to help insure the availability of new housing
to a burgeoning population. Plaintiff challenged the validity of the
agreement on the ground that the town held the property in trust for
the public's benefit and could not sell it for non-public purposes.
What judgment?

5.   The state's wetlands act, adopted in 1970, made it unlawful
for a riparian landowner to dredge or fill any wetlands without first
obtaining a license from the state wetlands commission. A license
holder would have to compensate the state for the use of wetlands.
Plaintiff, a landowner, whose property contained a large expanse of
wetlands, challenged the state's right to demand payment, contending
that for 220 years extensive landfilling had taken place in navigable
waters throughout the state without the state asserting any right to
compensation. The state insisted that under existing law it held title
to submerged land under navigable waters and could demand compensation. What judgment?

Chapter 22

COASTAL ZONES AND OCEANS

The need to protect the nation's coastal zones and abutting oceans from damage and destruction has only recently attracted the interest of environmentalists. The general failure to appreciate the full extent of the injury done and continuing to be done to these resources must in part be ascribed to their respective sizes. The United States is the beneficiary of a vast expanse of coastal area. The adjacent oceans and the Gulf of Mexico are so immense that their very presence tends to dwarf the importance of the proposition that they have to be cared for. Conventional thinking perceived our coastal zones to be infinite and the oceans as bottomless receptacles for refuse and sewage. Fresh knowledge has made it clear that our coastal zones and abutting waters must be safeguarded if their offerings are to be available for future use.

In the Submerged Lands Act of 1953 Congress addressed itself to the question of state's rights in the navigable waters which bounded them. It "approved and confirmed * * * [t]he seaward boundary of each [of the] original coastal States * * * as a line three geographical miles distant from its coast line or, in the case of the Great Lakes, to the international boundary."[1] In 1960 the Supreme Court of the United States was asked to pass on the import of the Act.[2] The Court asserted that it had already ruled "that paramount rights in the marginal sea are an attribute of the national rather than state sovereignty irrespective of the location of the state seaward boundaries."[3] This placed jurisdiction over the waters which adjoined states in the hands of the federal government. Congress, in the exercise of its "constitutional power to dispose of federal property" could set the outermost limit of state jurisdiction in submerged lands at three miles seaward and retain for the federal government jurisdiction over submerged land beyond that. The Court noted that vis-à-vis the United States and other nations the federal government claimed jurisdiction over the continental shelf which extends to a distance of two hundred miles seaward.

The Submerged Lands Act expressly reserves to the United States any rights it might otherwise have "to the natural resources of that portion of the subsoil and seabed of the Continental Shelf" which lies more than three miles from shore.[4] Congress declared it

1. 43 U.S.C.A. § 1312.

2. United States v. Louisiana, Texas, Miss., Ala. & Fla., 80 S.Ct. 961, 363 U.S. 1, 4 L.Ed.2d 1025. In Alabama v. Texas, 74 S.Ct. 481, 347 U.S. 272, 98 L.Ed. 689 (1954) the Court ruled the Act constitutional.

3. United States v. California, 67 S.Ct. 1658, 332 U.S. 19, 91 L.Ed. 1889 (1947).

4. 43 U.S.C.A. § 1302.

to be "in the public interest that * * * title to and ownership of the" submerged lands be in the States abutted by the Atlantic and Pacific Oceans and the Gulf of Mexico and that these States had "the right and power to manage, administer, lease, develop, and use * * * [such] lands and natural resources * * * in accordance with applicable State law * * *." [5] Congress expressly retained for the United States "all its navigational servitude and rights in and powers of regulation and control of said lands and navigable waters for the constitutional purposes of commerce, navigation, national defense, and international affairs, all of which * * * [Congress declared were] paramount to, but * * * not [to] be deemed to include, proprietary rights of ownership, or the rights of management, administration, leasing, use, and development of the lands and natural resources which * * * [were] specifically recognized, confirmed, established, and vested in and assigned to the respective States * * * [by the Act.]" [6]

The Act defines "outer Continental Shelf" as "all submerged lands lying seaward and outside of the area of lands beneath navigable waters" falling outside the jurisdiction of the States.[7] Congress declared "it to be the policy of the United States that the subsoil and seabed of the outer Continental Shelf appertain[s] to the United States and are subject to its jurisdiction, control, and power of disposition * * *." [8] Congress provided that "[t]he Constitution and laws and civil and political jurisdiction of the United States * * * [extended] to the subsoil and seabed of the outer Continental Shelf and to all artificial islands and fixed structures which may be erected thereon for the purpose of exploring, developing, removing, and transporting resources therefrom, to the same extent as if the outer Continental Shelf were an area of exclusive Federal jurisdiction located within a State: *Provided, however*, That mineral leases on the outer Continental Shelf shall be maintained or issued only under the provisions of * * * [the Act]." [9]

Congress vested in "[t]he United States district courts * * * original jurisdiction of cases and controversies arising out of or in connection with any operations conducted on the outer Continental Shelf for the purpose of exploring for, developing, removing or transporting by pipeline the natural resources, or involving rights to the natural resources of the subsoil and seabed of the outer Continental Shelf, and proceedings with respect to any such case or controversy may be instituted in the judicial district in which any defendant resides or may be found, or in the judicial district of the adjacent State nearest the place where the cause of action arose." [10]

5.   43 U.S.C.A. § 1311.

6.   43 U.S.C.A. § 1314(a).

7.   43 U.S.C.A. § 1331(a).

8.   43 U.S.C.A. § 1332(a).

9.   43 U.S.C.A. § 1333(a) (1).

10.   43 U.S.C.A. § 1333(b).

The task of granting or denying leases for the exploration, development, and removal of oil, gas, and sulphur from the outer Continental Shelf is entrusted to the Secretary of the Interior.[11] The Act specifies the procedures the Secretary must follow, the circumstances under which leases may be granted, and how leases are to be drawn.[12] "The issuance and continuance in effect of any lease, or of any extension, renewal, or replacement * * * [is] conditioned upon compliance with the regulations issued under * * * [the Act]."[13]

The Secretary is directed to "prescribe such rules and regulations as may be necessary to carry out * * * [the provisions of the Act]."[14] He is authorized to "prescribe and amend such rules and regulations as he determines to be necessary and proper in order to provide for the prevention of waste and conservation of the natural resources of the outer Continental Shelf, and the protection of correlative rights therein, * * *." [15]

The Act makes it a misdemeanor, "punishable by a fine of not more than $2,000 or by imprisonment for not more than six months, or by both such fine and imprisonment, * * * [with] each day of violation * * * [being] deemed to be a separate offense * * * [for a]ny person * * * [to] knowingly and wilfully * * * [violate] any rule or regulation prescribed by the Secretary for the prevention of waste, the conservation of the natural resources, or the protection of correlative rights * * *." [16] When enforcing "conservation laws, rules, and regulations the Secretary is authorized to cooperate with the conservation agencies of the adjacent States."[17]

Outraged over the damage already done, and fear of the damage which might occur in the future as a result of the intentional or unintentional dumping of oil into the navigable waters inside and adjacent to the United States, Congress, in 1970, declared "that it is the policy of the United States that there should be no discharges of oil into or upon the navigable waters of the United States, adjoining shorelines, or into or upon the waters of the contiguous zone."[18] It outlawed such discharge "in harmful quantities" except when permitted under "the International Convention for the Prevention of Pollution of the Sea by Oil, 1954, as amended" and "where permitted in quantities and at times and locations or under such circumstances or conditions as the President may, by regulation, determine not to be harmful."[19] Such regulations as might be issued must "be consistent

11.   43 U.S.C.A. §§ 1337(a) (c).

12.   43 U.S.C.A. §§ 1337(b), (d).

13.   43 U.S.C.A. § 1334(a) (2).

14.   43 U.S.C.A. § 1334(a) (1).

15.   43 U.S.C.A. § 1334(a) (1).

16.   43 U.S.C.A. § 1334(a) (2).

17.   43 U.S.C.A. § 1334(a) (1).

18.   33 U.S.C.A. § 1161(b) (1).

19.   33 U.S.C.A. § 1161(b) (2).

with maritime safety and with marine and navigation laws and regulations and applicable water quality standards."[20]   The President's regulations are required to "determine   *   *   *   those quantities of oil the discharge of which, at such times, locations, circumstances, and conditions, will be harmful to the public health or welfare of the United States, including, but not limited to, fish, shellfish, wildlife, and public and private property, shorelines, and beaches, except that in the case of the discharge of oil into or upon the waters of the contiguous zone, only those discharges which threaten the fishery resources of the contiguous zone or threaten to pollute or contribute to the pollution of the territory or the territorial sea of the United States may be determined to be harmful."[21]

"Any person in charge of a vessel or of an onshore facility or an offshore facility   *   *   *   [is required], as soon as he has knowledge of any discharge of oil from such vessel or facility in violation of   *   *   *   [law, to] immediately notify the appropriate agency of the United States Government of such discharge."[22]   One convicted of failure to do so may "be fined not more than $10,000, or imprisoned for not more than one year, or both."[23]   Such "notification received   *   *   *   as required by law or information obtained by exploitation of such notification   *   *   *   may not be used against any such person in any criminal case, except a prosecution for perjury or for giving a false statement."[24]

"Any owner or operator of any vessel, onshore facility, or offshore facility from which oil is knowingly discharged in violation of   *   *   *   law may be assessed a civil penalty by the Secretary of the department in which the Coast Guard is operating of not more than $10,000 for each offense   *   *   *.   Each violation is a separate offense.   The   *   *   *   civil penalty may be compromised by such Secretary.   In determining the amount of the penalty, or the amount agreed upon in compromise, the appropriateness of such penalty to the size of the business of the owner or operator charged, the effect on the owner or operator's ability to continue in business, and the gravity of the violation   *   *   *   are to be considered by such Secretary."[25]

"Except where an owner or operator can prove that a discharge was caused solely by (A) an act of God, (B) an act of war, (C) negligence on the part of the United States Government, or (D) an act or omission of a third party without regard to whether any such act or omission was or was not negligent, or any combination of the foregoing   *   *   *, such owner or operator of any vessel from which oil is discharged in violation of   *   *   *   [law is] liable to the Unit-

---

20.   33 U.S.C.A. § 1161(b) (2).

21.   33 U.S.C.A. § 1161(b) (3).

22.   33 U.S.C.A. § 1161(b) (4).

23.   33 U.S.C.A. § 1161(b) (4).

24.   33 U.S.C.A. § 1161(b) (4).

25.   33 U.S.C.A. § 1161(b) (5).

ed States Government for the actual costs incurred   *   *   *   for the removal of such oil by the United States Government in an amount not to exceed $100 per gross ton of such vessel or $14,000,000 whichever is lesser, except that where the United States can show that such discharge was the result of willful negligence or willful misconduct, within the privity and knowledge of the owner, such owner or operator   *   *   *   [is] liable to the United States Government for the full amount of such costs."[26] The same standard of liability is laid down for owners and operators of an offshore facility. They too are "liable to the United States for the actual costs incurred   *   *   *   for the removal of such oil by the United States Government [but] in an amount not to exceed $8,000,000, except that where the United States can show that such discharge was the result of willful negligence or willful misconduct within the privity and knowledge of the owner, such owner or operator   *   *   *   [is] liable to the United States Government for the full amount of such costs."[27]

Legislators in a number of states, fearful that the natural resources offered by coastal areas would be irreparably damaged unless protective governmental action were taken, have enacted laws designed to protect this unique reservoir of resources. State laws have been passed so as to keep beach areas intact, to insulate coastland residential areas from industry, to limit the extent to which industry can be carried on in coastal zones, to curb the discharge of sewage and wastes into coastal waters, and to curtail the discharge of oil onto the water seaward from the coast within the three mile zone established by Congress.

In some coastal areas nature itself is the despoiler of the environment. Erosion causes the disappearance of beachland and valuable coastal areas. Forceful protective state action is necessary if this source of danger to the environment is to be effectively dealt with.

That vast ocean region beyond the outer Continental Shelf of North America and all of the other ocean areas which are beyond the jurisdiction of the United States or any other single nation, pose environmental regulation problems which can be resolved only through multinational efforts. This sphere of environmental law invites United Nations' action. Already this world body has manifested an interest in identifying sources of ocean pollution and the formulation of viable and generally acceptable ways in which such pollution can be curtailed. Only if nations act collectively to enforce meaningful standards of environmental control can meaningful steps be taken to prevent extensive damage to the world's oceans. Oceans are a vital source of food. They contain an array of other resources which can be of benefit to all of mankind. The desirability of prompt and effective worldwide action is obvious.

26.   33 U.S.C.A. § 1161(f) (1).   27.   33 U.S.C.A. § 1161(f) (3).

GOLDEN v. BOARD OF SELECTMEN OF FALMOUTH

Supreme Judicial Court of Massachusetts, 1970.
265 N.E.2d 573, —— Mass. ——.

[The plaintiff, owner of a tract of land extending from the edge of a pond through a tidal marsh to upland property, applied to the Falmouth Board of Selectmen as required by § 36 of the Town's zoning by-law for a special permit to construct in the tidal marsh a 24 foot wide channel in which to dock his two boats. As required by a State Act he also filed with the State Director of Marine Fisheries a notice of intention to carry out the project. The Director issued an "Order of Conditions" authorizing the project. The Board denied the plaintiff's request. He appealed to the Superior Court. The Court ruled that the Board had exceeded its authority, annulled its decision, and ordered the issuance of a permit subject to the conditions imposed by the State Director. The Board appealed.]

KIRK, JUSTICE. * * * The only issue presented by the appeal is whether the [State] Act deprives the board, acting under a local zoning by-law, of the power to forbid the filling, dredging, or excavating of coastal wetlands in the town despite the approval of the undertaking by the Director of Marine Fisheries acting under the Act.

The purpose of the Act is to regulate the removal, filling, and dredging of areas bordering on coastal waters. It has been held to be valid legislative enactment.

In construing the Act the judge ruled that the board *acting pursuant to the Act* had the authority only to *make recommendations* to the appropriate State agencies and had no power to prevent the plaintiff from making the channel once the Director of Marine Fisheries approved it. We read this ruling to be entirely based on the proposition that the Act in and of itself does not permit boards of selectmen to regulate local coastal wetlands once regulation by the director has been imposed. The ruling is framed within the context of the Act and it considers only whether the Director of Marine Fisheries or the board has the ultimate authority under the Act. We do not so view the case. The board made its decision pursuant to § 36 of the zoning by-law, not pursuant to the Act.

Section 36 of the Falmouth zoning by-law is a permissible exercise of municipal zoning power. * * * In the *MacGibbon* case, this court held that a zoning by-law having the same purposes as § 36, the one before us (protecting the town's natural resources along its coastal areas) and similar operative provisions (requiring a permit prior to obstructing streams or tidal rivers or dredging and filling wetlands and marsh areas), was expressly authorized by the Zoning Enabling Act, G.L. c. 40A, § 2. The board, therefore, had the power to deny the permit as long as its decision was not "based on a legally untenable ground, or * * * [was not] unreasonable, whimsical, capricious or arbitrary." There is nothing before us showing that the board's decision did not comply with this standard.

Having upheld the validity of § 36 we turn to the question whether in enacting the Act the Legislature intended to repeal existing laws relating to the same subject. We find nothing in the language of the Act expressly, impliedly or inferentially suggesting that municipalities are deprived or preempted from exercising regulatory control of wetlands situated therein by means of zoning by-laws. The Act establishes a regulatory machinery at the State level in which local boards of selectmen, the Department of Public Works and the Director of Marine Fisheries each has a role. There is no express reference in the statute that municipalities may or may not otherwise undertake wetlands control independent of the Act.

Similarly, we do not construe the Act as impliedly precluding regulation by municipalities. Although it is an established rule of statutory construction that "[T]he enactment of a statute which seems to have been intended to cover the whole subject to which it relates impliedly repeals all existing statutes touching the subject," this rule has been applied with caution. * * * In applying this test, the court endeavors to determine whether the Legislature intended to repeal earlier related laws, including existing town by-laws, as well as whether there is a need for uniformity in the subject of the legislation.

We see no repugnance between the provisions of the Act and § 36 of the Falmouth zoning by-law. Each confers a separate and distinct type of authority upon the respective governmental bodies involved. * * *

* * * There is nothing to suggest, * * * that the board acting under the zoning by-law is powerless to refuse initial authorization.

Our construction of the Act logically permits each of the respective governmental bodies, the local board of selectmen under the Act, the Director of Marine Fisheries, the Department of Public Works, and the local board acting under the zoning by-law to carry out effectively the legislative and local policy of preserving and protecting coastal wetlands. * * * The advances thus far made in this Commonwealth with regard to environmental control would be reversed if local communities were prevented from exercising regulatory authority. It is apparent to us that the Legislature in enacting the Act did not attempt to cover the entire field of coastal wetlands regulations to the exclusion of regulation by local authority. The Act does not attempt to create a uniform statutory scheme. It establishes minimum State-wide standards leaving local communities free to adopt more stringent controls.

It follows that the decree must be reversed. A new decree is to be entered stating that the decision of the board of selectmen was within its jurisdiction and no modification of it is required.

* * *

UNITED STATES v. RAY AND ACME GENERAL CONTRACTORS INC., ATLANTIS DEVELOPMENT CORPORATION, LTD.

United States Court of Appeals, Fifth Circuit, 1970.
423 F.2d 16.

[The defendants, desirous of transforming two coral reefs 4½ miles off the Florida coast into an independent nation, built caissons on the reefs and dredged material from the seabed and deposited it inside the caissons. The United States brought an action to enjoin the defendants, alleging that they were causing irreparable injury to the reefs and their activities were prohibited by the Rivers and Harbors Act of 1899. Atlantis intervened, alleging it wished to start a new nation and claimed superior title to the reefs. The District Court found (1) the defendants' activities were unlawful, (2) the reefs were subject to the Outer Continental Shelf Lands Act, and (3) together with the attached organisms the reefs are natural resources under the Act and the Geneva Convention on the Continental Shelf. It denied the defendants' and intervenor's claims, recognized the sovereign rights of the plaintiff, but concluded that since the United States had less than a property right in the reefs a trespass action could not lie and therefore denied an injunction. All parties appealed.]

AINSWORTH, CIRCUIT JUDGE:

* * *

The District Court correctly concluded that the past and proposed activities of defendants and intervenor were unlawful in the absence of a statutory permit from the Secretary of the Army. Section 10 of the Rivers and Harbors Act, prohibits construction in navigable waters of the United States unless the work has been "recommended by the Chief of Engineers and authorized by the Secretary of the Army." The authority of the Secretary of the Army is extended to the Outer Continental Shelf by the Outer Continental Shelf Lands Act: * * *

* * * the structures herein involved interfere with the exclusive rights of the United States under the Convention to explore the Continental Shelf and exploit its natural resources. * * *

It is clear that the reefs in question are within the area designated as the Continental Shelf by both national (Outer Continental Shelf Lands Act) and international (Geneva Convention on the Continental Shelf, executed in 1958 and effective in 1964) law.

* * *

* * * The District Court's finding that the reefs are part of the "seabed" of the Shelf is fully supported by substantial evidence of record.

The same national and international laws * * * explicitly recognize the sovereign rights of the United States and the exclusiveness of those rights to explore the Shelf and exploit its natural resources.

* * *

* * * The right of the United States to control those resources is implicit in Article 2, paragraphs 1, 2 and 3, supra, of the Geneva Convention on the Continental Shelf, and explicitly recognized in the Submerged Lands Act, * * *.

* * *

Article 2, paragraph 4, of the Geneva Convention on the Continental Shelf includes in its definition of "natural resources" both living and non-living resources, * * *.

Having thus concluded that the United States has the exclusive right for purposes of exploration and exploitation of the reefs, there remains only the question of whether injunctive relief was improperly denied to the Government * * *.

Although the complaint is inaccurately framed in terms of trespass * * * the Government repeatedly stresses that it is not claiming ownership of the reefs. We do not question the District Court's conclusion that the Government's interest, being something less than fee simple, cannot support a common law action for trespass * * *.

Neither ownership nor possession is, however, a necessary requisite for the granting of injunctive relief. This principle is implicit in the * * * decisions of the Supreme Court, in which injunctive relief was granted to protect "paramount rights" of the United States beyond territorial limits * * * to distances farther out in international waters than that involved here and at a time when those rights had not yet been statutorily established.

* * * The test for such relief * * * [is] "whether the United States * * * [has] an interest to protect or defend." * * *

The evidence overwhelmingly shows that the Government has a vital interest, from a practical as well as an aesthetic viewpoint, in preserving the reefs for public use and enjoyment. The protective underwater crannies of the reefs serve as a haven and spawning ground for myriad species of tropical and game fish. The unique and spectacular formations of the submerged coral deposits attract scores of water sports enthusiasts, skin divers, nature students, and marine researchers. * * * The reefs protect the inland waters from the heavy wave action of the open sea, thus making the area conducive to boating and other water sports. * * * the evidence shows that protective action by the Government to prevent despoliation of these unique natural resources is of tantamount importance. There was convincing evidence that the activities of defendants in dredging and filling the reefs has and would continue to kill the sensitive corals by smothering them; that the construction would constitute a navigational hazard to pleasure craft, and would destroy a very productive marine area and other natural resources. Obviously the United States has an important interest to protect in preventing the establishment of a new sovereign nation within four and one-half miles of the Florida Coast, * * *.

The rights of the United States in and to the reefs and the vital interest which the Government has in preserving the area require full and permanent injunctive relief against any interference with those rights by defendants and intervenor.

* * *

Affirmed in part, reversed in part.

PROBLEMS

1. Several months after Congress enacted the Water Quality Improvement Act of 1970 which subjected owners and operators of vessels or onshore or offshore facilities to liability for the sum of money expended by the federal government in cleaning up an oil spill unless it was caused by an act of God, war, negligence by the government, or the act or omission of a third party, a state legislature enacted an "Oil Spill Prevention and Pollution Control Act." The Act imposed liability on one who discharged oil into water on entering or leaving a state port or in the course of operating an onshore or offshore terminal facility. The Act did not recognize any of the defenses contained in the federal legislation. Plaintiff, charged with violating the state law, challenged its constitutionality. What judgment?

2. Plaintiff who operated a summer resort fronting on an ocean beach brought an action to enjoin the United States Department of Interior from exploring offshore oil deposits two miles seaward from his hotel and beach on the ground that the agency had not prepared an impact statement. What judgment?

3. Should states which have an extensive coastline use a single state agency or local agencies for the purpose of formulating and enforcing environmental coastal policy?

4. A city with extensive port facilities enacted an ordinance barring the docking of vessels which did not have prescribed sewage treatment facilities on board. The city maritime commissioner, after discovering that a United States Navy vessel and a Brazilian Navy vessel lacked the requisite facilities, directed that the vessels leave. When the commanding officers of the vessels refused to obey the or-

der, the city brought an action in the federal district court for an order directing them to do so. What judgment?

5. Should nations which abut on the world's oceans have the power to dike large areas of tidelands for use as sea farms to raise fish to the exclusion of other nations? Should sea farms be subject to common ownership by all nations? Should one international agency be entrusted with overseeing the exploitation of all of the resources found in or beneath the earth's oceans?

6. The United States brought an action to enjoin 15 communities located along a state's shoreline from discharging sewage into the Atlantic Ocean. The district court granted a permanent injunction. It found that the practice constituted an immediate and irreparable harm, produced a destructive impact upon marine life and the environment generally, and posed a dangerous health hazard to thousands of shoreline residents. The court rejected the defendants' argument that they had no place to store the sewage and to force them to transport their sewage seaward would impose a grave financial hardship on their taxpayers. The defendants appealed. What judgment?

EPILOGUE

The foundations of our national, state, and local environmental policies are already in place. A substantial part of the observable and significant portions of the superstructure of these policies is now complete. Construction continues. For the remainder of this decade it is certain to be vigorous. It will then slacken, to proceed in sloth-like fashion. The task of environmental policy-building will never come to an end. Continuous change in a plethora of factors will demand innovative responses on the heels of careful re-evaluation of existing programs and approval of worthy and workable modifications and additions. Prompt and brisk extensive cooperative environmental policy-making and enforcement on a multinational basis is urgently needed. There has been a devastating dearth of such action. These undertakings will be laborious and the work tedious, but they must be forthcoming. Hopefully, they will be fruitful. Whatever the rate of progress may be, regardless of the level on which the activity takes place, concern for the environment makes it essential that there be output and that it be effective.

Several matters demand immediate attention. They require a critical re-appraisal of some long accepted shibboleths, the structuring of a new scale of acceptable values, and a re-ordering of society's priorities. Some persons have concluded that our planet's limited spatial accommodations and finite quantity of usable resources call for the promulgation of a national, and in time a worldwide, population management policy. In addition to dealing with the issue of population size this policy may take into account such questions as what are and what are not "desirable" individual human characteristics and how "desirable" characteristics can be maintained and "undesirable" ones eliminated. Already a call has been sounded for the formulation of a new definition of "life" and a new attitude toward euthanasia. Too often a concomitant of a highly advanced technology is damage to the environment. To date the legal system is generally utilized to curb or bar the use of a technological application only after it has caused environmental injury. It is not unreasonable to conclude that in the not too distant future the federal government will establish a body charged with the task of assessing the probable impact of technology and technological applications before they may be put to use. Environmental considerations may preclude the utilization of particular forms of technology or technological applications. To facilitate the implementation of environmental policies use may be made of an environmental ombudsman. Charged with the responsibility of prodding officials to perform their assigned duties, an ombudsman can grease the wheels of officialdom which often grind too slowly, if at all. An ombudsman may instigate action required by law which would otherwise not be forthcoming. As increased atten-

236

tion is paid to environmental considerations the more pressing it becomes to arrive at a satisfactory answer to the query: "Who is to pay the cost of pollution control?" Some suggest that the polluter should pay the entire cost, government outlawing what is currently being done or imposing a tax at a rate which would insure behavior that would bring an end to the pollution causing activity. Others insist that the public should pay, government financing the cost of pollution abatement. Absent the express formulation of policy, in most instances it is the public and the consumer who bear the cost. The public pays the cost of undoing the damage caused by the polluter. The consumer pays more for products produced by pollution free means. A socially responsible business enterprise patently has an obligation aside from the law's commands to act with candor and vim to avoid damaging the environment, even if this means reduced profits. To prosper business too needs a satisfactory environment in which to operate.

In the future new and presently unforeseeable environmental problems will require the adoption of trenchant environmental protection policies. In quest for a solution society will turn to the law. Law will be used as the prime and critical problem-solving tool. It will be the obligation of those who play a role in the on-going operation of the legal process to see to it that the law's adjective and substantive mandates are such that our legal system can successfully meet the challenge.

*

INDEX

DATE DUE

HiGHSMiTH 45-220